Operations Research
for Immediate Application
A Quick & Dirty Manual

Operations Research for Immediate Application A Quick & Dirty Manual

Assembled somehow by

ROBERT E. D. WOOLSEY

and

HUNTINGTON S. SWANSON

Department of Mineral Economics, Colorado School of Mines
Rocky Mountain Fire Brigade, Inc., Golden, Colorado
Fire Brigade Consulting Ltd., Waterloo, Canada
Systemas Analyticas de Mexico, S.C., Monterrey, Mexico

HARPER & ROW, PUBLISHERS
New York, Evanston, San Francisco, London

Sponsoring Editor: John Greenman
Project Editor: Cynthia Hausdorff
Designer: Gayle Jaeger
Production Supervisor: Stefania J. Taflinska

**OPERATIONS RESEARCH FOR IMMEDIATE APPLICATION:
A QUICK & DIRTY MANUAL**
Copyright © 1969, 1975 **by R. E. D. WOOLSEY**

Library of Congress Cataloging in Publication Data
Woolsey, Robert E   D   1936–
    Operations research for immediate application.
    Includes index.
    1. Operations research. I. Swanson, Huntington S.,
joint author. II. Title.
T57.6.W66   1975   658.4′034   74-22328
ISBN 0-06-047233-2

There is neither a friend nor an enemy
that I have not repaid in full
                    SULLA

Contents

Two QUICK & DIRTY METHODS IN INVENTORY CONTROL 38

Preface

Before you plunge into this Quick & Dirty manual, I would like to say a few words as to what it is and how it came about.

For some time now, I and a few other practitioners in the areas of operations research, management science, and industrial engineering, have had the feeling that our profession is turning more and more inward and is talking less and less to the managers who have real problems.

This trend is exemplified by the appearance of papers in the journals of the profession that seem to be cures searching for a disease. On the rare occasions when a real problem is presented, it is usually disguised by a level of mathematical jargon that is beyond the potential user.

Over a period of years as a consultant, this author discovered that some of the simple methods for selected real-world problems, which have been known by the academics in this field for some time, were totally unknown to the people who really needed them. Study of this problem showed that the main reason was that the academics, naturally, wrote about the methods in such a manner as to ensure acceptance in academic journals. Unfortunately, the degree of mathematical rigor and fashionable notation required by these journals assured that the methods were incomprehensible to the final consumer.

This Quick & Dirty manual is an attempt to bridge this gap in communication. With rare exceptions, this author has simply taken the creative work he has learned from others and presented it in what he hopes to be plain English.

This manual is, frankly, a cookbook. This means that using the recipes herein may cause acute corporate (or governmental) indigestion if some careful thought is not given to the actual circumstances of the problem. Thoughtful consideration of the references supplied is a requirement for meaningful use of this manual.

The basic format for each chapter is a general discussion and brief summary of each Quick & Dirty, followed by the Quick & Dirtys themselves, each with an example and a reference. In a number of cases conversational FORTRAN programs are supplied to show how the methods may be implemented in practice. Some chapters, however, are rather more concerned with *how* a given quantitative approach may be introduced into an organization. For example, Chapter Three, on capital budgeting, has *The Prince* of Niccolo Machiavelli as its principal inspiration. It is the contention of this author that *defining* the model is often the easiest part of the optimization problem. The most difficult part is convincing someone with the problem to *use* your solution. For this reason, various apparently cynical comments and suggestions for practical use of the methods and programs in this book are scattered throughout the text. Some chapters are really essays on case studies in which the author, at worst, has hit the wall at high speed or, at best, has done a little better than break even. I realize that the implication that this author has not always done splendidly in his professional work breaks with the usual scholarly tradition that authors of operations research texts never admit error. However, after a few years of professional experience, this author must confess that you win a few and you lose a few. It is painfully clear that the best way to be unbeaten, untied, and unscored is simply not to play.

To the academic reviewers of this book, I can only say that this book is not for you, but rather for your students—who are often turned loose on the world knowing all about the problem but who are unable to find the answer.

Let me define operations research/management science as I see it:

Operations research is the application of logic and mathematics to a real-world problem in such a way that the method doesn't get in the way of common sense.

Robert E. D. Woolsey

This book was *not* supported by the National Science Foundation.

Instructions for Industry

This book should not be considered a cure for all ills. The probability that any one of the Quick & Dirtys or one of the programs will exactly fit a real-world situation is extremely small. The Quick & Dirtys are, at best, a guide for developing a rule of thumb to fit the situation at hand. The programs are only examples of how a given method might be presented in order to help its acceptance in the real-world situation at hand. As is sometimes suggested in the text, forms may be easily constructed to accomplish the desired objective without a computer. Whenever possible, this should be the goal and some examples of this are provided. People will use a nomogram or a chart long before they will consider using a computer. Say, for example, that a nomogram is constructed that will tell an inventory controller when to reorder so that total costs are minimized. Acceptance of this chart is helped by (1) making it look just like the form he has been using for years, (2) making it easy to read, and (3) if it is to be placed on a wall, having a full-color pin-up above the chart to ensure that it will not be misplaced.

Instructions for Students

This book should be used as a supplement to the usual college course in operations research or management science. Some problems are provided in this text, but they are not keyed to any given chapter. Experience has shown this author that problems at the end of Chapter X are usually attacked with the methods to be found in Chapter X. The student will notice considerable commentary on the fact that the data fed into most models is usually not accurate. This was brought home to this author most strongly when he realized that an operations research group in an oil company was worried about the third decimal place in a linear programming output, when the data on viscosity of the input stream had been obtained by a refinery worker rubbing it between his fingers! Indeed, one of the bigger problems faced by the young management scientist is to construct a model for which data may be obtained quickly and at reasonable cost. Woolsey's bean-counter theorem states that: "Either the data is not present, or if it is present, it is not in the right form." The student is strongly encouraged to include in his school program sufficient accounting so that he can use data with some understanding of the assumptions under which it was collected. For example, many economic order quantity models require that an inventory holding cost for some item be obtained before the model may be implemented. The budding analyst who asks the accounting organization to give him the holding cost will discover that they will give it to him every time. The good accountant will ask the analyst if he wants a first-in first-out, last-in first-out, lower-of-cost-or-market, or a how-we-do-it figure. If the analyst states that his model needs only one number, the usual reaction of the bean counter is to "give 'em what they want" just to get rid of the interruption. The student is therefore encouraged to give his instructors a bad time by asking questions on how the data is to be collected for models, assuming that such data *can* be collected if it exists. Finally, the student is encouraged to inquire as to how to "sell" the model once it is defined. It the instructor feels that this is of no importance, because the method is so elegant that it will "sell itself," *ask for evidence*. If the instructor states that he is interested only in the theory, you must decide if that is also your interest and make plans accordingly. There is no question that theory is important as a conceptual tool; however, to allow a student to think that he is a competent management scientist because he has earned a degree in it on the basis of good absorption of theory is tragic. The student should therefore examine what is presented to him as "useful" theory with care.

Instructions for Teachers

This manual can best be used for teaching in the following way. The presentation of Quick & Dirtys in this text should be contrasted with the presentation that appears in journals or other books. The methods presented here are deficient in that mathematical rigor and elegance of presentation is ignored. The original articles contain carefully listed assumptions concerning the conditions under which optimality may be proven. The purpose of the original presentation was to provide a conceptual base for further development. The presentation here is solely on the basis of maximizing utility, an inelegant diety at best. After exposing students to, say, the two- and three-machine job-shop methods, homeworks are suggested in which the students have to construct their own Quick & Dirty for a case where different machine orderings are allowed. The Quick & Dirty must be written so that a person *with that problem* can understand and use it. Then take it to a man with that problem. Assign a grade of F to anything he finds difficult to understand. Assign a grade of C to anything he can *read*. Assign a grade of A to the few he would like to put on a wall and *use*. The instructor will find that only a few homeworks like this will do wonders for the student's ability to communicate effectively. Occasionally a student will argue that he is only being trained to deal with dumb bastards, and as since he does not expect to be dealing with such people too often, this form of homework is not necessary. It should be gently but firmly pointed out to such a student that God must have loved the dumb bastards, because he made so many more of them then he did students like himself.

Operations Research
for Immediate Application
A Quick & Dirty Manual

one

A Survey of Quick & Dirty Methods for Production Scheduling

General Discussion
A Note on the Shop Scheduling Program

For some years there has been a communication gap of some magnitude between the theory of production scheduling and its day-to-day implementation. Elegant formulations of production scheduling appear in journals but for some reason never seem to be implemented. The academic who ventures into a real-world situation is often made to feel as Sir Isaac Newton must have felt the first time he informed a major of the Royal Artillery that "The cannon ball will fall right *there,* neglecting air resistance." The major's reply has not, alas, been recorded for posterity. However, there is little doubt as to its content. As a result, Sir Isaac went back to Cambridge and the major went back to doing it the way he had always done it—both with a solid contempt for the other.

Unfortunately, much the same situation still exists today in production scheduling. The academics cheerfully go on designing total systems that seem to work only with at least a 5-megabuck computer, three management scientists to explain the printout, and ten programmers to keep it working. The author recently had the unnerving experience of being asked to demonstrate some of the simple-minded programs in this book, on his Brand X mini-computer, for the production-scheduling organization of a large plant manufacturing Brand Y computers. Upon close questioning, the head production-scheduling supervisor admitted that the overall system really didn't work too well in practice. The reason given was that because the system considered *everything,* no one group was ever able to figure out why they should follow it.

What was wanted was something that *they* could use and understand. At this point the author proceeded to pass out copies of the "Quick & Dirty" methods to be found later in this book. It can be seen that implementation of these techniques on a teletype on the shop floor is quite straightforward. For this purpose some programs with examples are provided. By looking at the sample program one can see that the basic idea is that of *conversation.* That is, there is no barrier between the user and the computer. The computer can be made to get the data needed from the scheduler in English, and to return the answer in the same language.

A NOTE ON THE SHOP SCHEDULING PROGRAM

The shop scheduling program examples that follow the Quick & Dirtys allow the user to do conversationally the eight different shop scheduling methods covered in this chapter. The program will first ask the user how many processes (machines) the jobs have to go through Note that a whole shop may be considered as one process if desired. If the user answers that there is only one process, the program then goes into the subroutine for one-process scheduling and proceeds to request how many jobs are to be processed over the one machine or process. After the user gives an answer, the program will then allow the user to choose which of five different criteria to use to optimize the schedule. After the appropriate criterion is chosen, the program will then request such data as is needed for optimization of the schedule. When the schedule is optimized, the answer is printed out in the form of the sequence that is optimum for the criterion chosen. The program then will ask if it is desired to "optimize this problem another way?" If the answer is yes, the program will return to the place where the user is asked which of the criteria he wishes to choose.

If the user inputs two different processes, the program branches to the Johnson two-machine method discussed in the first Q & D. However, if the answer to the next question, "All jobs processed in same order thru the shop?," is "no," the program then branches to the Q & D that considers the two-machine case with technological ordering. In this case not only the processing time data is required but also the order that each job is to be processed through the two machines.

If the user inputs that there are three or more processes, the program branches to the Q & D based on the method of Gupta, and proceeds accordingly. The program itself (Program 1.1) will be found in the appendix.

The following 'Quick & Dirty' methods are, of course, severly restricted in their applications. Most assume that in-process inventory is available, and that no passing of jobs is allowed. Others assume that all jobs have equal priority. Candor compels the author to admit that the only place he ever found where all jobs had the same priority was the County Clerk's office of Jefferson County, Colorado.

The methods presented here are not to be considered as panaceas, but only as methods that work (under the conditions stated) and that are simple to teach and to understand. All that this author has accomplished here is to act as a translator. The following Quick & Dirtys are the creative work of the referenced authors only.

Q & D TO MINIMIZE TOTAL PROCESSING TIME FOR N JOBS ON TWO MACHINES

This method, due to S. M. Johnson [1], is probably one of the most referenced papers in production scheduling. It makes the usual amusing assumptions about inventory being present when needed, no passing of jobs, set-up and tear-down time included, no breakdowns, and no strikes. However, the importance of this method is that it requires only that the user can read, can tell when one number is larger than another, and knows left from right.

Q & D TO MINIMIZE TOTAL PROCESSING TIME FOR N JOBS ON THREE MACHINES (SPECIAL CASE)

This method, also due to Johnson [1], is the natural extension of the above problem to the three-machine case. In this extension, Johnson shows that if the minimum processing time over all jobs on the first process is greater than or equal to the maximum processing time on the second process, then an equivalent two-machine job shop problem can be constructed. Further, another equivalent two-machine problem can be constructed if the minimum processing time on the third process is greater than or equal to the maximum element in the second process. In short, if the second process is dominated by either the first or the last, we can solve the problem as an equivalent two-machine problem.

Q & D TO MINIMIZE TOTAL PROCESSING TIME FOR N JOBS ON M MACHINES

With three or more machines, we leave the world of optimal solutions and enter the area of heuristic techniques. The procedure presented here was extensively explored by Dudek and Ghare [2], and shows that the logical extension of Johnson's three-machine special case to more machines is a reasonable and easy-to-use heuristic. This method is presented here, but careful note should be made of another approach to this problem, presented later in this manual, based on the method of J. N. D. Gupta. Gupta's method is perhaps easier for hand computation; however, the programming of both methods is quite straightforward.

Q & D TO MINIMIZE THE NUMBER OF LATE JOBS FOR N JOBS ON ONE MACHINE

This method is due to Moore [3] and is one of two methods presented in his paper. The method assumes that all jobs are of equal priority, and makes the usual above-stated assumptions on inventory, and so forth. The method is extremely simple, and a form can be easily designed for scheduling use. The most obvious application is to treat the whole shop as one process and operate from there. A sample of the program for conversational mode treatment is provided.

This method has its greatest potential in its use as a defensive weapon for production schedulers in their continuing war with the marketing or sales departments. Let us now explore how this method can be used to sandbag the opposition into letting the production run optimally. Let us assume that our production scheduler had used this method to come up with an optimum schedule that will make only one job late out of six jobs to be done. The law of scheduling states that: "The late job is the one that becomes the hot job." Now we usually assume that all accounts are equal, but we know that they never are. As soon as the optimal schedule is posted, the salesman whose job is to be late will scream. He will usually bring pressure to bear higher up, which will force the production scheduler to place his job in the sequence in such a way that it is on time. This, naturally, means that somebody else is going to be late. He will scream in turn, forcing another change in the schedule, and so on. However, the alert production scheduler can use this situation to his own advantage in the following way. The scheduler resequences the jobs in such a way that the late job is now on time. This will cause, say, two other jobs to be late. The scheduler then sends a memo to the person whose job *was* late, stating that his job will now be on time at the expense of making two other salesman's jobs late. A copy of this memo is also sent to the two salesmen whose orders will *now* be late. These two people will usually form a coalition against the first salesman. They will take the memo to the sales manager, who must then determine the relative priorities. He is, of course, confronted with the following facts: (1) Two salesmen are getting shafted to benefit one, and (2) the two salesmen would get off his back if he allowed the *optimal* schedule to stand. The scheduler has adroitly called for the basin by presenting an original optimal schedule and then, reluctantly, changing it. This is known as "doing a Pontius Pilate." This same procedure can be adapted to most of the methods in this study, if the scheduler is sure what the criterion of operation actually *is*. If, for example, the criterion is to minimize the maximum tardiness that can take place over all possible sequences that may be considered, then the reader should consider the Q & D to do that, which appears later in this book. Under these conditions we can consider that the latter Q & D would really be minimizing the maximum scream that would take place whenever a particular job would be late. The proper choice of the method, however, will always depend upon the circumstances of the particular situation, especially the politics at that time.

Q & D TO MINIMIZE TOTAL PROCESSING TIME FOR N TECHNOLOGICALLY ORDERED JOBS ON TWO MACHINES

We consider the problem of scheduling a batch of technologically ordered jobs through two machines in such a way as to minimize total processing time. By technological ordering we mean that (1) some jobs are done on machine A or B only, (2) some jobs are done on both machines in order A, B, and (3) some jobs are done on both machines in order B, A. The usual assumption is made that all the necessary inventory to do the jobs is present when you need it, and that all the jobs are of equal importance. The method used is due to Jackson and, because it is an optimum method, should properly be called a Quick & *Clean*. Again it should be noted that the "goodness" of the answer is directly related to the accuracy of the estimated processing times supplied to the method. In this author's experience, forecasts can be amazingly accurate when the method is used by the man who will have to do the work. Conversely, forecasts tend to have large error when the data is collected from one man, processed elsewhere, and returned to the first man. For a discussion of this and related phenomena, the reader is directed to the author's paper, "On Lying to Industrial Engineers and Other Traditional Shop Practices" (*forthcoming*).

Q & D TO MINIMIZE TOTAL PROCESSING TIME FOR TWO TECHNOLOGICALLY ORDERED JOBS ON M MACHINES

This Quick & Dirty considers the case where you have two high-priority jobs that must be processed on each of M machines, but *not* in the same order. The method shown is due to Akers and Friedman [4], and was extended by Szwarc [5]. The method assumes that the total processing time on job 1 is greater than or equal to the total processing time on job 2. When this is the case, the best schedule can be shown to be the one with the least number of vertical segments. For justification, the author refers the reader to p. 783 in reference [5]. It should be noted that this method is really a Quick & *Clean* if the method in [5] is used. *This* Q & D will not always find the "optimal" schedule.

Q & D TO MINIMIZE SET-UP TEAR-DOWN TIME
ON ONE MACHINE

This Quick & Dirty looks at the problem of processing a batch of jobs on one machine with large set-up tear-down times relative to processing times. We essentially assume that the time to peel the steel, once the job is set up, is pretty much a constant. Our only problem is to find a sequence of jobs such that the machine operator has to do the minimum of set-up and tear-down to get all the jobs done in the least amount of time. The author should point out that students have some difficulty understanding the fact that when a machinist has the job running, he cannot be expected to use his time for the benefit of the company in some other set-up or machine operation. When this problem arises, this author refers to the "least measurable instant of time law," which states: "The least measurable instant of time is the time that elapses between the time a foreman tells a machinist to pick up a paint brush and the time everybody is out on strike."

Q & D TO MINIMIZE TOTAL PROCESSING TIME
FOR N JOBS ON M MACHINES (FLOWSHOP SCHEDULING)

This Quick & Dirty considers the case where you have N jobs that must move through the same sequence of M machines in the same order. A method for this problem was presented by this author earlier. However, the recent brilliant work of the production scheduler J. N. D. Gupta has supplied a much more compact and quicker method, which is reproduced here. Upon comparison with the first method, it can be seen that this method can be eye-balled with considerably less effort than the previous one. Again we assume small transfer times, inventory present when necessary, no breakdowns, good estimates, and a sense of humor.

Q & D TO MINIMIZE THE SUM OF COMPLETION TIMES
OR SUM OF WAITING TIMES ON ONE PROCESS
Q & D TO MINIMIZE THE WEIGHTED SUM OF COMPLETION TIMES
OR WEIGHTED SUM OF WAITING TIMES ON ONE PROCESS

In this part of the survey we consider the one-process case, scheduling with two different criteria. We assume that we have a batch of jobs with known or estimated processing times. The problem of optimizing from among the possible sequences is examined from two points of view. The first point of view is that all the jobs are of equal importance, and we wish to find the sequence that minimizes the sum of completion times. The second point of view is that the jobs are *not* of equal importance and that we can rank them in some way; in this case we wish to find the sequence that will minimize the weighted sum of completion times. It was shown by Smith [6] that the sum of completion times and the sum of waiting times differ by a constant. Therefore, if we minimize the sum of completion times, we automatically minimize the sum of waiting times. This author does not assert that the criterion of minimizing sum of completion times is especially good, but the reader is directed to the study of optimality criteria for flowshops by Gupta and Dudek [7]. In this study 190 flowshop problems were generated, ranging in size from four jobs–four machines to 40 jobs–40 machines. The statistical analysis of this study showed that a ranking of criteria from best to worst is as follows:

1. Job waiting cost + penalty cost.
2. Job waiting cost + machine idle cost.
3. Penalty cost + machine idle cost.
4. Penalty cost.
5. Job waiting cost.
6. Make-span.
7. Machine idle cost.

In the same study, comparison of the above criteria was made against a criterion of total opportunity cost, which was a composite of the above criteria. It is not hard to see why the first criterion above should do well. In most small job shops within this author's experience, penalty cost dominates almost all other costs. And job waiting cost gets a lot of attention, because pallets of in-process inventory tend to attract the attention of supervisors and the bean-counter types from accounting. As a further comment on penalty costs, consider the proverb: "If things are on time, I get no points, because after all that's my job; but if things are late, I'm in trouble."

The reason for this state of affairs is simply that an on-time job is good news, but a late job is a *problem*. I tell my students that if the plant supervisor tells you, "Being on time often enough balances out being late," *don't believe it*.

Q & D TO MINIMIZE THE MAXIMUM TARDINESS
ON ONE PROCESS (DUE DATE RULE)

This Quick & Dirty assumes that you have a batch of jobs with known due dates and known or estimated processing times. The criterion in this case is that we wish to minimize tardiness on any given job. In the real shop situation we assume that if any given job is late, then someone will scream. We further assume that the scream is proportional to the lateness of the job. Our desire, therefore, is to find the sequence of jobs that will minimize the loudest scream. It should also be noted that this method guarantees that all other screams will be less than or equal to the loudest one (which is minimized.)

All three of the above Quick & Dirties are *optimal;* the proofs are found in reference [6].

Q & D TO MAXIMIZE THE MINIMUM TARDINESS ON ONE PROCESS (SLACK RULE)

Stated as above, the slack rule provokes the usual reaction that "No one in their right mind would want to do *that!*" When confronted with a shop situation, however, it seems intuitively "right." The reason is simply that the job with the least difference between when it is due and how long it will take to complete is the job that seems most likely to be *late*. By getting that job done first, we "get it out of our hair," confident that we have now minimized our worries. The assumption here that all jobs are equally important is seldom the case. And further adjustment using priorities is strongly suggested.

Q & D FOR N JOBS ON TWO MACHINES, ARBITRARY START AND STOP LAGS, COMMON SEQUENCE

In 1959 L. G. Mitten of the University of British Columbia made a very useful extention of S. M. Johnson's two-machine job shop problem. It very nicely takes care of the common industrial problem of overlapping production, or the problem of accumulating a minimum necessary backlog of materials before proceeding to the next portion of a job. Also, as pointed out by Mitten, transport time between machines can easily be incorporated in the start and stop lags. As an example, if the second process needs product from the first process, proper setting of the start and stop lags can insure that the second machine is not idle due to lack of material. The Quick & Dirty presented here is a slightly modified version of the one found in Mitten's original paper, done by Mr. Robert Bass.

Q & D FOR REDUCING FLOW TIME WITHOUT INCREASING MAXIMUM TARDINESS

In an earlier Quick & Dirty it was shown that the sequence that minimizes maximum tardiness on one process results simply from arranging the jobs in increasing order of due dates. Of course, it is realized that if this sequence were adhered to strictly, some jobs with far-off due dates would be continually delayed. Often, we want to apply a *secondary criteria* to improve a sequence that is already optimum in some sense. This Quick & Dirty assumes that we have already minimized maximum tardiness and now wish to minimize the sum of completion times, such that no job is made later than the present latest job. The proof of optimality is found in the reference at the bottom of the Quick & Dirty. The presentation here is due to Judith Grange.

Q & D METHOD TO MINIMIZE MAXIMUM TARDINESS ON ONE PROCESS SUBJECT TO PRECEDENCE CONSTRAINTS

The above Quick & Dirty concerns itself with reducing flow time *after* a due-date ordering has ben used to minimize maximum tardiness. This Quick & Dirty is used to minimize maximum tardiness on one process when we have the additional requirement that some jobs must be done before others. Note that this procedure will indeed minimize the maximum tardiness on a given job; however, it can also result in a majority of the jobs being close to the tardiness of the latest job. Stated another way, if we minimize the maximum lateness that can take place, we *may* increase the mean lateness of other jobs. In short, the latest job may not be very late by this method, but we trade off this advantage by possibly increasing the number of late jobs.

CITED REFERENCES

[1]   Johnson, S. M., "Optimal Two and Three Stage Production Schedules with Set-Up Times Included," *Naval Research Logistics Quarterly,* Vol. 1, 1954, pp. 61–68.

[2]   Dudek, R. A., and Ghare, P. M., "Make-Span Sequencing on M-Machines," *Journal of Industrial Engineering,* Vol. 18, No. 2, Jan. 1967, pp. 131–134.

[3]   Moore, J. M., "An N Job, One Machine Sequencing Algorithm for Minimizing the Number of Late Jobs," *Management Science,* Vol. 15, No. 1, Sept. 1968, pp. 102–109.

[4]   Akers, S. B., and Friedman, J., "A Non-Numerical Approach to Production Scheduling Problems," *Operations Research,* Vol. 3, 1955, pp. 429–442.

[5]   Szwarc, W., "Solution of the Akers-Friedman Scheduling Problem," *Operations Research,* Vol. 8, 1969, pp. 782–788.

[6] Smith, W. E., "Various Optimizers for Single Stage Production," *Naval Research Logistics Quarterly,* Vol. 3, 1956, pp. 59–66.

[7] Gupta, J. N. D., and Dudek, R. A., "An Optimality Criteria for Flowshop Schedules," *AIIE Transactions,* Vol. 3, No. 3, Sept. 1971, pp. 199–205.

Quick & Dirty TO MINIMIZE TOTAL PROCESSING TIME
N JOBS ON TWO MACHINES

Method

To find the sequence of jobs on two processes, that minimizes total elapsed time:

1. Set up a table of the processing time as shown in the example below.

i	A_i	B_i
1	9	1
2	8	3
3	5	4
4	7	11
5	6	8
6	2	9

where

A_i = processing time for job i
 on machine A, and

B_i = processing time for job i
 on machine B.

2. Find the smallest A_i or B_i in the table. (In the example, it is $B_1 = 1$). Ties may be broken arbitrarily.
3. If the smallest value is to your left, schedule this job *first* on machine A. If the value is to your right, schedule this job *last* on machine B.
4. Cross off the assigned job and go to step 2.

Example

It should be noted that if we Gantt chart the above problem, as shown below, in the sequence 1, 2, 3, 4, 5, 6, we shall get a total of 57 hr elapsed time with 19 hr of idle time on machine B.

A	9		8		5		7		6	2			
B	/////////	1	////////	3	/	4	//	11			8	9

However, by using the above sequencing procedure we get the optimal sequence 6, 5, 4, 3, 2, 1. When Gantt charted, below, we obtain 38 hr elapsed time with 2 hr of idle time on machine B.

A	2	6	7	5	8		9			
B	//	9	8		11		4	3	1	

Reference

Johnson, S. M., "Optimal Two and Three Stage Production Schedules with Set-Up Times Included," *Naval Research Logistics Quarterly*, Vol. 1, 1954, pp. 61–68.

CONVERSATIONAL LIST FOR THE Q & D TO MINIMIZE TOTAL PROCESSNG TIME, *N* JOBS ON TWO MACHINES

```
APICS SHOP SCHEDULING

HOW MANY PROCESSES ARE THERE?:2

 2 PROCESS SCHEDULING TO MINIMIZE TOTAL TIME THRU SHOP

HOW MANY JOBS ARE THERE?:6

ALL JOBS PROCESSED IN SAME ORDER THRU THE SHOP?:YES

PLEASE ENTER PROCESSING TIME FOR EACH JOB ON PROCESS
1 THRU  2 SEPARATED BY COMMAS
JOB  1:9,1
JOB  2:8,3
JOB  3:5,4
JOB  4:7,11
JOB  5:6,8
JOB  6:2,9

OPTIMUM SEQUENCE TO

MINIMIZE TOTAL PROCESSING TIME IS:
 6
 5
 4
 3
 2
 1

DO MORE SCHEDULING?:NO
```

Quick & Dirty TO MINIMIZE TOTAL PROCESSING TIME, N JOBS ON THREE MACHINES (SPECIAL CASE)

Method

Johnson, in the reference cited below, shows that if certain conditions were met, one can generate an optimal schedule for the three-machine case. Assume a table of processing times as shown:

i	A_i	B_i	C_i	where A_i = processing time for job i on machine A, and
1	7	8	10	B_i = processing time for job i on machine B, and
2	8	2	10	
3	6	7	9	C_i = processing time for job i on machine C.
4	13	1	8	
5	6	2	11	

If the minimum element in column A_i is greater than or equal to the maximum element in column B_i

or

If the minimum element in column C_i is greater than or equal to the maximum element in column B_i

then

From the three-machine problem above, form the two-machine problem by summing all the $A_i + B_i$, and the $B_i + C_i$. Then solve as a two-machine problem.

Example

i	$A_i + B_i$	$B_i + C_i$
1	15	18
2	10	12
3	13	16
4	14	9
5	8	13

The two-machine table generated from the above problem is

The optimal sequence, by the two-machine method, is 5, 2, 3, 1, 4. This optimal sequence will result in a total elapsed time of 56 hr with 8 hr idle time on machine C and 21 hr idle time on machine B. However, if we sequence the jobs in the sequence 1, 2, 3, 4, 5, we get 63 hr of elapsed time, 15 hr idle time on machine C and 41 hr idle time on machine B.

Reference

Johnson, S. M., "Optimal Two and Three Stage Production Schedules with Set-Up Times Included," *Naval Research Logistics Quarterly*, Vol. 1, 1954, pp. 61–68.

Quick & Dirty TO MINIMIZE TOTAL PROCESSING TIME, N JOBS ON M MACHINES

Method

Let

$$t_{ij} \begin{cases} i = 1, \ldots, N \\ j = 1, \ldots, M \end{cases}$$

represent the time for processing the ith job on the jth machine in an N-job, M-machine make-span sequencing problem. The p auxiliary N-job, two-machine problems can be defined as follows: In the kth auxiliary problem, where k is the sequence number and is equal to or less than p, let:

$$A_{i1}k = \sum_{j=1}^{k} t_{ij} = \text{the processing time for the } i\text{th job on the "first machine"}$$

$$A_{i2}k = \sum_{j=m+1-k}^{m} t_{ij} = \text{the processing time for the } i\text{th job on the "second machine"}$$

It should be noted that the model for auxiliary problems limits the number of auxiliary problems to $M - 1$ or less, that is, $p \leq M - 1$.

For each auxiliary problem, S. M. Johnson's N-job, two-machine method is used to determine the optimal sequences, thus generating $S_1, S_2, \ldots, S_p$ for the p auxiliary problems. The best sequence among these is chosen on the basis of minimum total processing time.

Reference

Campbell, H. G., "A Heuristic Technique for Near Optimal Production Schedules," unpublished MS thesis, Texas Technological College, 1966.

Quick & Dirty TO MINIMIZE THE NUMBER OF LATE JOBS, N JOBS ON ONE MACHINE

Assume that you have a batch of N jobs with known due dates (d_i), and known or estimated processing times (p_i).

Method

1. Order the jobs from left to right in order of increasing due dates. That is, the job with the earliest due date is ordered first and the job with latest due date is ordered last. This is the current sequence.
2. Using the current sequence, find the first late job. If one is found, go to step 3. If no job is late, stop. The sequence is optimal.
3. Look at the subsequence up to and including the late job. Find the job in this subsequence with the largest processing time and reject it. Consider the resulting sequence as the current sequence. Go to step 2.

Example

Consider the six jobs below with due dates and process times:

i	1	2	3	4	5	6
d_i	9	13	16	22	35	40
p_i	6	8	4	7	21	11
Total	6	14*				

The first late job, as indicated by the asterisk, is the second. It also has the largest processing time, so reject it.

We then have the new sequence:

i	1	3	4	5	6	2
d_i	9	16	22	35	40	13
p_i	6	4	7	21	11	8
Total	6	10	17	38*		

The first late job is the fifth. Again, it has the largest processing time and is rejected.

The optimal sequence results, which is 1, 3, 4, 6, 2, 5. Four jobs are on time; two are late.

Reference

Moore, J. M., "An N Job, One Machine Sequencing Method for Minimizing the Number of Late Jobs," *Management Science,* Vol. 15, No. 1, Sept. 1968, pp. 102–109.

CONVERSATIONAL LIST FOR THE Q & D TO MINIMIZE THE NUMBER OF LATE JOBS, N JOBS ON ONE MACHINE

APICS SHOP SCHEDULING

HOW MANY PROCESSES ARE THERE?:1

ONE PROCESS SCHEDULING

HOW MANY JOBS ARE THERE?:6

CHOOSE ONE OF THE FOLLOWING TO OPTIMIZE:

1. MINIMIZE SUM OF COMPLETION TIMES

2. MINIMIZE WEIGHTED SUM OF COMPLETION TIMES

3. MINIMIZE MAXIMUM TARDINESS

4. MAXIMIZE MINIMUM LATENESS

5. MINIMIZE NUMBER OF LATE JOBS

INPUT A 1, 2, 3, 4, OR 5 AS WANTED:5

INPUT PROCESSING TIMES FOR EACH JOB, SEPARATED BY COMMAS
AND ENDING WITH A CARRIAGE RETURN
6,8,4,7,21,11

INPUT DUE DATES FROM NOW FOR EACH JOB, SEPARATED BY COMMAS
AND ENDING WITH A CARRIAGE RETURN
9,13,16,22,35,40

LATE JOB IS 2
LATE JOB IS   5
OPTIMUM SEQUENCE TO

5. MINIMIZE NUMBER OF LATE JOBS
  1
  3
  4
  6
  2
  5

  4 JOBS ON TIME,   2 JOBS LATE

OPTIMIZE THIS JOB ANOTHER WAY?:NO

DO MORE SCHEDULING?:NO

Quick & Dirty TO MINIMIZE TOTAL PROCESSING TIME FOR N TECHNOLOGICALLY ORDERED JOBS ON TWO MACHINES

Assume that you have a batch of jobs to be processed on two machines, A and B. Some jobs are to be processed only on machine A; some only on machine B. Some are to be processed on both machines A and B in the order A, B; and some are to be processed on both machines A and B in the order B, A. We want to minimize total processing time.

Method

1. Put the jobs to be done only on machine A in any order.
2. Put the jobs to be done only on machine B in any order.
3. Find the best ordering of the jobs to be processed on both machines in order A, B by Johnson's method.
4. Find the best ordering of the jobs to be processed on both machines in order B, A by Johnson's method.
5. On machine A, the optimal order should be the ordering found from step 3, followed by the ordering from step 1, followed by the ordering from step 4.
6. On machine B, the optimal order should be the ordering found from step 4, followed by the ordering from step 2, followed by the ordering from step 3.

Example

The following nine jobs have estimated processing times and orderings:

Job	Mill (A)	Lathe (B)	Order
1	20	0	M
2	70	40	M–L
3	30	60	M–L
4	0	70	L
5	10	30	M–L
6	30	10	L–M
7	20	70	L–M
8	0	40	L
9	40	0	M

1. Put the jobs to be done on the mill only in the order (1, 9).
2. Put the jobs to be done on the lathe only in the order (4, 8).
3. Build a table of processing times for the jobs to be done on both machines in the order: mill, lathe.

Job	Mill	Lathe
2	70	40
3	30	60
5	10	30

Now, using Johnson's rule, we find that the job with the least processing time is job 5. As the least processing time is on the *left*, we therefore schedule job 5 *first*. The next smallest processing time is again on the left in job 3, so job 3 is scheduled as the second job, leaving job 2 as the last one. Thus the order is (5, 3, 2).

4. Johnson's rule is used again on the jobs to be done on both machines in the order lathe, mill. The table of processing times is:

Job	Lathe	Mill
6	10	30
7	70	20

Johnson's rule gives the ordering (6, 7).

5. The optimal ordering on machine A (the mill) is:

	(5, 3, 2)	(1, 9)	(6, 7)
From:	step 3	step 1	step 4

6. The optimal ordering on machine B (the lathe) is:

	(6, 7)	(4, 8)	(5, 3, 2)
From:	step 4	step 2	step 3

References

Johnson, S. M., "Optimal Two and Three Stage Production Schedules with Set-Up Times Included," *Naval Research Logistics Quarterly*, Vol. 1, 1954, pp. 61–68.

Jackson, J. R., "An Extension of Johnson's Result on Job-Lot Scheduling," *Naval Research Logistics Quarterly*, Vol. 3, No. 3, Sept. 1956, pp. 201–204.

CONVERSATIONAL LIST FOR THE Q & D TO MINIMIZE TOTAL PROCESSING TIME FOR *N* TECHNOLOGICALLY ORDERED JOBS ON TWO MACHINES

```
APICS SHOP SCHEDULING

HOW MANY PROCESSES ARE THERE?:2

 2 PROCESS SCHEDULING TO MINIMIZE TOTAL TIME THRU SHOP

HOW MANY JOBS ARE THERE?:9

ALL JOBS PROCESSED IN SAME ORDER THRU THE SHOP?:NO

PLEASE ENTER PROCESSING TIMES FOR EACH JOB ON PROCESS
1 AND 2 SEPARATED BY COMMAS

ENTER ORDER AS:   1,2 OR 2,1 OR 1,0 OR 0,2

JOB  1:20,0
ORDER?:1,0

JOB  2:70,40
ORDER?:1,2

JOB  3:30,60
ORDER?:1,2

JOB  4:0,70
ORDER?:0,2

JOB  5:10,30
ORDER?:1,2

JOB  6:30,10
ORDER?:2,1

JOB  7:20,70
ORDER?:2,1

JOB  8:0,40
ORDER?:0,2

JOB  9:40,0
ORDER?:1,0


OPTIMAL ORDER ON MACHINE 1 IS:
    5   3   2   1   9   6   7

OPTIMAL ORDER ON MACHINE 2 IS:
    6   7   4   8   5   3   2

DO MORE SCHEDULING?:NO
```

Quick & Dirty TO MINIMIZE TOTAL PROCESSING TIME FOR TWO TECHNOLOGICALLY ORDERED JOBS ON M MACHINES

Assume that you have two priority jobs that must be processed on each of M machines, but *not* in the same order. Consider the example below.

Job 1	Order of machines	A	C	E	F	B	D	G
	Processing times	1	2	2	4	3	1	1
Job 2	Order of machines	C	F	A	E	G	D	B
	Processing times	3	3	2	1	1	1	2

Method

1. On a piece of graph paper, lay out the processing times of job 1, in order of processing on the $(X–X)$ horizontal axis. Lay out the processing times of job 2 in order of processing on the $(Y–Y)$ axis. (Total time on job 1 $\geq$ Total time on job 2.)
2. Find the oblong area where the processing time on the first machine required by job 1 crosses the processing time required by that same machine on job 2. Crosshatch this area. This area is the time when both jobs require the same machine.
3. Complete step 2 for all remaining machines.
4. Starting at the origin, draw (if possible) a 45° line until you hit an oblong. Follow the edge of the oblong until you can again go at 45°.[1] Continue until you have completed all processing. (*Justification:* If we started at the origin and went to the right, job 1 would be done, letting job 2 wait. And if we went straight up, job 2 would be done, letting job 1 wait. *Therefore* a 45° line through a square indicates progress on *both* jobs.)
5. Starting at the origin, count each square through which the line passes. This is the time for the optimal schedule. Check to see which job has to wait by looking for horizontal (job 2 waits) or vertical (job 1 waits) lines.

[1] If you hit the *corner* of an oblong, follow both edges, generating alternative solutions. Pick the line that gives the least processing time.

Example

Following the above steps for the example we create Figure 1. Note that as we *do* hit a corner, we must examine *both* routes. The upper route will take 4 hr of idle time on job 2, and the lower, 2 hr, therefore the lower route is the best solution. *Remember:* The optimal schedule is the one with the least number of vertical segments.

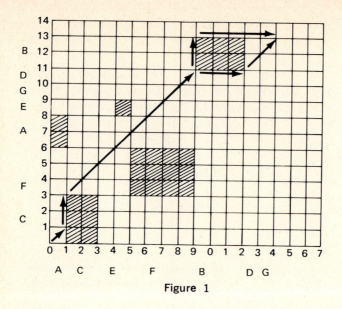

Figure 1

Reference

Akers, S. B., and Friedman, J., "A Non-Numerical Approach to Production Scheduling Problems," *Operations Research*, Vol. 3, 1955, pp. 429–442.

Quick & Dirty TO MINIMIZE SET-UP TEAR-DOWN TIME ON ONE MACHINE

Assume that you have a batch of N jobs to be processed on one machine. The set-up tear-down times are very large relative to processing times. Because some of the jobs use the same jigs or part of the set-up as another job, different set-up tear-down times occur in going between different jobs. Also, the time needed to go from job A to job B may not be the same as the time to go from B to A. We would like to find a Quick & Dirty sequence of jobs to minimize the set-up tear-down time for these jobs.

Method

1. First set up a table of set-up tear-down times to go from one job to another. Arrange the table so that the first row shows the time to go from the first job to all of the other jobs, and so on for the other rows. You might have a table like the one below:

To job	1	2	3	4	5
From job					
1	✕	1	5	7	3
2	✕	✕	2	4	6
3	✕	8	✕	6	3
4	✕	5	4	✕	8
5	✕	8	2	3	✕

2. Reduce the table by subtracting the minimum element in each row from all other elements in the row. For the example we would have the table below:

To job	1	2	3	4	5
From job					
1	✕	0	4	6	2
2	✕	✕	0	2	4
3	✕	5	✕	3	0
4	✕	1	0	✕	4
5	✕	6	0	1	✕

3. Start at the X in row 1, column 1. Draw a horizontal line to the smallest number in that row and circle it. If there are two smallest numbers, pick either one.
4. Draw a vertical line from the circled number to the X in that column.
5. Draw a horizontal line to the smallest number in *that* row and circle it. (Once a number is circled in a column, no more assignments can be made in that column. So go to the next smallest number and circle *it*.)
6. Repeat steps 3 and 4 until all jobs are assigned in a sequence. The sequence follows the line to the circled numbers in the columns.

For the above example the sequence is (1, 2, 3, 5, 4) with a time of 9 units of time.

Reference

Gavett, J. W., "Three Heuristic Rules for Sequencing Jobs to a Single Production Facility," *Management Science,* Vol. 11, No. 8, June 1965, pp. 166–176.

Quick & Dirty TO MINIMIZE TOTAL PROCESSING TIME FOR N JOBS ON M MACHINES (FLOWSHOP SCHEDULING)

Assume that you have a batch of jobs to be processed on 1, 2, . . ., M machines as in the example below. All jobs must be processed on the machines in the same order. We want to minimize total processing time for all jobs.

1. Form a table of processing times as shown in the example below.

   Machine A_i B_i C_i D_i E_i where A_i = processing time for job i on machine A

Job 1	4	3	7	2	8
2	3	7	2	8	5
3	1	2	4	3	7
4	3	4	3	7	2

   M_i = processing time for job i on machine M

2. For each job determine the "job value" (JV_i) as follows:

$$JV_i = \frac{K}{\text{minimum of } [(A_i + B_i) \text{ or } (B_i + C_i) \text{ or } \ldots (L_i + M_i)]}$$

   where

   $K = +1$ *if* processing time on first machine $\geq$ processing time on last machine (i.e., $A_i \geq M_i$)

   $K = -1$ *if* processing time on first machine $<$ processing time on last machine (i.e., $A_i < M_i$)

3. Now put these job values in order from smallest to largest. This is the answer.

Example

For the above example we already have the table of processing times, so we may proceed at once to step 2 and determine JV_1, . . . , JV_4 as follows:

$$JV_1 = \frac{-1}{\min[(4+3), (3+7), (7+2), (2+8)]} = -\tfrac{1}{7}, \quad \text{as } 4 < 8, (A_i < E_i)$$

$$JV_2 = \frac{-1}{\min[(3+7), (7+2), (2+8), (8+5)]} = -\tfrac{1}{9}, \quad \text{as } 3 < 5, (A_i < E_i)$$

$$JV_3 = \frac{-1}{\min[(1+2), (2+4), (4+3), (3+7)]} = -\tfrac{1}{3}, \quad \text{as } 1 < 7, (A_i < E_i)$$

$$JV_4 = \frac{+1}{\min[(3+4), (4+3), (3+7), (7+2)]} = +\tfrac{1}{7}, \quad \text{as } 3 \geq 2, (A_i \geq E_i)$$

From step 3 we have the order $-\frac{1}{3}$, $-\frac{1}{7}$, $-\frac{1}{9}$, $+\frac{1}{7}$, or the schedule 3, 1, 2, 4. Total elapsed time for this schedule is 34 hr versus 33 hr for the optimum schedule.

Reference

Gupta, J. N. D., "A Functional Heuristic Algorithm for the Flowshop Scheduling Problem," *Operational Research*, Vol. 22, No. 1, March 1971, pp. 39–48.

CONVERSATIONAL LIST FOR THE Q & D TO MINIMIZE TOTAL PROCESSING TIME FOR N JOBS ON M MACHINES (FLOWSHOP SCHEDULING)

```
AFICS SHOP SCHEDULING

HOW MANY PROCESSES ARE THERE?:5

 5 PROCESS SCHEDULING TO MINIMIZE TOTAL TIME THRU SHOP

HOW MANY JOBS ARE THERE?:4

PLEASE ENTER PROCESSING TIME FOR EACH JOB ON PROCESS
1 THRU  5 SEPARATED BY COMMAS
JOB  1:4,3,7,2,8
JOB  2:3,7,2,8,5
JOB  3:1,2,4,3,7
JOB  4:3,4,3,7,2

OPTIMUM SEQUENCE TO

MINIMIZE TOTAL PROCESSING TIME IS:
 3
 1
 2
 4

DO MORE SCHEDULING?:NO
```

Quick & Dirty TO MINIMIZE SUM OF COMPLETION TIMES OR SUM OF WAITING TIMES ON ONE PROCESS

Assume that we have a batch of jobs with known or estimated processing times. We wish to sequence jobs in such a way that (1) the sum of completion times or (2) the sum of waiting times is minimized. Both of the above may be taken care of at once, because it can be shown that these sums differ by a constant value.

Method

1. Order the jobs from left to right in order of increasing processing time.
2. Stop; the optimal sequence has been found.

Example

Consider the eight jobs given below with processing times as shown:

Job no.	1	2	3	4	5	6	7	8	
Processing time	7	2	3	4	9	11	5	4	(sum of
Total time	7	9	12	16	25	36	41	45	completion times = 191)
Waiting time	0	7	9	12	16	25	36	41	(sum of waiting time = 146)

(completion time
  — waiting time = 45)

Now, by using step 1 above, we have the following schedule:

Job no.	2	3	4	8	7	1	5	6	
Processing time	2	3	4	4	5	7	9	11	(sum of
Total time	2	5	9	13	18	25	34	45	completion times = 151)
Waiting time	0	2	5	9	13	18	25	34	(sum of waiting time = 106)

(completion time
  — waiting time = 45)

Notice that application of the method has reduced both sums by 40.

Reference

Smith, W. E., "Various Optimizers for Single-Stage Production," *Naval Research Logistics Quarterly*, Vol. 3, 1956, pp. 59–66.

CONVERSATIONAL LIST FOR THE Q & D TO MINIMIZE SUM OF COMPLETION TIMES OR SUM OF WAITING TIMES ON ONE PROCESS

```
APICS SHOP SCHEDULING

HOW MANY PROCESSES ARE THERE?:1

ONE PROCESS SCHEDULING

HOW MANY JOBS ARE THERE?:8

CHOOSE ONE OF THE FOLLOWING TO OPTIMIZE:

1.   MINIMIZE SUM OF COMPLETION TIMES

2.   MINIMIZE WEIGHTED SUM OF COMPLETION TIMES

3.   MINIMIZE MAXIMUM TARDINESS

4.   MAXIMIZE MINIMUM LATENESS

5.   MINIMIZE NUMBER OF LATE JOBS

INPUT A 1, 2, 3, 4, OR 5 AS WANTED:1

INPUT PROCESSING TIMES FOR EACH JOB, SEPARATED BY COMMAS
AND ENDING WITH A CARRIAGE RETURN
7,2,3,4,9,11,5,4

OPTIMUM SEQUENCE TO

1.   MINIMIZE SUM OF COMPLETION TIMES
2
3
4
8
7
1
5
6


OPTIMIZE THIS JOB ANOTHER WAY?:NO

DO MORE SCHEDULING?:NO
```

Quick & Dirty TO MINIMIZE WEIGHTED SUM OF COMPLETION TIMES OR WEIGHTED SUM OF WAITING TIMES ON ONE PROCESS

Assume that we have a group of jobs with known or estimated processing times (P_i). Some jobs are more important than others, so we assign a positive weight (w_i) to each of the jobs. The greater the weight, the more important the job. We wish to sequence the jobs in such a way that the weighted sum of completion times is minimized.

Method

1. Order the jobs from left to right in order of the increasing ratio P_i/w_i.
2. Stop; this is the optimal sequence.

Example

Consider the six jobs given below with processing times as shown:

Job no.	1	2	3	4	5	6	
Processing time	2	4	7	6	3	2	
Completion time	2	6	13	19	22	24	
Weight	4	6	2	1	5	3	(sum of weighted
w_i Compl. T_i	8	36	26	19	110	72	completion times = 271)

Now, by the use of step 1 above, we have the following sequence. The ratio of processing time to weight for the jobs 1, 2, . . . , 6 are ½, ⅔, ½, 6, ⅗, ⅔, giving

Job no.	1	5	2	6	3	4	
Processing time	2	3	4	2	7	6	
Completion time	2	5	9	11	18	24	
Weight	4	5	6	3	2	1	(sum of weighted
w_i Compl. T_i	8	25	54	33	36	24	completion times = 180)

It is now interesting to see the result if the jobs had been scheduled simply in order of importance (i.e., decreasing weight).

Job no.	2	5	1	6	3	4	
Processing time	4	3	2	2	7	6	
Completion time	4	7	9	11	18	24	
Weight	6	5	4	3	2	1	(sum of weighted
w_i Compl. T_i	24	35	36	33	36	24	completion times = 188)

Let the reader beware that this example result does not confirm any present opinions, because it is very easy to construct examples where the last ordering is a disaster *when using this priority rule.*

Reference

Smith, W. E., "Various Optimizers for Single-Stage Production," *Naval Research Logistics Quarterly,* Vol. 3, 1956, pp. 59–66.

CONVERSATIONAL LIST FOR THE Q & D TO MINIMIZE SUM OF COMPLETION TIMES OR SUM OF WAITING TIMES ON ONE PROCESS

```
APICS SHOP SCHEDULING

HOW MANY PROCESSES ARE THERE?:1

ONE PROCESS SCHEDULING

HOW MANY JOBS ARE THERE?:6

CHOOSE ONE OF THE FOLLOWING TO OPTIMIZE:

1.   MINIMIZE SUM OF COMPLETION TIMES

2.   MINIMIZE WEIGHTED SUM OF COMPLETION TIMES

3.   MINIMIZE MAXIMUM TARDINESS

4.   MAXIMIZE MINIMUM LATENESS

5.   MINIMIZE NUMBER OF LATE JOBS

INPUT A 1, 2, 3, 4, OR 5 AS WANTED:2

INPUT PROCESSING TIMES FOR EACH JOB, SEPARATED BY COMMAS
AND ENDING WITH A CARRIAGE RETURN
2,4,7,6,3,2

INPUT WEIGHTS ON JOBS, SEPARATED BY COMMAS
AND ENDING WITH A CARRIAGE RETURN
4,6,2,1,5,3

OPTIMUM SEQUENCE TO

2.   MINIMIZE WEIGHTED SUM OF COMPLETION TIMES
  1
  5
  2
  6
  3
  4

OPTIMIZE THIS JOB ANOTHER WAY?:NO

DO MORE SCHEDULING?:NO
```

Quick & Dirty TO MINIMIZE THE MAXIMUM TARDINESS ON ONE PROCESS (DUE DATE RULE)

Assume that we have a batch of jobs with known due dates, counted from today, and known or estimated processing times. Out of all the possible ways to sequence these jobs we wish to choose the sequence that will minimize the maximum tardiness on any given job.

1. Order the jobs from left to right in order of increasing due date.
2. Stop; the optimal sequence has been found.

Example

Consider the seven jobs shown below with due dates and processing times as shown:

Job no.	1	2	3	4	5	6	7
Due date	21	18	15	2	7	9	25
Processing time	4	7	2	1	6	5	9
Total time	4	11	13	14	20	25	34

Note that if this sequence is used, the lateness of the jobs is as follows (OT = on time):

Job no.	1	2	3	4	5	6	7
	OT	OT	OT	12	13	16	9

The first three jobs are on time, and the maximum lateness occurs for job 6 and is 16.

Now, by step 1 above, we have the following schedule:

Job no.	4	5	6	3	2	1	7
Due date	2	7	9	15	18	21	25
Processing time	1	6	5	2	7	4	9
Total time	1	7	12	14	21	25	34
Lateness	OT	OT	3	OT	3	4	9

Maximum lateness occurs for job 7 and is 9.

Reference

Smith, W. E., "Various Optimizers for Single-Stage Production," *Naval Research Logistics Quarterly,* Vol. 3, 1956, pp. 59–66.

CONVERSATIONAL LIST FOR THE Q & D TO MINIMIZE THE MAXIMUM TARDINESS ON ONE PROCESS (DUE DATE RULE)

```
APICS SHOP SCHEDULING

HOW MANY PROCESSES ARE THERE?:1

ONE PROCESS SCHEDULING

HOW MANY JOBS ARE THERE?:7

CHOOSE ONE OF THE FOLLOWING TO OPTIMIZE:


1.  MINIMIZE SUM OF COMPLETION TIMES

2.  MINIMIZE WEIGHTED SUM OF COMPLETION TIMES

3.  MINIMIZE MAXIMUM TARDINESS

4.  MAXIMIZE MINIMUM LATENESS

5.  MINIMIZE NUMBER OF LATE JOBS

INPUT A 1, 2, 3, 4, OR 5 AS WANTED:3

INPUT DUE DATES FROM NOW FOR EACH JOB, SEPARATED BY COMMAS
AND ENDING WITH A CARRIAGE RETURN
21,18,15,2,7,9,25

OPTIMUM SEQUENCE TO

3.  MINIMIZE MAXIMUM TARDINESS
 4
 5
 6
 3
 2
 1
 7


OPTIMIZE THIS JOB ANOTHER WAY?:NO


DO MORE SCHEDULING?:NO
```

Quick & Dirty TO MAXIMIZE THE MINIMUM TARDINESS ON ONE PROCESS (SLACK RULE)

Assume that we have a batch of jobs with known due dates, counted from today, and known or estimated processing times. Out of all the possible ways to sequence these jobs, we wish to choose the sequence that will maximize the minimum tardiness (or lateness).

Method

1. Order the jobs from left to right in order of increasing (due date minus processing time).
2. Stop; the optimal sequence has been found.

Example

Consider the three-job problem below with all six sequences.

	1			2			3		
Job no.	1	2	3	1	3	2	2	1	3
Due date	4	3	9	4	9	3	3	4	9
Processing time	15	7	4	15	4	7	7	15	4
Total time	15	22	26	15	19	26	7	11	26
Lateness	11	19	17	11	10	23	4	18	17
Tardiness	11	19	17	11	10	23	4	18	17

	4			5			6		
Job no.	2	3	1	3	1	2	3	2	1
Due date	3	9	4	9	4	3	9	3	4
Processing time	7	4	15	4	15	7	4	7	15
Total time	7	11	26	4	19	26	4	11	26
Lateness	4	2	18	−5	15	23	−5	8	18
Tardiness	4	2	18	0	15	23	0	8	18

If we form the quantity $(d_i - p_i)$ for jobs 1, 2, and 3, we get −11, −4, 5, respectively. This can be seen to generate the first sequence above, or 1, 2, 3. The minimum lateness for these six sequences is (11, 10, 4, 2, −5, −5). Maximizing the minimum lateness is done by sequence 1, 2, 3. The minimum tardiness for these six sequences is (11, 10, 4, 2, 0, 0). Maximizing the minimum tardiness is again done by sequence 1, 2, 3.

Reference

Conway, R. W., Maxwell, W. L., and Miller, L. W. *Theory of Scheduling,* Addison-Wesley, Don Mills, Ontario, 1967, pp. 31–32.

CONVERSATIONAL LIST FOR THE Q & D TO MAXIMIZE THE MINIMUM TARDINESS ON ONE PROCESS (SLACK RULE)

APICS SHOP SCHEDULING

HOW MANY PROCESSES ARE THERE?:1

ONE PROCESS SCHEDULING

HOW MANY JOBS ARE THERE?:7

CHOOSE ONE OF THE FOLLOWING TO OPTIMIZE:

1. MINIMIZE SUM OF COMPLETION TIMES

2. MINIMIZE WEIGHTED SUM OF COMPLETION TIMES

3. MINIMIZE MAXIMUM TARDINESS

4. MAXIMIZE MINIMUM LATENESS

5. MINIMIZE NUMBER OF LATE JOBS

INPUT A 1, 2, 3, 4, OR 5 AS WANTED:4

INPUT PROCESSING TIMES FOR EACH JOB, SEPARATED BY COMMAS
AND ENDING WITH A CARRIAGE RETURN
6,8,4,7,21,11,13

INPUT DUE DATES FROM NOW FOR EACH JOB, SEPARATED BY COMMAS
AND ENDING WITH A CARRIAGE RETURN
9,13,16,22,35,40,50

OPTIMUM SEQUENCE TO

4. MAXIMIZE MINIMUM LATENESS
  1
  2
  3
  5
  4
  6
  7

OPTIMIZE THIS JOB ANOTHER WAY?:NO

DO MORE SCHEDULING?:NO

Quick & Dirty FOR N JOBS, TWO MACHINES, ARBITRARY START AND STOP LAGS, AND COMMON SEQUENCE

Assume that you have a batch of jobs that must be processed on two machines, A and B. Each job must be run first on machine A, then on B. Associated with each job are start and stop lags. The start lag is the minimum time that must elapse between starting a job on machine A and starting it on machine B. The stop lag is the minimum time that must elapse between finishing a job on machine A and finishing it on machine B. We desire to find the sequence such that total time to complete all jobs on both machines is a minimum.

Method

Let a_i = start lag for job i. A_i = processing time for job i on the first machine

Let b_i = stop lag for job i. B_i = processing time for job i on the second machine

Fill in the form below with the above data.

1	2	3	4	5	6	7	Running order
i	a_i	A_i	b_i	B_i			
1	1	4	3	5	2	3	1
2	4	7	1	4	4	1	5
3	4	3	6	4	5	6	2
4	6	2	4	4	6	8	3
5	4	6	3	4	5	3	4

1. If $a_i > A_i + b_i - B_i$, enter column 6 with a_i and column 7 with $a_i + B_i - A_i$.
   Otherwise, enter column 6 with $A_i + b_i - B_i$ and column 7 with b_i.
2. Now solve columns 6 and 7 as a two-machine job shop.

Example

From the above example, we fill in columns 6 and 7 as shown. The Johnson two-machine job shop method gives the optimum sequence: 1,3,4,5,2.

Reference

Mitten, L. G., A Scheduling Problem, *Journal of Industrial Engineering*, Vol. X, No. 2, March–April 1959, pp. 131–135.

Quick & Dirty FOR REDUCING FLOW TIME
WITHOUT INCREASING MAXIMUM TARDINESS

After a shop scheduler has used the preceding Q & D to minimize maximum tardiness on one process, he may use this technique to reduce total flow time without making any job later than the present latest job.

Method

1. Fill in a form as shown in the example below with processing times and due dates, figured in terms of days from now. Then calculate the completion times and tardiness for each job and enter these in the appropriate rows as shown.
2. Find the largest value of lateness, circle it, and call it T_{max}.
3. Find the difference between the sum of the processing times for all jobs and the due date for each job. Enter this number in the first blank row.
4. Circle numbers in this last row that are less than or equal to T_{max}.
5. If there are *no* circled numbers in the last row, write the last job number in the last remaining blank on the Order Line. If there *are* circled numbers, write the job number of the job with the largest processing time in the last remaining blank on the Order line.
6. Cross out the job that was just assigned a position in the schedule. Return to step 3, until all jobs are assigned in the schedule. (Note that the sum of the processing times has now changed as a job has been eliminated from consideration.)

Example

Job no.	1	2	3	4	5	6	... N
Processing time	5	8	3	13	7	1	
Due date	3	5	17	21	22	27	
Completion time	5	13	16	29	36	37	
Tardiness	2	8	0	8	(14)	10	
$\Sigma p_i - d_i$	34	32	20	16	15	(10)	
$\Sigma p_i - d_i$	33	31	19	15	(14)		
$\Sigma p_i - d_i$	26	24	(12)	(8)			
$\Sigma p_i - d_i$	(13)	(11)	(-1)				
$\Sigma p_i - d_i$	(5)		(-9)				
$\Sigma p_i - d_i$			(-14)				
Order	3	1	2	4	5	6	

Note that the largest tardiness occurs for job 5 and $T_{max} = 14$. We discover that only job 6 has a $\Sigma p_i - d_i$ less than or equal to T_{max}. Therefore job 6 is indeed last. With job 6 crossed out, total processing time equals 36; only job 5 satisfies the requirements and it is put last. The next pass circles two jobs. Choosing on the basis of greatest p_i gives job 4. Continuing we find that the optimum sequence is 3 1 2 4 5 6.

Reference

Heck, H., and Roberts, S., A Note On The Extention Of A Result On Scheduling With Secondary Criteria, *Naval Research Logistics Quarterly*, Vol. 19. No. 2, June 1972, pp. 403–405.

Quick & Dirty TO MINIMIZE MAXIMUM TARDINESS ON ONE PROCESS SUBJECT TO PRECEDENCE CONSTRAINTS

Assume that we have a batch of jobs with known due dates, counted from today, and known or estimated processing times. Also, we have arbitrary precedence constraints that require some jobs to be done before others. We wish to find the sequence that will minimize the maximum tardiness on any given job.

1. Order the jobs from *last to first*, always choosing next from among the jobs currently available (i.e., jobs that have no jobs to be done after them) a job with the latest possible due date.

Example

Consider the following group of jobs to be done:

Job	Due date	Processing time	Jobs that must follow this one
1	4 days	1 days	4, 5
2	7	3	3, 4
3	5	2	6
4	6	2	none
5	5	3	none
6	4	2	none

Note: There are two optimal sequences; both will have the same maximum tardiness of 7 days for job 4.

To start we first note that jobs 4, 5, and 6 have no jobs following, and so are currently available. We choose the one with the latest due date, putting job 4 last. This leaves 5 and 6 currently available. Choosing again on latest due date puts job 5 next to last. However, we note that job 6 and job 1 are now available because jobs 4 and 5, *which must follow job 1,* have been selected. Note that we have a tie, which may be broken arbitrarily in favor of job 1. As job 6 is the only available job, it is chosen next. Only job 3 is now eligible; it is chosen, thus leaving job 2 to go first. This process is demonstrated below. (Circle indicates chosen job.)

Jobs currently available	④ 5 6	⑤ 6	① 6	⑥	③	②
Deadline	6 5 4	5 4	4 4	4	5	7
Day chosen job finished	13	11	8	7	5	3
Days chosen job late	7	6	4	3	0	0

Note that at step 3 we could just as easily have chosen job 6, resulting in another optimum solution as mentioned above.

Reference

Lawler, E. L., Optimal Sequencing of a Single Machine Subject To Precedence Constraints, *Management Science*, Vol. 19, No. 5. Jan. 1973, p. 544.

two

Quick & Dirty Methods in Inventory Control

The Economic Order Quantity

How to Use the EOQ

Discussion of Individual Q & D's

Q & D EOQ for Constant Demand, No Shortages Allowed

Q & D EOQ for Constant Demand, Shortages Allowed

Q & D EOQ for Uncertain Demand, Shortages Allowed, Discrete Units

Q & D for Finding Optimal Range of Shortage Costs for the EOQ for Uncertain Demand, Shortages Allowed, Discrete Units

Q & D for Finding the EOQ for Varying Forecasted Demand, No Shortages Allowed

Q & D for Finding the EOQ for Varying Forecasted Demand, Where All Stock Needed in a Period Must Be Available at Start of Period

Q & D To Decide Whether or Not to Stock an Item

Q & D To Decide Whether or Not to Stock an Item (Health Care and Hospital Version)

Q & D for Economic Packaging Frequency for Items Jointly Replenished

For some time, the textbooks have considered the Wilson economic order quantity (EOQ) equation as the cornerstone of inventory theory. In its most basic form, one representation can be shown as

$$\text{total expected cost} = \frac{CIQ}{2} + \frac{FS}{Q}$$

where

Q = the economic order quantity in pieces
S = the reorder or set-up cost in dollars
C = the unit cost in dollars per piece
F = the usage rate in pieces per unit time
I = the inventory carrying cost in dollars per piece per unit time

There are as many representations of this model as there are authors in the field. It is very rare for two authors to use the same notation for this model. Examination of the model shows that we are really finding the trade-off point between increasing carrying costs and decreasing set-up costs as Q gets larger. A graph can easily be drawn (see Figure 2) of the two pieces of the above model, the two pieces added together to give the total cost curve, and the minimum point found by inspection.

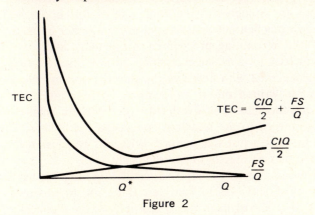

Figure 2

An application of geometric programming, discussed elsewhere in this work, shows that at the optimum solution, the contribution of carrying cost and the contribution of set-up cost to total cost should be equal. Differentiation of the above equation will generate the usual formula:

$$Q^* = \sqrt{\frac{2FS}{CI}}$$

A glance at the formula will show why it is often referred to as "the square-root rule." Many elaborate methods have been defined to calculate the optimum reorder point for inventory problems, but the Wilson EOQ seems to "hang in there" on day-to-day operations. Why is this? The best justification for this model is that it is jolly robust in the face of gross goofs in the forecasted demand. It is usually the case that the curve is very flat in the vicinity of the optimum order quantity. The result is that if a large error is made in the number ordered, only a small difference will result in the total expected cost.

However, the basic problem with the Wilson EOQ is that the input data is often so bad that even a sociologist would not consider using it to base conclusions on. Let us look for a moment at I, the inventory carrying cost in dollars per piece per unit time. Where does this number come from? We are really attempting to evaluate the proportional expense of having one piece of this item sit on the shelves of the company for some specific time. We know at once that the holding cost is at least the value of the money earned if we took the unit cost and placed it at interest in a bank. And, assuming that the company in question has a rate of gain greater than that of the local bank, a better lower bound on this inventory carrying cost would be the rate of profit of the corporation at large. In short, if we cannot be better off by paying the inventory carrying cost on the item than we would be if we put its cost out at interest, we shouldn't hold any. In the Instructions for Students at the beginning of this book, we pointed out that how this figure is arrived at requires a rather intimate understanding of the accounting procedures in the individual situation. If the student tries to consider everything, he will discover that he must become concerned with how fast the shelving and inventory control equipment is written off, to say nothing of how much the time clocks cost and the amount of overhead in the workers' salaries. He will usually be forced to the reluctant conclusion that "There is no damn reason for it, it's just our policy." With this conclusion let us now consider another cost factor in the same light.

If we consider S, the reorder or set-up cost, we discover that we have a whole new group of variables to consider. If we are to sit down and determine the *actual* cost incurred to reorder, we must consider the cost of the forms used, the hourly rate of every person involved, the internal charge for computer time to process the order (including the rate at which the computer equipment is being written off), to say nothing of the proportion of the written-off cost of the building. If we are dealing with a set-up cost for production, we at once enter the morass of labor agreements, standard time measurements, machine breakdowns, strikes, and other minor difficulties. The reader should beware of considering such costs as being "too small to consider seriously." Many a small businessman has gone under because the small costs ate him alive. However, a good rule to use is the following: "If the cost of gathering the data is greater than the expected saving generated by the right use of the data, *don't do it.*" Now that this author has planted some seeds of doubt in the mind of the reader with respect to the use of the EOQ, he is forced to say how the EOQ *should* be used.

HOW TO USE
THE EOQ

The EOQ can best be used to test the opinions on the values of the costs given by the user. By this we mean that if the user says that he is using a carrying charge per year of 20 percent and a set-up cost of $3245.63 per run, *plug in what he is doing and see if I and S come out that way.* In short, don't solve the model for the optimum EOQ (Q*). Take two different orders in recent company history done by this man, say Q_1 and Q_2, using the total costs actually generated, and solve for the values of I and S. If you do this and come out with value of $S = \$2134.45$ and $I = 35$ percent, you might have reason to believe that he is not doing either (1) what he told you he was doing or (2) what he *thinks* he is doing. In this author's experience, the *EOQ* is *never* followed exactly in practice, because priority changes, machine breakdowns, or anticipated or real labor troubles always militate against it. Economic order quantities concerned with more complex forms and situations, such as price breaks, obsolescence costs, or multicommodity cases, are not considered here because they are, by definition, beyond the scope of this manual. Now that the user has been sufficiently warned against careless use of the EOQ, we present the two most basic forms for discussion.

Q & D FOR EOQ FOR CONSTANT DEMAND,
NO SHORTAGES ALLOWED

In this form the problem is often referred to as the "Jato bottle problem." We assume that a contractor has signed a contract with the federal government to supply Jato bottles to a local Air Force base. The rate at which he must supply them is defined in his contract. However, if he runs short, the fat, sole-source, cost-plus-140% contract is instantly terminated and given to another senator's brother-in-law. He is thus highly motivated to make sure that he has no shortages, and must use a model that will assure him that he will never be short. For derivation of this model the reader is referred to Churchman, Ackoff, and Arnoff, referenced at the end of the Quick & Dirty for this case. This model has appeared in numerous forms with different symbols in virtually every book on production and inventory control and operations research. Again, its principal virtue is ease of use for the unsophisticated. Indeed a series of slide-rule-type calculators have been made and distributed for years for EOQ calculations by such firms as Van De Mark Associates of Dallas. The method is effective as long as the real situation is allowed to override the answer found by using this method.

Q & D FOR EOQ FOR CONSTANT DEMAND,
SHORTAGES ALLOWED

This form is really an expanded form of the above case. Those readers so inclined can show, by using limits, that the formulas for the optimum values of the EOQ and the total expected cost for this case will collapse to those of the first case above if the shortage cost is allowed to approach infinity. With this model we have introduced yet another ill-defined variable cost. The "shortage" cost per unit of goods for a specified period can be very difficult to pin down. In usual operations research jargon, this can be called a "lost opportunity cost." That is, if we are short, we have not only lost the profit we could have made from the sale, but we may have lost some customer good will. By this we mean that the customer may be sufficiently discouraged by our not having the item on hand that he will shop elsewhere next time. It is easily seen that the difficulties of accurately determining the cost of the lost good will is nontrivial. It becomes even more difficult when one considers the fact that lost good will will usually affect not just one item, but rather may determine whether the customer will return for *anything*.

Q & D FOR EOQ FOR UNCERTAIN DEMAND,
SHORTAGES ALLOWED, DISCRETE UNITS
Q & D FOR FINDING OPTIMAL RANGE OF SHORTAGE COSTS
FOR THE EOQ FOR UNCERTAIN DEMAND,
SHORTAGES ALLOWED, DISCRETE UNITS

We would probably use this model mostly in the area of finding the optimum number of replacement parts to stock. Optimum in the sense used here means that we wish to stock the level that minimizes both shortage cost and inventory holding cost. This model also requires a history of demand or failure rate over time that may be very difficult to obtain. Clearly, data on such matters supplied by the vendor should be viewed with some suspicion.

This model has another useful attribute. Once a given level of inventory has been chosen, it can be plugged back into the model to show an upper and lower bound on shortage cost for which that level is optimum. The user should consider that these bounds tell him how much "insurance" he is buying by stocking to the given level. Thus it may be found that it is very cheap (or very expensive) to increase the stock level to obtain more insurance. This attribute is shown in the example in the Quick & Dirty.

A perfect example of this kind of model took place in a nameless iron and steel company a few years ago. An overhead gantry of immense size provided the means by which a series of blast furnaces were charged. The operation of the gantry was controlled by a driver who sat in a control room at the top. The planetary gear in the drive train disintegrated without warning. The pieces were removed, but no spare was available. By the time a spare was obtained, two blast furnaces had cooled. Now, when a blast furnace cools, you must rebuild it. To forstall this ever happening again, ten of these gears, at roughly $250, were ordered. This leads us immediately to the question: If none is too few, how many in inventory is too many? The derivation of this model may be found in the appropriate reference. Again, we may have some difficulty estimating the shortage cost. In this case the problem lies in the fact that it may be very hard to estimate correctly the damage or loss of production by the part not being present when needed. At best, a lower bound on loss can be calculated.

Q & D FOR FINDING THE EOQ FOR VARYING FORECASTED DEMAND, NO SHORTAGES ALLOWED

Q & D FOR FINDING THE EOQ FOR VARYING FORECASTED DEMAND, WHERE ALL STOCK NEEDED IN A PERIOD MUST BE AVAILABLE AT START OF PERIOD

As mentioned earlier, the greatest failing of deterministic EOQ's is that they cannot take into consideration large variations of demand over time. These two Quick & Dirtys are based on the brilliant work of Silver and Meal and effectively solve this problem, given that you can trust your cost figures as before. The real danger with these methods is that the forecast may be *really* bad. However, it may be seen that the methods are relatively insensitive to gross errors in forecasting if these variations are known and prepared for by the user. That is, the user must have sense enough to distrust the source of his forecast

Q & D FOR DECIDING WHETHER OR NOT TO STOCK AN ITEM

Usually when a firm has demand for a given item, the decision to stock is automatic unless the item is so costly that the inventory holding cost could be significant. Once the decision has been made to stock the item, we would like to think that some optimum economic order quantity should be established through either EOQ or MRP methods. However, experience shows that usually no real consideration is given to the decision of stocking or not stocking in the first place. The authors contend that this is the case because no simple procedure for evaluation of such decisions is generally known. The method presented here is due to Fenske, as modified by Silver, and the derivations are found in the appropriate references cited below.

Let:
R = selling price per item
P = production cost per item ($P = 0$ if wholesaler or retailer)
N = average order size
G = estimated percent of sales lost if item is *not* stocked (decimal fraction)
H = holding cost per item per year
T = annual production rate (if manufacturing)
S = set-up cost per production run (if manufacturing)
  = ordering cost per order (if wholesaler or retailer)

Rule: Calculate D_c according to one of the following methods:
1. Manufacturing

$$D_c = \frac{2SH}{A^2 + 2SH/T}$$

2. Wholesaler or retailer

$$D_c = \frac{2SH}{A^2}$$

where, in both cases, $A = G(R - P) + (1 - G)(S/N)$.
If the item has an annual demand less than D_c, do *not* stock it.
Needless to say, this Quick & Dirty should be used with care, and the D_c calculated by this rule should not be considered hard and fast because of the considerable uncertanties introduced by variations in the demand and manufacturing rates and in G. Some experimentation will show that the value of G can make a profound difference in the value of D_c, and a number of independent estimates

should be taken and the variation compared before a final decision is made.

Q & D FOR DECIDING WHETHER OR NOT TO STOCK AN ITEM (HEALTH CARE AND HOSPITAL VERSION)

This Quick & Dirty came about because an industrial engineer from a hospital in Ontario, Canada asked if the previous Quick & Dirty could not be modified to apply to the problem inventory of a hospital. By "problem" inventory we mean that we are dealing with inventory that is (1) expensive, (2) perishable, (3) hard to get, (4) hard to store, or (5) all of the above. Notice that in order to use the concepts of the last Q & D for not stocking, we have to move ourselves out of the profit-oriented world. As an example of some of the differences, note that whereas before we had a "production cost per item," we now have a "cost of item to the hospital." And whereas before we could consider "percent of sales lost if item not stocked," we now have to consider that a stockout could result in loss of life. This results in the "emergency use" designation in *this* Q & D as being equivalent to 100 percent loss of sales (lives). We realize that the value of a life may not be set, as the sociologists do, at plus infinity. However, it would take a damned secure hospital administrator to set it (publicly) at any less.

Q & D FOR ECONOMIC PACKAGING FREQUENCY FOR ITEMS JOINTLY REPLENISHED

We concern ourselves here with the problem of determining how often we should do a production run for an item that is sold in packages of different sizes and types. The model used is the usual EOQ model discussed before, extended to the case of M different package types. We assume that each package will have a different set-up and holding cost, and an annual demand that is constant over time. We further assume that we will have a major set-up cost incurred each time any or all of the different package types are run. The author of this method, S. K. Goyal, makes the extremely important point that if application of a method such as this does not reduce costs, a likely reason is that the costs of the system to "do it better" may be eating up all the savings that could be made. This is a point that, to our knowledge, has never before appeared in the journal *Operations Research*. He is to be congratulated for sneaking it past the editors. The Quick & Dirty here is due to Franklin E. Grange II.

Quick & Dirty EOQ FOR CONSTANT DEMAND, NO SHORTAGES ALLOWED

Method

Assume that the inventory holding cost per unit per unit time (C_1) is known, as well as the set-up cost per production run (C_s). We are required to supply R units at a constant rate over time T with no shortages. If Q^* is the defined economic order quantity (EOQ) such that total expected cost is minimized, then the formula to be minimized is:

Total expected cost = inventory holding cost + set-up cost

$$= \frac{C_1 T Q}{2} + \frac{C_s R}{Q}$$

The optimum (least cost) EOQ is

$$Q^* = \sqrt{\frac{2 C_s R}{C_1 T}}$$

A production run should be run every

$$t^* = \sqrt{\frac{2 C_s T}{C_1 R}} \text{ time units}$$

The total expected cost is

$$TEC^* = \sqrt{2 C_1 T C_s R}$$

Example

Say that C_1 is \$0.17 (holding cost per item per day), set-up cost per production run is $C_s = \$3000$, the requirement is 5500 items ($R = 5500$), and we require them at a constant rate over 365 working days ($T = 365$). At once, from above we have that the EOQ is

$$Q^* = \sqrt{\frac{2(3000)(5500)}{0.17(365)}} = 730 \text{ units}$$

A production run should be run every

$$t^* = \sqrt{\frac{2(3000)(365)}{0.17(5500)}} = 49 \text{ days}$$

The total expected cost for this schedule is

$$TEC = \sqrt{2(0.17)(365)(3000)(5500)}$$
$$= \$45250$$

Reference

Churchman, C. W., Ackoff, R. L., Arnoff, E. L. *Introduction to Operations Research,* Wiley, New York, 1957.

CONVERSATIONAL LIST FOR THE Q & D FOR THE EOQ FOR CONSTANT DEMAND, NO SHORTAGES ALLOWED (PROGRAM 2.1)

```
INVENTORY MODEL, NO SHORTAGES ALLOWED

PLEASE INPUT HOLDING COST PER ITEM PER DAY
AS A DECIMAL FRACTION PERCENTAGE OF ITEM SELLING PRICE:0.17

PLEASE INPUT SETUP COST PER PRODUCTION RUN:3000

HOW MANY ITEMS ARE NEEDED:5500

OVER HOW MANY DAYS:365

OPTIMAL INTERVAL BETWEEN PRODUCTION RUNS IS   48 DAYS.

OPTIMAL ORDER QUANTITY IS      729 UNITS.

COST OF THIS PRODUCTION SCHEDULE IS $  45250.97

DO ANOTHER?:NO

THANK YOU AND GOODBYE
```

Quick & Dirty EOQ FOR CONSTANT DEMAND, SHORTAGES ALLOWED

Method

Assume that the inventory holding cost per unit per unit time (C_1), the set-up cost per production run (C_s), and the shortage cost per unit per unit time (C_2) are all known. We are required to supply R units at a constant rate over time T with shortages allowed. If S is the desired inventory level at the start of a cycle and Q is the economic order quantity, the formula to be minimized is

Total expected cost = inventory holding cost + shortage cost + set-up cost

$$= \frac{C_1 T S^2}{2Q} + \frac{(Q-S)^2 C_2 T}{2Q} + \frac{C_s R}{Q}$$

The optimum (least cost EOQ) is

$$Q^* = \sqrt{\frac{2C_s R}{C_1 T} \cdot \frac{C_1 + C_2}{C_2}}$$

The desired inventory level is

$$S^* = \sqrt{\frac{2C_s R}{C_1 T} \cdot \frac{C_2}{C_1 + C_2}}$$

A production run should be run every

$$t^* = \sqrt{\frac{2TC_s}{RC_1} \cdot \frac{C_1 + C_2}{C_2}} \text{ time units}$$

The total expected cost is

$$TEC^* = \sqrt{2C_1 TC_s R} \sqrt{\frac{C_1 + C_2}{C_2}}$$

Example

Say that we have $C_1 = \$0.17$ (holding cost per item per day), $C_2 = \$5.00$ (shortage cost per item per day), $R = 5500$ (requirement), $C_s = \$3000$ (set-up cost per production run), $T = 365$ days. From the above we have that the EOQ is

$$Q^* = \sqrt{\frac{2(3000)(5500)}{0.17(365)} \cdot \frac{0.17 + 5.00}{5.00}} = 743 \text{ units}$$

A production run should be run every

$$t^* = \sqrt{\frac{2(3000)(365)}{0.17(5500)} \cdot \frac{0.17 + 5.00}{5.00}} = 50 \text{ days}$$

The total expected cost for this schedule is

$$TEC = \sqrt{2(0.17)(365)(3000)(5500)\frac{(0.17 + 5.00)}{5.00}}$$

$$= \$44500$$

Note further that as $S^* = 706$ units, we will run short $(Q - S) = (743 - 706) = 37$ units at the end of each scheduling period.

Reference

Churchman, C. W., Ackoff, R. L., and Arnoff E. L., *Introduction to Operations Research,* Wiley, New York, 1957.

CONVERSATIONAL LIST FOR THE Q & D FOR THE EOQ FOR CONSTANT DEMAND, SHORTAGES ALLOWED (PROGRAM 2.2)

```
INVENTORY MODEL WITH SHORTAGES

PLEASE INPUT HOLDING COST PER ITEM PER DAY
AS A DECIMAL FRACTION PERCENTAGE OF ITEM SELLING PRICE:0.17

PLEASE INPUT SETUP COST PER PRODUCTION RUN:3000

HOW MANY ITEMS ARE NEEDED:5500

OVER HOW MANY DAYS:365

PLEASE INPUT SHORTAGE COST PER ITEM PER DAY (IN $):5.00

OPTIMAL INTERVAL BETWEEN PRODUCTION RUNS IS      51 DAYS.

OPTIMAL ORDER QUANTITY IS      777 UNITS.

SHORTAGE AT END OF PRODUCTION CYCLE IS      24 UNITS.

COST OF THIS PRODUCTION SCHEDULE IS $   46672.81

DO ANOTHER?:NO

THANK YOU AND GOODBYE
```

Quick & Dirty EOQ FOR UNCERTAIN DEMAND, SHORTAGES ALLOWED, DISCRETE UNITS

We assume that a company has a crucial part, with a well-recorded history of failure, that can stop a production line completely if it is not on hand when needed. We further assume that the cost of purchasing spares (C_1) and the estimated cost of being short (C_2) are known. If S^* is the required inventory level to minimize total cost, the formula to be minimized is

$$\text{Total expected cost} + C_1 \sum_{r=0}^{S} P(r)(S-r) + C_2 \sum_{r=S+1} P(r)(r-S)$$

where S = number of parts in stock
  r = number required
  $P(r)$ = probability that r will be required

Method

1. From the history table of past number of replacements needed, construct a table of probabilities that S or less parts would be required, $P(r \leq S)$.
2. Calculate the value of $C_2/(C_1 + C_2)$.
3. Looking at the table generated by step 1, find the value of S for which

$$P(r \leq S-1) < \frac{C_2}{C_1 + C_2} < P(r \leq S)$$

This is S^*.

Example

Vidrio De Mexico, S. A., a glass company, has a motor-driven conveyer for moving plate glass from the oven to the shearing station. The conveyer has one crucial part that costs $250. On the one occasion when the part failed at Vidrio, the losses in production and so forth until a new one was obtained were estimated at $49,750. A history of replacements for 1000 conveyers, supplied by the vendor, follows:

No. replacements needed (r)	0	1	2	3	4	5	6	7	8	9	10
No. parts replaced	914	20	16	15	12	9	6	5	2	1	0

By summing the number of parts replaced (1000) and dividing into each entry, we create a table of probabilities that exactly r parts are needed. Now, summing from the left we can create, at once, a table of probabilities that the requirements are $r \leq S$:

No. replacements needed (r)	0	1	2	3	4	5	6	7	8	9	10
Probability of needing r	.914	.020	.016	.015	.012	.009	.006	.005	.002	.001	.000
Probability of needing $r \leq S$	.914	.934	.950	.965	.977	.986	.992	.997	.999	1.00	1.00

As $C_2/(C_1 + C_2) = 49{,}750/50{,}000 = 0.995$, we have at once that

$$P(r = 6) < 0.995 < P(r = 7)$$

which implies that $S^* = 7$ parts.

Reference

Churchman, C. W., Ackoff, R. L., and Arnoff, E. L., *Introduction to Operations Research,* Wiley, New York, 1957.

Quick & Dirty FINDING OPTIMAL RANGE OF SHORTAGE COSTS FOR EOQ FOR UNCERTAIN DEMAND, SHORTAGES ALLOWED, DISCRETE UNITS

Consider the example in the last Quick & Dirty. For $C_1 = 250$, $C_2 = 49{,}750$, and the associated history table, we discovered that the optimum level of inventory was 7 parts. Now let us say that we would like to know just how much "insurance" this level of inventory has purchased for us.

Method

Given S^*, the optimum level of inventory, and C_1 and the table of $P(r \leq S)$ from the last example, assume that C_2 is unknown and solve for C_2 by using the following:

$$P(r \leq S^* - 1) < \frac{C_2}{C_1 + C_2} < P(r \leq S^*)$$

Example

Because $P(r \leq 6) = 0.992$ and $P(r \leq 7) = 0.997$, we have, from the equation above,

$$0.992 < \frac{C_2}{\$250 + C_2} < 0.997$$

The upper bound on insurance is found from $C_2 < 0.997(\$250 + C_2)$ or $C_2 < \$83,073$. The lower bound on insurance is found from $C_2 > 0.992(\$250 + C_2)$ or $C_2 > \$31,000$.

Now, say that we wish to know how much more insurance stocking one more item would yield for our peace of mind. We operate just as before, but now $S^* = 8$ parts.

Example

Because $P(r \leq 7) = 0.997$ and $P(r \leq 8) = 0.999$, we have, as before,

$$0.997 < \frac{C_2}{\$250 + C_2} < 0.999$$

The upper bound on insurance is found from $C_2 < 0.999(\$250 + C_2)$ or $C_2 < \$249,750$. The lower bound on insurance is found from $C_2 > 0.997(\$250 + C_2)$ or $C_2 > \$83,073$. We thus conclude that an additional outlay of \$250 for another part would result in an additional \$166,667 of insurance against disaster. This works out to \$666.67 of insurance for each dollar spent. An appealing sum to the foreman, but not, perhaps, to the company accountant. Because this is a political question, its resolution is left as an exercise for the user.

Reference

Churchman, C. W., Ackoff, R. L., and Arnoff E. L., *Introduction to Operations Research,* Wiley, New York, 1957.

CONVERSATIONAL LIST FOR THE Q & D FOR FINDING THE OPTIMAL RANGE OF SHORTAGE COSTS FOR THE EOQ FOR UNCERTAIN DEMAND, SHORTAGES ALLOWED, DISCRETE UNITS (PROGRAM 2.3)

```
INVENTORY FOR SPARE PARTS WITH HISTORY

PLEASE INPUT COST OF SPARE PURCHASED WITH ASSEMBLY:250

PLEASE INPUT SHORTAGE COST:49750

PLEASE INPUT HISTORICAL DATA CONSISTING OF THE NUMBER OF
ASSEMBLIES REQUIRING THE NUMBER OF REPLACEMENT PARTS INDICATED.
BEGIN WITH ZERO REPLACEMENTS; DATA FOR 1, 2, 3, AND SO FORTH
MUST FOLLOW.

DATA ENDS WHEN ZERO FOUND IN 2ND COLUMN.

        *****HISTORY TABLE*****
# PARTS REPLACED       # ASSEMBLIES
        0                  :914
        1                  :20
        2                  :16
        3                  :15
        4                  :12
        5                  :9
        6                  :6
        7                  :5
        8                  :2
        9                  :1
        10                 :0

OPTIMAL STOCK LEVEL IS     7

DO YOU WISH TO DETERMINE THE RANGE OF SHORTAGE COST
FOR WHICH A GIVEN STOCK LEVEL HOLDS TRUE:YES

WHAT IS THE GIVEN STOCK LEVEL:7

STOCK   7 UNITS WHEN THE SHORTAGE COST IS GREATER THAN $  31000.02
BUT LESS THAN $  83083.58

DO YOU WISH TO DETERMINE THE RANGE OF SHORTAGE COST
FOR WHICH A GIVEN STOCK LEVEL HOLDS TRUE:YES

WHAT IS THE GIVEN STOCK LEVEL:8

STOCK   8 UNITS WHEN THE SHORTAGE COST IS GREATER THAN $  83083.58
BUT LESS THAN $ 249751.36

DO YOU WISH TO DETERMINE THE RANGE OF SHORTAGE COST
FOR WHICH A GIVEN STOCK LEVEL HOLDS TRUE:NO
```

Quick & Dirty FOR FINDING THE EOQ FOR VARYING FORECASTED DEMAND, NO SHORTAGES ALLOWED

We assume that we have one product for which the unit cost (C), the carrying charge, expressed as a decimal fraction of C per period (I), and the set-up or ordering cost (S) are all known. Further, we have a forecast of demand for some number of periods in advance: $D(1), D(2), \ldots, D(N)$. Forecasts tend to vary greatly with different periods, so the usual assumption that average inventory over time is Q/2 is not usable. Further, bitter experience has shown that forecasts are usually found to be better measures of the sales manager's optimism than actual sales. The P & IM manager therefore wishes to have a method (1) with the ability to keep the bean counters off his back by minimizing inventory and (2) with the ability to allow large variations in forecasted demand without blowing delivery dates.

Method

1. Calculate $M = 2S/CI$ from historical data.
2. For each period, starting with period 1, calculate (period)² * (demand in the period). As soon as this calculation gives a number larger than M, go to step 3. If the number is smaller than M, calculate step 2 again using the next period.
3. Find T, the time this EOQ should last, by the formula:
   $T = \sqrt{M/(\text{demand in last period})}$, where the last period is the one that forced us to step 3.
4. The EOQ will be the number of units that would last thru time T.

Example

Say that $C = \$10.00$, $I = 0.10$, $S = \$150$, and the (present) forecast for the next six months is:

Period	1	2	3	4	5	6
Demand	10	10	15	20	70	180

Calculation of the first replenishment:
1. $M = 2 * 150/10 * 0.1 = 300$ period-pieces.
2. Period 1: $(1)^2 * (10) = 10$, Bigger than 300? No, go to next period.
   Period 2: $(2)^2 * (10) = 40$. Bigger than 300? No, go to next period.
   Period 3: $(3)^2 * (15) = 135$. Bigger than 300? No, go to next period.
   Period 4: $(4)^2 * (20) = 320$. Bigger than 300? Yes, go to step 3.
3. $T = \sqrt{300/20} = \sqrt{15} = 3.87$ time periods.

4. The optimum order quantity that will last through 3.87 time periods is

$$Q = D(1) + D(2) + D(3) + 0.87 * D(4)$$
$$= 10 + 10 + 15 + 0.87 * 20 = 52 \text{ pieces}$$

Calculation of the second replenishment:
1. Same as above.
2. Period 1: $(0.13)^2 * (20)$. Bigger than 300?   No, go to next period.
   Period 2: $(1.13)^2 * (70)$. Bigger than 300?   No, go to next period.
   Period 3: $(2.13)^2 * (180)$. Bigger than 300? Yes, go to step 3.
3. $T = \sqrt{300/180} + 3.87 = 5.16$ (that is, this replenishment should run out 5.16 time periods from the starting time.
4. $Q = 0.13 * (4) + D(5) + 0.16 * D(6) = 0.13 * 20 + 70 + 0.16 * 180 = 102$ pieces. Order the 102 items so that they arrive at time zero for the second replenishment.

Reference

Silver, E. A., and Meal, H. C., "A Simple Modification of the EOQ for the Case of a Varying Demand Rate," *P & IM Journal,* Vol. 10, No. 4, 1969 pp. 52–65.

Quick & Dirty FOR FINDING THE EOQ FOR VARYING FORECASTED DEMAND, WHERE ALL STOCK NEEDED IN A PERIOD MUST BE AVAILABLE AT START OF PERIOD

We assume that we have one product for which the unit cost (C), the carrying charge (I), and the set-up or ordering cost (S) are all known. Further, we have a forecast of demand for some number of periods in advance: $D(1), D(2), \ldots, D(N)$. Due to varying demands and outright lies by the sales manager, the usual assumption that the average inventory is $Q/2$ is hilarious. Further replenishments may only be made at the start of a time period, and all items needed in that period must be on hand at the start of the period. The P & IM manager therefore wishes to be able to calculate EOQ's that will satisfy the above conditions and also minimize cost.

Method

1. Calculate $M = S/CI$ from historical data, set $T(\text{period}) = 1$, set $G = M$, set $EOQ = D(1)$.
2. Is (present period number)^2 * (demand in *next* period) larger than G? If No, go to step 3; If Yes, go to step 4.

3. Advance to next period (set $T = T + 1$). Set EOQ = EOQ + demand in present period. Set $G = G +$ (present period minus 1) * (demand in present period). Go to step 2.
4. Present value of EOQ is optimum order quantity, and will last through the end of period T.

Example

Say that $C = \$10.00$, $I = 0.10$, $S = \$150$, and the (present) forecast for the next six months is

Period	1	2	3	4	5	6
Demand	10	10	15	20	70	180

1. $M = 150/10 * 0.1 = 150$, $T = 1$, $G = 150$, EOQ = $D(1) = 10$.
2. $T^2 * D(2) = (1)^2 * (10) = 10$, which is not larger than $G = 150$. Go to step 3.
3. $T = 2$, EOQ = $10 + D(2) = 10 + 10 = 20$, $G = 150 + (2 - 1) * D(2) = 150 + 10 = 160$. Go to step 2.
2. $T^2 * D(3) = (2)^2 * (15) = 60$, which is not larger than $G = 160$, Go to step 3.
3. $T = 3$, EOQ = $20 + D(3) = 35$, $G = 160 + (3 - 1) * D(3) = 160 + 30 = 190$. Go to step 2.
2. $T^2 * D(4) = (3)^2 * (20) = 180$, which is not larger than $G = 190$. Go to step 3.
3. $T = 4$, EOQ = $35 + D(4) = 55$, $G = 190 + (4 - 1) * D(4) = 190 + 60 = 250$. Go to step 2.
2. $T^2 * D(5) = (4)^2 * (70) = 1120$, which is larger than $G = 250$. Go to step 4.
4. EOQ = 55 is the optimum order quantity. It will last for 4 time periods and should be ordered so that it will come in at the start of the first period.

Reference

Silver, E. A., and Meal, H. C., "In Defense of 'A Simple Modification of the EOQ for the Case of a Varying Demand Rate,'" Working Paper No. 62, Dept. of Management. Sciences, University of Waterloo, Waterloo, Ontario, Jan. 1972.

CONVERSATIONAL LIST FOR THE Q & D FOR FINDING THE EOQ UNDER CONDITIONS OF VARYING DEMAND (SILVER AND MEAL METHOD) (PROGRAM 2.4)

```
SILVER AND MEAL EOQ FOR TIME-VARYING DEMAND

DO YOU WANT THE TUTORIAL:YES

THIS PROGRAM WILL CALCULATE THE EOQ FOR ONE ITEM UNDER
CONDITIONS OF TIME-VARYING DEMAND.

YOU WILL BE ASKED TO ENTER THE FOLLOWING INFORMATION:

(1) THE COST OF THE ITEM,
(2) THE CARRYING CHARGE PER PERIOD OF TIME, EXPRESSED
AS A DECIMAL FRACTION OF THE ITEM COST,
(3) THE SET-UP OR ORDERING COST,
(4) THE NUMBER OF TIME PERIODS IN ADVANCE FOR WHICH YOU HAVE THE DEMAND
INFORMATION,
(5) THE FORECASTED DEMAND IN EACH PERIOD,
AND (6) WHETHER OR NOT ALL STOCK NEEDED IN A PERIOD MUST BE AVAILABLE
AT THE START OF EACH PERIOD.


ENTER THE COST OF THE ITEM:10

ENTER THE CARRYING CHARGE (DECIMAL FRACTION):0.10

ENTER THE SET-UP OR ORDERING COST:150

ENTER THE NUMBER OF TIME PERIODS
FOR WHICH YOU HAVE FORECASTED DATA:6

ENTER DEMAND FOR PERIODS 1 THROUGH  6, SEPARATED BY COMMAS:
10,10,15,20,70,180

MUST ALL STOCK NEEDED IN A PERIOD BE AVAILABLE
AT THE START OF THE PERIOD:NO

OPTIMUM EOQ IS      52 PIECES.

THIS WILL RUN OUT   3.87 TIME PERIODS FROM THE STARTING DATE.


DO YOU WISH TO CALCULATE THE NEXT REPLENISHMENT:YES

OPTIMUM EOQ IS     102 PIECES.

THIS WILL RUN OUT   5.16 TIME PERIODS FROM THE STARTING DATE.
```

DO YOU WANT TO LOOK AT ANOTHER ITEM:YES

ENTER THE COST OF THE ITEM:10

ENTER THE CARRYING CHARGE (DECIMAL FRACTION):0.10

ENTER THE SET-UP OR ORDERING COST:150

ENTER THE NUMBER OF TIME PERIODS
FOR WHICH YOU HAVE FORECASTED DATA:6

ENTER DEMAND FOR PERIODS 1 THROUGH 6, SEPARATED BY COMMAS:
10,10,15,20,70,180

MUST ALL STOCK NEEDED IN A PERIOD BE AVAILABLE
AT THE START OF THE PERIOD:YES

OPTIMUM EOQ IS   55 PIECES.

THIS WILL RUN OUT   4.00 TIME PERIODS FROM THE STARTING DATE.

DO YOU WISH TO CALCULATE THE NEXT REPLENISHMENT:YES

OPTIMUM EOQ IS   70 PIECES.

THIS WILL RUN OUT   5.00 TIME PERIODS FROM THE STARTING DATE.

DO YOU WANT TO LOOK AT ANOTHER ITEM:NO

Quick & Dirty TO DECIDE WHETHER OR NOT TO STOCK AN ITEM

Method

1. Calculate 2 * (set-up or ordering cost) * (holding cost per item per year). Put this number on line A.   A _____
2. If ordering (out of house), enter 0 (zero) on line B; if manufacturing item in house, enter the number on line A divided by the yearly rate of production.   B _____
3. Determine selling price per item minus production cost per item.   C _____
4. Multiply line C by percent of sales lost if the item is not stocked.   D _____
5. Calculate set-up or ordering cost divided by average order size.   E _____
6. Multiply line E by 1—(percent of sales lost if item is not stocked).   F _____
7. Add line D to line F.   G _____
8. Square the number on line G.   H _____
9. Add the number in line B to the number on line H.   I _____
10. Divide the number in line A by the number on line I.   J _____

If line J is greater than your annual demand, don't stock it.

Example

Say that the annual demand (use) of an item is 20, the set-up or ordering cost is $10 per order, estimated holding cost is $30 per item per year, selling price is $50, item cost is $25, average order size is $2\frac{1}{2}$ items per order, and you figure to lose 5 percent of your sales if the item is not on hand. Should you stock or not?

1.	$2 * 10 * 30 =$	A	600
2.	Since we are ordering,	B	0
3.	$50 - 25 =$	C	25
4.	$25 * 0.05 =$	D	1.25
5.	$10/2.5 =$	E	4
6.	$4 * 0.95 =$	F	3.8
7.	$1.25 + 3.8 =$	G	5.05
8.	$(5.05)^2 =$	H	25.5
9.	$0 + 25.5 =$	I	25.5
10.	$600/25.5 =$	J	23.5

Now, since line J is 23.5 and annual demand is 20, do not stock the item.

References

Fenske, R. W., "Non-stocking Criterion," *Management Science*, Vol. 14, No. 12, Aug. 1968, pp. 705–714.
Silver, E. A., "A Note on the Non-stocking Criterion," *Management Science*, Vol. 15, No. 8, April 1969, pp. 359–360.

CONVERSATIONAL LIST FOR THE Q & D TO DECIDE WHETHER OR NOT TO STOCK AN ITEM (PROGRAM 2.5)

```
THIS PROGRAM DETERMINES IF A GIVEN ITEM SHOULD BE
STOCKED OR NOT STOCKED

PLEASE INPUT THE FOLLOWING DATA

HOLDING COST PER ITEM PER YEAR?:30

SELLING PRICE PER ITEM?:50

PRODUCTION COST PER ITEM?:25

YEARLY DEMAND?:20

AVERAGE ORDER SIZE?:3

ESTIMATE PER CENT OF SALES LOST IF ITEM NOT STOCKED?:5

IF ITEM IS MANUFACTURED, ENTER M; IF ORDERED, ENTER O:O

ENTER ORDERING COST PER ORDER?:3

ITEM SHOULD NOT BE STOCKED

STOCK IT IF ANNUAL DEMAND IS AT LEAST     37 ITEMS

DO AGAIN?:YES

THIS PROGRAM DETERMINES IF A GIVEN ITEM SHOULD BE
STOCKED OR NOT STOCKED

PLEASE INPUT THE FOLLOWING DATA

HOLDING COST PER ITEM PER YEAR?:30

SELLING PRICE PER ITEM?:80

PRODUCTION COST PER ITEM?:7

YEARLY DEMAND?:310

AVERAGE ORDER SIZE?:28

ESTIMATE PER CENT OF SALES LOST IF ITEM NOT STOCKED?:15

IF ITEM IS MANUFACTURED, ENTER M; IF ORDERED, ENTER O:M

ENTER SETUP COST PER PRODUCTION RUN?:165

ANNUAL PRODUCTION RATE?:422

ITEM SHOULD BE STOCKED

DO NOT STOCK IT IF ANNUAL DEMAND FALLS BELOW     35 ITEMS

DO AGAIN?:NO
```

Quick & Dirty TO DECIDE WHETHER OR NOT TO STOCK AN ITEM (HEALTH CARE AND HOSPITAL VERSION)

If it is decided to stock an item, the EOQ can be calculated by various methods so as to minimize the sum of holding and ordering costs. One would think, however, that we should first have a simple way to decide if the item should be stocked at all. The following Q & D allows the hospital to make this decision quickly and cheaply.

Method

1. Find 2 * (cost to order and process the item) * (item cost * interest rate for hospital). Put this number on line A.   A _____
2. Put (price item sold for − cost of item to hospital) on line B.   B _____
3. If item is for emergency use, line C = box B, otherwise put 0 on line C.   C _____
4. Enter (cost to order and process the item/average order size) on line D.   D _____
5. If item is for emergency use, line E = 0, otherwise line E = line D.   E _____
6. Enter line F with sum of line C and line E.   F _____
7. Square line F and enter onto line G.   G _____
8. Enter line H with (line A/line G).   H _____

If line H is greater than your annual demand, *don't* stock it.

Example

Say that your annual demand for an item is 480 bottles, your ordering price (cost) and processing cost together are $5 per order, your holding cost is $20 * 0.10 = $2 per year per item, the selling price is $30, the item cost is $20, and the average order is 40 bottles. The item is *not* an emergency item. Should you stock it or not?

1. 2 * 5 * 2 =   A   20
2. 30 − 20 =   B   10
3. not emergency = C   0
4. 5/40 =   D 0.125
5. not emergency = E 0.125
6. line C + line E = F 0.125

7. square line F =   G <u>0.016</u>

8. line A/line F =   H <u>1250</u>

Line H is 1250 bottles and annual demand is 480 bottles, so do *not* stock it, but order as needed. Further, you should not stock the item until demand reaches 1250 bottles per year.

Reference

Fenske, R. H., "Non-stocking Criterion," *Management Science,* Vol. 14, No. 12, Aug. 1968, pp. 705–714.
Silver, E. A., "A Note on the 'Non-stocking Criterion,'" *Management Science,* Vol. 15, No. 8, April 1969, pp. 359–360.

Quick & Dirty ECONOMIC PACKAGING FREQUENCY FOR ITEMS JOINTLY REPLENISHED

Some products, like detergents and oils, are sold in packages of different types and sizes to appeal to different markets. Just as a homemaker doesn't want a 10-gallon can of floor wax, a janitor doesn't want a 16-ounce "giant economy-size" bottle of floor wax, either. These different markets, furthermore, will obviously have different demands, and the packaging runs for different containers will have quite different set-up costs.

M = number of package types whose inventories may be jointly replenished
S_j = packaging set-up cost for package type j
Q_j = annual demand for type j
h_j = holding cost per unit per year for type j
S = cost of a manufacturing run set-up

Method

1. Determine the total number of manufacturing set-ups, N.

$$N = \sqrt{\frac{h_1Q_1 + h_2Q_2 + \cdots + h_MQ_M}{2(S + S_1 + S_2 + \cdots + S_M)}}$$

2. For each packaging type j, compute the packaging frequency

$$K_j = N\sqrt{\frac{2S_j}{h_jQ_j}}$$

and round-off K to the nearest non-zero whole number. If $K = 1$, the package type is produced at every manufacturing run; if $K = 2$, at every other run; and so on.

3. Compute the total cost.

$$\text{Total cost} = NS + \frac{NS_1}{K_1} + \frac{NS_2}{K_2} + \cdots + \frac{NS_M}{K_M} + \frac{h_1Q_1K_1}{(2N)}$$
$$+ \frac{h_2Q_2K_2}{(2N)} + \cdots + \frac{h_MQ_MK_M}{(2N)}$$

Example

	Item	Annual demand, units	Packaging set-up cost	Holding cost, $/unit-yr	K_j
	1	100,000	$80	0.16	0.67; rounds to 1
	2	80,000	80	0.16	0.75; rounds to 1
$S = \$125$	3	60,000	75	0.16	0.84; rounds to 1
	4	30,000	70	0.16	1.14; rounds to 1
	5	10,000	70	0.16	1.98; rounds to 2

1. $N = \sqrt{\dfrac{(0.16)(280,000)}{(2)(125 + 375)}} = 6.69$ runs/yr

2. As shown above.
3. Total cost = $6578.71

Reference

Goyal, S. K., "Economic Packaging Frequency for Items Jointly Replenished," *Operations Research*, Vol. 21, No. 2, March–April 1973, p. 644.

three

Quick & Dirty Methods in Time-Shared Capital Budgeting

In the operations research (O.R.) literature, the capital budgeting field gives the usual appearance of great progress due to the emphasis on optimum algorithm construction. The author contends that the real problem in capital budgeting is simply getting someone to use the models. The author will explore the use of conversational programs, using both heuristic and optimum integer programming (I.P.) methods, to sell people on capital budgeting models. These programs assume that the customer has never used a computer before and is, in fact, generally hostile to the whole idea. The source programs are found in the appendix. Conversational outputs of two sample programs to do this appear at the end of the chapter.

MARKETING THE MODEL

The first hard lesson that should be learned by any budding O.R. man is that the most difficult optimization problem is getting someone to *use* an optimization model. It is interesting that the many papers written in the area of capital budgeting (to say nothing of general O.R.) assume that the decision maker greets the O.R. analyst with open arms and instantly accepts his sage counsel with only minor protests. In point of fact, the best way to break in the usual O.R. graduate is to send him down to the usual decision maker, who rightfully sizes up the newcomer as a young smartass and treats him accordingly. What we should realize is the fact that, for any O.R. model to succeed, it must have some forces within it that motivate the customer to use it. From his own experience the author offers the following three motivators with, of course, a considerable acknowledgment to Niccolo Machiavelli [1]:

1. Desire for status
2. Greed
3. Fear

It can be shown that these three motivators, working together, can accomplish wonders of efficiency even in organizations that have absolutely no desire to operate efficiently, such as state, local, and federal governments. The first question the decision maker should ask the O.R. analyst is the classic: "What's in it for *me?*" O.R. types without a ready answer to this question, *in terms that the decision maker can understand,* should be fired at once.

The O.R. analyst confronted with a large, inefficient organization has the usual problem of deciding where to start. As a possible suggestion, the author asks him to consider starting with a "shark," now at the lowest level of management. By a "shark" we mean a person who is highly motivated to rise in the hierarchy, *by any means necessary.* In the author's experience, there is usually at least one of these in any given organization. The author has now, admittedly, loaded the dice somewhat by providing the O.R. analyst with someone who is motivated to move up the hierarchy. The problem is still to convince this person that capital budgeting will ensure his desired growth in power, prestige, status, and money. Let us further assume that our lower-level manager is embedded in a large research and development division where payoffs for projects are almost impossible to measure. We now ask the manager to rank all the projects he is

1.   Now working on,
2.   Must be working on, and
3.   Would *like* to be working on.

By rank we mean that he simply lists them in some order of importance that is meaningful to *him*. Say that he comes up with ten projects in all. We then ask him to assign 100 youdels of satisfaction to the completion of the first project. We then ask him to assign some reasonable number of youdels to the next most important project, keeping in mind that the first one got 100 youdels. When this process is completed for all the projects, we proceed to the next step. If we assume that all projects are go–no go, we have really formed an objective function for a capital budgeting problem in the usual form. That is, we have defined a group of go–no go variables called *projects,* say we call them $p_1, p_2, \ldots, p_n$. We have also defined a group of weights of importance, $w_1, w_2, \ldots, w_n$. If we knew for certain what these weights *were,* we would have the case where the weights would be net present value or annual cost of the projects. But because we are assuming that we are in a R & D environment where these things can *not* be known with certainty, we shall stick to youdels for now. After the above ranking has been carried out, let us pause to consider the way in which we asked the question about the projects. Note that the question asked for the projects in three separate groups. This author contends that the three groups requested comprise the total universe of projects to be considered at any given time. It should be reasonably clear that some projects are being done because upper management has shoved them down the throat of the lower-level manager.

Also, the person proposing to inject capital budgeting methods into a large organization should beware of doing it from the top down. Too often, in this author's experience, upper management tends to view this new tool as the answer to all ills. In the initial burst of enthusiasm, the upper manager will sell it to his peers and embody this new method in the policy manual before the analyst is really aware of what may happen. The inexperienced analyst will view the embodiment of his technique with great joy, not yet realizing that for his method to *work,* the data must be supplied and implemented in the model by *lower* management. At some point in this process the phrase, "Let's now disseminate this to lower management," will be used by the big dog who has been sold on the method. Let us list the steps of dissemination in order.

1. The new method is shoved down the throat of lower management.
2. Lower management appears to comply.
3. The usual capital budgeting process grinds to a halt.
4. The upper manager points out that "lower management in this company is against progress."
5. The method dies (at least as far as this company is concerned).

We should note, however, that if we start from the bottom and go up, the shark we have chosen sees implementation of the method as a way to get ahead. Therefore we are assured of implementation, at least at this level of management.

After the objective function above has been defined, we must determine what are the constraining factors that prevent the shark from doing all of the projects. These can usually be divided into constraints of men, money, or materials. If we first ask the shark to inform us as to how his budget is divided up, we can usually learn quite a bit about how the organization functions. The usual division encountered by this author is division into (1) cost of a project consumed neither by salaries nor by capital investment, (2) cost of a project in salaries of similar-type personnel, and (3) cost of a project considered a capital cost. For purposes of this discussion let us call these three costs "bucks," "man-years," and "corporate burden." We now ask the shark to tell us what kind of requirement he would expect each project to have on these three costs over the next fiscal period. In short, we ask such questions as, "How many bucks will this project require next year?" After all this information has been obtained, we then ask how much of these three resources the manager is supplied with for the forecasted year. At this point we have assembled all the information we need to proceed with an optimization method, such as integer programming. We have now constructed a model in the following form:

Maximize:
  (weight on project 1) * (go–no go variable 1) $+ \cdots + w_n * p_n$

Subject to:
  bucks: (bucks to do project 1) * (go–no go variable 1)
  $$+ \cdots + b_n p_n \leq \text{total bucks}$$
  man-years: (man-years for project 1) * (go–no variable 1)
  $$+ \cdots + m_n p_n \leq \text{total man-years}$$
  corporate burden: (capital cost for project 1) * (go–no go variable 1)
  $$+ \cdots + c_n p_n \leq \text{total capital available}$$

The analyst or the user should beware of running this model immediately. Rather often the simple layout of the model on a form will reveal some unexpected and useful bits of information. The first thing the user should do is to look at the columns of the model *separately*. Consider the following example:

Maximize:
  $\ldots 30 * p_4 + 15 * p_5 \ldots$

Subject to:
  bucks: $\ldots \$10,000 * p_4 + \$1000 * p_5 \ldots$
  man-years: $\ldots 5 * p_4 + 10 * p_5 \ldots$
  corporate burden: $\ldots 0 * p_4 + 0 * p_5 \ldots$

Note that on a payoff basis, the first project is twice as good as the second. However, the first project is ten times as costly as the second on a bucks basis, but again, half as costly on a man-years basis. At this point let us introduce the concept of "bang-for-buck ratio." To obtain this we simply divide the resource needed for a particular project into the expected payoff for that project. In the above case the bang-for-buck ratios for the two projects are 3×10^{-3}, and 15×10^{-3}, respectively. We can at once see that the second project is five times as effective with regard to the resource considered as is the first. If we now calculate the bang-per-man-year ratios, we get 6×10^{-3} and 1.5×10^{-3}. This information tells us that the first project is four times as effective as the second with respect to man-years. It can be seen that to make project 1 look as good as project 2 with respect to bucks, we must make the payoff on project 1 be 150. This kind of example can be considered as partial justification to the au-

Quick & Dirty Project Selection

Project No.	1	2	3	4	5	6	·	· ·	N	Limit L	Requirement R	Slack R−L
Payoff	500	900	300	600	100	300						
Resource 1 needed	1	4	5	7	5	6				16	28	12
Resource 2 needed	5	3	2	8	4	9				16	31	15
. . .												
Resource M needed												

Senju and Toyoda Effectiveness Calculation

Resource 1 × (R − L)	1×12 / 12	4×12 / 48	5×12 / 60	7×12 / 84	5×12 / 60	6×12 / 72						
Resource 2 × (R − L)	5×15 / 75	3×15 / 45	2×15 / 30	8×15 / 120	4×15 / 60	9×15 / 135						
. . .												
Resource M × (R − L)												
Sum of above rows	87	93	90	204	120	207						
Payoff/ sum = effectiveness	5.7	9.7	3.3	2.9	0.8	1.4						

Selection of Projects Calculation

Projects in/out	OUT / 5	OUT / 6	OUT / 4	IN / 5						
R − L total for resource 1	12-5 / 7	7-6 / 1	1-7 / -6	-6+5 / -1						
R − L total for resource 2	15-4 / 11	11-9 / 2	2-8 / -6	-6+4 / -2						
. . .										
R − L total for resource M										

Instructions

1. For each project, fill in the expected payoff and the amount of each resource it will require in the fiscal period we are looking at.
2. For each resource, fill in the total amount available in the Limit column and the total required to do all the projects in the Requirement column.
3. Put the difference between what we *have* (L) and what we *need* (R) in the Slack column.
4. For each project, multiply each resource requirement by the appropriate Slack entry. Enter the product in the project column, and sum the result for each project.
5. For each project, divide the payoff by the sum found in step 4. This is the Effectiveness.
6. Choose the project with the smallest effectiveness and remove the amount of resources it requires from the Slack for each resource. Record that it is *not* to be done.
7. If the adjusted slacks are all ≤ 0, go to step 8, otherwise go to step 6.
8. Check to see if any project that has been removed can be added back in and still keep the resource slacks negative or zero. Look first at the most effective and then down to the least effective. If none can be added, *stop. Do* the indicated projects.

Figure 3

thor's contention that *gross changes in the payoff values often don't change the result.*

At this point the reader should have asked: "How does the analyst get the shark to put down this kind of information?" Because we assume that the shark is a budding bureaucrat, we do the thing most natural to a bureau. We create a form for him to fill out, as in the worked-out example in Figure 3.

The first rule of justification is: "If the user doesn't *want* any, *shut up.*" Unfortunately, many O.R./M.S. types feel obliged to beat the simplex method into the skull of some poor character who just wants an *answer*. As a rule, the usual customer will take sufficient examples for a proof that the method works. Now all of us mathematically brainwashed types will agree that an example is not a proof. But beyond our ivied walls, the usual proof is *not* understood, and definitely not appreciated. Very often the customer asks something like: "Draw me a picture." For this method we *can* draw him a picture.

If we assume that we have two resources that are limited by L_1 and L_2, we could draw the picture shown in Figure 4. Starting from the

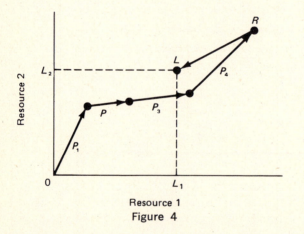

Resource 1

Figure 4

origin, if we decided to *do* the first project, we would step off the amount of the two resources on the appropriate axis and draw an arrow to that point. If we decided then to do project 2, we would step off the resources used from the last point and so on. Eventually we would step out of our limit, and if we continued we would finally get to the point R, the amount of the resources we would require to do *all* the projects. If we now drew a line from R (our total requirement) to L (our total limit), this is the direction to which we would like to stay as close as possible to get back within our limit. The nearer a project is to this line is its effectiveness. If the effectiveness is large, the project is near the line; if the effectiveness is small, the project is not near the line and therefore should be removed. So we remove projects until we get back within our limit. After we "get back in," we look to see if there are any projects that have been dropped that we might add back in without going "out" again. If not, we stop.

The method we are using here is that of Senju and Toyoda [2]. This method has the advantage that it *can* be explained by drawing a picture for each step of the method. Of course, the disadvantage of the method is that it is *not* an optimal method. (At this point the purist will go lie down.) The question now arises: "If it is not an optimal method, why do you use it?" The answer is that it should be used because (1) the method and the justification are easy for a layman to follow, and (2) it usually gives better answers than were obtained before and provides insights into the problem not obvious before. As further justification, the author offers two more rules garnered from painful experience:

Rule 1. A manager would rather live with a problem that he cannot solve than accept an answer that he cannot understand.

Rule 2. Managers usually don't want (and will not pay for) the optimum solution. They just want to be better off than they are *now* (as cheaply as possible).

MARKETING THE COMPUTER MODEL

Eventually, your shark will get tired of doing the calculations on the form by hand every time he wants to change something. You may then provide a *conversational* program to do the dog work such as appears on page 73. Note that the program expects only that the user can spell "yes," "no," and can count. Note further that he is asked if he wants the tutorial before anything else. The wise analyst will provide an input as close to that of the form used as possible so as to minimize future shock in going from the by-hand method to the computer.

The short form of this program will be found in the Appendix (Program 3.1). It was originally written in the FOCAL language for the Digital Equipment PDP-8. The fact that capital budgeting problems of interesting size can be run on a computer costing less than \$10,000 and about the size of a large attache case is very significant. The effect of placing a teletype on the user's desk, plugging the machine into the wall, and telling him to go ahead has proved a very powerful incentive for acceptance.

Eventually, of course, your user will want to have bells and whistles. These are provided by substituting the next program, called (naturally) EXECUTIVE, for the long-form Senju and Toyoda program (Program 3.2).

A worked-out example may be found on pages 74–76. The method used is a modified form of the method of Senju and Toyoda [1], and is also a heuristic method. Again, the program is given in the Appendix. It will be found that it is *now* rather easy to get the user to move up to an optimum code [3], because we have first allowed him to crawl, then walk. We can now be confident that he will run by himself. Indeed, in this author's experience, the user will use up many happy hours changing the values just to see what will happen. One of the most meaningful examples is when there is a sudden budget cut, and a quick decision must be made as to which projects to throw out, which to keep, and which to start up. It can be seen that EXECUTIVE takes care of this problem by simply subtracting the reduction from the amount of resource available and running the model again. Then an intersection of projects in the two cases may be taken to estimate better the effect of the reduction.

Sooner or later our shark will realize that "If I can see what would happen in a reduction by subtracting some resource, I can see what would happen if I had *more* resource by just adding it on." As soon as he discovers that he can double his payoff if he just had one more man and $3756.34, I wouldn't be surprised if he looks around to see if there just might be some place to *steal* it. At this point his peers had better make sure that they are as well set up to justify their needs as our shark.

This will be left as an exercise for the reader.

CITED REFERENCES

[1] Machiavelli, N., *The Prince,* Florence, 1532 A.D.
[2] Senju, Shizuo, and Toyoda, Yoshiaki, "An Approach to Linear Programming with 0–1 Variables," *Management Science,* Vol. 15, No. 4, Dec. 1968, pp. B-196–207.
[3] Balas, E., "An Additive Algorithm for Solving Linear Programs with 0–1 Variables," *Operations Research,* Vol. 13, 1965, pp. 517–549.

CONVERSATIONAL LIST FOR THE Q & D FOR THE SWANSON AND WOOLSEY CAPITAL BUDGETING METHOD (PROGRAM 3.1)

```
SWANSON & WOOLSEYS CAPITAL BUDGETING QUICK & DIRTY

DO YOU WANT THE TUTORIAL:YES

THIS PROGRAM ASSUMES THAT YOU HAVE A GROUP OF PROJECTS THAT
ARE CONSTRAINED BY A GROUP OF SCARCE RESOURCES, SUCH AS MEN,
MONEY, OR MATERIALS.  YOU DESIRE TO CHOOSE FROM THESE PROJECTS
IN SUCH A WAY AS TO MAXIMIZE YOUR PAYOFF.  YOU WILL BE ASKED
TO INPUT THE NUMBER OF PROJECTS, THE NUMBER OF  RESOURCES, THE
PAYOFF ASSOCIATED WITH EACH PROJECT, THE AMOUNT OF EACH RESOURCE
AVAILABLE, AND THE AMOUNT OF EACH RESOURCE THAT EACH PROJECT
REQUIRES.

HOW MANY PROJECTS ARE THERE?:10

HOW MANY DIFFERENT RESOURCES ARE THERE?:2

LIST THE PAYOFF VALUES FOR THE PROJECTS, SEPARATEL BY COMMAS
120,140,230,78,34,56,178,124,302,235

WHAT IS THE AVAILABILITY OF RESOURCE  1:600

LIST THE AMOUNT OF RESOURCE  1 NEEDED FOR THE PROJECTS SEPARATEL
BY COMMAS
65,67,146,53,68,20,53,45,67,295

WHAT IS THE AVAILABILITY OF RESOURCE  2:40

LIST THE AMOUNT OF RESOURCE  2 NEEDED FOR THE PROJECTS SEPARATEL
BY COMMAS
12,14,23,5,17,4,9,14,32,13

PROJECT OUT
PROJECT OUT
PROJECT OUT
PROJECT OUT
PROJECT OUT
PROJECT OUT
PROJECT OUT
PROJECT OUT
PROJECT OUT

OPTIMUM FOUND, PAYOFF=    380.00

DO THE FOLLOWING PROJECTS

PROJECT  4
PROJECT  9
```

CONVERSATIONAL LIST FOR THE Q & D FOR $$$EXECUTIVES$$$
CAPITAL BUDGETING METHOD (PROGRAM 3.2)

$$$ EXECUTIVE $$$

DO YOU WANT THE TUTORIAL:YES

THIS PROGRAM ASSUMES THAT YOU HAVE A GROUP OF PROJECTS (UP TO 20) THAT
ARE CONSTRAINED BY A GROUP OF SCARCE RESOURCES, SUCH AS MEN, MONEY, OR
MATERIALS. YOU DESIRE TO CHOOSE FROM THESE PROJECTS IN SUCH A WAY AS
TO MAXIMIZE YOUR NET PRESENT VALUE OF FUTURE CASH FLOWS (PAYOFFS).

YOU WILL BE ASKED TO INPUT THE NUMBER OF PROJECTS, THE NUMBER OF
RESOURCES, THE NET PRESENT VALUE OF FUTURE CASH FLOWS (PAYOFF) ASSOCI-
ATED WITH EACH PROJECT, THE AMOUNT OF EACH RESOURCE AVAILABLE, AND THE
AMOUNT OF EACH RESOURCE THAT EACH PROJECT REQUIRES.

HOW MANY PROJECTS ARE THERE:6

HOW MANY DIFFERENT RESOURCES ARE THERE:2

LIST THE PAYOFF VALUES FOR THE PROJECTS, SEPARATED BY COMMAS:
120,145,178,345,256,189

WHAT IS THE AVAILABILITY OF RESOURCE 1:600

LIST THE AMOUNT OF RESOURCE 1 NEEDED FOR
EACH PROJECT, SEPARATED BY COMMAS:
56,67,102,234,156,106

WHAT IS THE AVAILABILITY OF RESOURCE 2:27

LIST THE AMOUNT OF RESOURCE 2 NEEDED FOR
EACH PROJECT, SEPARATED BY COMMAS:
2,4,8,13,9,4

OPTIMUM PAYOFF IS   888.00

DO THE FOLLOWING PROJECTS
  1
  2
  3
  5
  6

THE AMOUNT OF RESOURCE 1 NOT ALLOCATED IS   113.00 UNITS.

THE AMOUNT OF RESOURCE 2 NOT ALLOCATED IS   0.00 UNITS.

DO YOU WANT TO CHANGE SOME OF THE OLD DATA AND RERUN
THIS PROBLEM:YES

DO YOU WANT TO CHANGE ANY PAYOFF VALUES:YES

LIST THE PROJECTS FOR WHICH YOU WANT TO CHANGE THE PAYOFFS,
SEPARATED BY COMMAS:4

PAYOFF FOR PROJECT 4 IS NOW   345.00.

NEW PAYOFF FOR PROJECT 4 IS:400

DO YOU WANT TO CHANGE THE AVAILABILITY OF ANY RESOURCE:YES

LIST THE RESOURCES FOR WHICH YOU WANT TO CHANGE THE AVAILABILITY,
SEPARATED BY COMMAS:1,2

AVAILABILITY OF RESOURCE 1 IS NOW   600.00 UNITS.

NEW AVAILABILITY OF RESOURCE 1 IS:540

AVAILABILITY OF RESOURCE 2 IS NOW   27.00 UNITS.

NEW AVAILABILITY OF RESOURCE 2 IS:26

DO YOU WANT TO CHANGE THE RESOURCE REQUIREMENTS FOR ANY PROJECTS:YES

FOR WHICH PROJECTS DO YOU WANT TO CHANGE THE RESOURCE REQUIREMENTS:
2

FOR WHICH RESOURCES WILL PROJECT 2'S REQUIREMENTS CHANGE:
2,1

PROJECT 2 NOW REQUIRES   4.00 UNITS OF RESOURCE 2.

NEW REQUIREMENT OF PROJECT 2 IS:6

PROJECT 2 NOW REQUIRES   67.00 UNITS OF RESOURCE 1.

NEW REQUIREMENT OF PROJECT 2 IS:74

OPTIMUM PAYOFF IS   854.00

DO THE FOLLOWING PROJECTS
  1
  2
  4
  6

THE AMOUNT OF RESOURCE 1 NOT ALLOCATED IS   70.00 UNITS.

THE AMOUNT OF RESOURCE 2 NOT ALLOCATED IS   1.00 UNITS.

PROJECTS SELECTED IN BOTH THE RERUN AND THE PREVIOUS RUN ARE AS FOLLOWS
  1
  2
  6

DO YOU WANT TO PRESERVE THE RERUN SELECTION, CHANGE SOME OF THE
DATA, AND RERUN THE PROBLEM:NO

DO YOU WANT TO RUN AN ENTIRELY NEW PROBLEM:NO

A Tutorial on Markov Chains

INTRODUCTION

The Society of Marijuana and Opium Growers (SMOG) is trying to decide which of two new cigars to market—El Hempo Ropo or El Stinko Grande. Due to limited production facilities and the technology involved, it is feasible to market only one of them.

Based on a previous market survey, SMOG has observed certain traits in customer buying habits: If a customer bought a particular brand on his previous purchase there is a certain probability that he will "repeat" and buy that brand again. Likewise, if on the previous purchase he did not buy Brand X, there is a certain probability that he will switch to it.

The problem, then, is how to use this "brand switching model" to decide which cigar to market.

How does this model differ from previous stochastic inventory models?

1. Demand varies from period to period.
2. Demand is dependent on past demand.

We can depict this model by a matrix:

| | | Current Purchases | |
		Brand X	Others
Previous Purchase	Brand X	P11	P12
	Others	P21	P22

This process is *state dependent;* that is, probabilities of demands depend on the current "state of the system" (customer).

The authors gratefully acknowledge that the introductory material in this chapter is freely adapted from lecture notes of Dr. William G. Lesso, Mechanical Engineering Department, University of Texas.

We can also depict this model by a transition diagram.

$$P_{11} \; \underset{P_{21}}{\overset{P_{12}}{\boxed{\text{Brand X}} \rightleftarrows \boxed{\text{Others}}}} \; P_{22}$$

This type of process is known as a *Markov process*. Formally, we can define a Markov process in terms of the probability of being a given state S at time T as follows:

$$\text{prob}(S_t = k | S_{t-1}, S_{t-2}, S_{t-3}, \ldots, S_1, S_0)$$
$$= \text{prob}(S_t = k | S_{t-1})$$

that is, the probability of being in a given state at time T depends *only* on the previous state the system was in.

To see how this process can be used, let us return to SMOG. Performing a small-scale sales experiment, SMOG found that El Hempo Ropo (EHR) has the following transition probabilities:

	EHR	Others
EHR	0.5	0.5
Others	0.7	0.3

We shall assume that the "customer population" is 500,000 cigar smokers and that their buying habits can be assumed to be fairly regular. In fact, on the average, each smoker consumes (some have found it better to eat rather than smoke the El Hempo Ropo) 10 cigars a week. SMOG makes $0.06 revenue on each cigar.

We shall define the states of the system as follows:

state 1: The previous purchase was EHR
state 2: The previous purchase was another brand

Then, in the first week of marketing El Hempo Ropo, the state vector is

$$S_0 = [0, \quad 500,000]$$

The sales are then

$$[0 \quad 500,000] \times \begin{bmatrix} 0.5 & 0.5 \\ 0.7 & 0.3 \end{bmatrix}, = [350,000, \quad 150,000]$$

The revenue is $350,000 \times 0.06 \times 10 = \$210,000$.
In the second week, sales are

$$[350,000 \quad 150,000] \times \begin{bmatrix} 0.5 & 0.5 \\ 0.7 & 0.3 \end{bmatrix} = [280,000, \quad 220,000]$$

The revenue is $280,000 \times 0.06 \times 10 = \$168,000$.

Repeating this process, we obtain

	State	Revenue
3rd week	[294,000, 206,000]	$176,400.00
4th week	[291,200, 208,800]	174,720.00
5th week	[291,760, 208,340]	175,056.00
6th week	[291,714, 208,386]	175,028.40
7th week	[291,727, 208,373]	175,036.20
8th week	[291,725, 208,375]	175,035.00
9th week	[291,726, 208,374]	175,035.60
10th week	[291,726, 208,374]	175,035.60

Thus, even with active brand switching, the effects dampen out to constant sales level.

Now let us look at the calculations in more detail:

$$S_1 = S_0 \begin{bmatrix} P_{11} & P_{12} \\ P_{21} & P_{22} \end{bmatrix} = [S_{10}, S_{20}] \begin{bmatrix} P_{11} & P_{12} \\ P_{31} & P_{22} \end{bmatrix}$$

$$= S_0 \cdot P$$

$$S_2 = S_1 \cdot P = [S_{11}, S_{21}] \begin{bmatrix} P_{11} & P_{12} \\ P_{21} & P_{22} \end{bmatrix}$$

$$= [S_{10}, S_{20}] \begin{bmatrix} P_{11} & P_{12} \\ P_{21} & P_{22} \end{bmatrix} \cdot \begin{bmatrix} P_{11} & P_{12} \\ P_{22} & P_{22} \end{bmatrix}$$

$$= S_0 \cdot P^2$$

$$S_N = S_0 P^N$$

We can find the state of the system at any period N by knowing the initial state and the Nth power of the transition matrix.

$$P = \begin{bmatrix} 0.5 & 0.5 \\ 0.7 & 0.3 \end{bmatrix} \qquad P^2 = \begin{bmatrix} 0.60 & 0.40 \\ 0.56 & 0.44 \end{bmatrix}$$

$$P^3 = \begin{bmatrix} 0.584 & 0.416 \\ 0.5844 & 0.4156 \end{bmatrix} \qquad P^4 = \begin{bmatrix} \cdots \end{bmatrix}$$

In general,

$$P^{i+1} = P \cdot P^i = \begin{bmatrix} P_{11} & P_{12} \\ P_{21} & P_{22} \end{bmatrix} \cdot \begin{bmatrix} P_{11}^i & P_{12}^i \\ P_{21}^i & P_{22}^i \end{bmatrix}$$

$$= \begin{bmatrix} P_{11}P_{11}^i + P_{12}P_{21}^i & P_{11}P_{12}^i + P_{12}P_{22}^i \\ P_{21}P_{11}^i + P_{22}P_{21}^i & P_{21}P_{12}^i + P_{22}P_{23}^i \end{bmatrix}$$

Also,

$$\lim_{N \to \infty} P^N = \bar{P}$$

For El Hempo Ropo,

$$\bar{P} = \begin{bmatrix} \frac{7}{12} & \frac{5}{12} \\ \frac{7}{12} & \frac{5}{12} \end{bmatrix}$$

Now, we can obtain the limiting form of P by one of two means:

1. We can continue to raise P to higher and higher powers until the values converge. This method can be tedious if P does not converge rapidly. However, we may be interested in how fast it does converge.

If El Stinko Grande has the following transition matrix, what are the limiting state vector sales revenue and $\tilde{P}$?

$$P = \begin{bmatrix} 0.6 & 0.4 \\ 0.75 & 0.25 \end{bmatrix}$$

2. The second method requires solving for the eigenvalues. Two results can be obtained:

$$P^N = \begin{bmatrix} \dfrac{b}{1-a+b} + \dfrac{(1-a)(a-b)^N}{1-a+b} & \dfrac{1-a}{1-a+b} + \dfrac{(1-a)(a-b)^N}{1-a+b} \\ \dfrac{b}{1-a+b} + \dfrac{b(a-b)^N}{1-a+b} & \dfrac{1-a}{1-a+b} + \dfrac{b(a-b)^N}{1-a+b} \end{bmatrix}$$

and

$$\lim_{N \to \infty} P^N = \frac{1}{1-a+b} \begin{bmatrix} b & 1-a \\ b & 1-a \end{bmatrix} \qquad \text{if } |a-b| < 1$$

where

$$P = \begin{bmatrix} a & 1-a \\ b & 1-b \end{bmatrix}$$

PROBLEM—
SERVICE STATION ADVERTISING

Given that there are three major oil companies whose service stations supply gasoline to a small community (closed system). If you represent one of these companies, given the following data, how can you best use a limited advertising budget to maximize your return on the advertising dollar?

Number of Customers

Company	June	July	Gain	Loss
Shell	200	220	60	40
Conoco	500	490	40	50
Frontier	300	290	35	45

Gains from

Company	Shell	Conoco	Frontier
Shell	0	35	25
Conoco	20	0	20
Frontier	20	15	0

If we now assume that the state (company used) of customers in a given month depends only on their state in the previous month, we can generate a one-step transition matrix that will become stationary over time if the probabilities in the one-step matrix do not change with time.

PROBLEM—
CALCULATING PROFESSOR SNARF'S MOODS

Professor Snarf, the celebrated S.O.B. on campus, has been the subject of considerable study by his long-suffering students. It has been observed that he arrives at work every morning at 9:00 A.M. in one of two moods: happy or browned off about something. Further observation has resulted in the following conclusions: If he arrived at work happy at 9:00, the probability that he will be still happy at 10:00 is 0.6. If he arrived at work browned off at 9:00, the probability that he will still be browned off at 10:00 is 0.8.

1.   Given that he arrived at work browned off, what is the probability of a favorable grade change for a student at noon?
2.   Given that he arrived at work happy, what is the probability that he will yell at his wife when he goes home at 6:00 P.M.

Quick & Dirty MARKOV CHAINS

Markov property The future, given the present, is independent of the past.

Definition

1. Given a set of states $i = 1, \ldots, M$, then P_{ij} is the percentage of time that state j is the outcome if the system starts in state i.
2. Given the *transition matrix P* (its elements are the P_{ij}'s above), the state of the system after n moves is described by numbers $p_{ij(n)}$—this is the percentage of the time that j is the outcome after n moves if the system starts in state i.

Facts

a. The $p_{ij(n)}$ is the (i, j) position in the matrix P_n.
b. As n becomes large $p_{ij(n)}$ approaches π_j; that is, all the numbers in a column become identical.

c. The π_j's may be computed from $\pi_j = \sum_{i=1}^{M} \pi_i P_{ij}$, where $\sum_{j=1}^{M} \pi_j = 1$, $\pi_j > 0$.

Limitations

1. For accurate π_j's the p_{ij}'s must be well determined.
2. The size of n for $p_{ij(n)}$ to be close to π_j may be quite large; the π_j's are useful only if the requisite size of n is reasonable for the problem at hand.

Reference

Hillier, F. S., and Lieberman, G. J., *Introduction to Operations Research*, Holden-Day, San Francisco, 1967.

CONVERSATIONAL LIST FOR THE Q & D FOR 2 × 2 MARKOV PROCESS (PROGRAM 4.1)

```
2X2 MARKOV PROCESS

IF IN STATE 1, P(STATE 1):0.5

IF IN STATE 2, P(STATE 1):0.7

TRANSITION MATRIX FOR TIME PERIOD  1

    P(1,1)= .5000    P(1,2)= .5000

    P(2,1)= .7000    P(2,2)= .3000

TRANSITION MATRIX (0 FOR NONE)?:2

TRANSITION MATRIX FOR TIME PERIOD  2

    P(1,1)= .6000    P(1,2)= .4000

    P(2,1)= .5600    P(2,2)= .4400

TRANSITION MATRIX (0 FOR NONE)?:0

STEADY-STATE MATRIX?:YES

STEADY-STATE MATRIX

    P(1,1)= .5833    P(1,2)= .4167

    P(2,1)= .5833    P(2,2)= .4167

DO YOU WISH TO ENTER A STATE VECTOR:YES

S1:0
S2:50000

VECTOR AT END OF PERIOD  1

S1=  35000.00   S2=  15000.00

VECTOR AT END OF PERIOD (0 FOR NONE)?:2

VECTOR AT END OF PERIOD  2

S1=  28000.00   S2=  22000.00

VECTOR AT END OF PERIOD (0 FOR NONE)?:0

DO YOU WISH THE STEADY-STATE VECTOR?:YES

S1=  29166.67   S2=  20833.33

DO 2X2 MARKOV AGAIN? :NO
```

five

Two Tutorials on Geometric Programming

BACKGROUND CONSIDERATIONS

In this chapter two free-standing tutorials are presented for the method of geometric programming. The first is a simplified engineering design problem; the second is concerned not only with a solution method that is new but also with a step-by-step formulation of a crude mathematical model. The rules for using geometric programming as a solution technique are repeated in both examples to ease the learning process for the reader.

The usual analytical approach for optimization of nonlinear programming problems is to use the calculus and/or Lagrange multipliers. With these methods, the optimal policy must first be determined and then plugged back into a cost function to determine if there is enough money to *do* the optimal policy. However, the geometric programming approach of Duffin, Peterson, and Zener [1] often gives the cost figure *first*. If this cost figure is found to be acceptable, the method can *then* be continued to deliver the optimum policy, with the sensitivity analysis thrown in automatically, for good measure.

EXAMPLE 1*

Dryhole Oil and Refining Company has a cylindrical oil storage tank that holds 3141.59 cubic yards of oil. It is massively underinsured, so naturally it catches fire and burns down to the cement foundation in 2.5×10^{-2} hr. The insurance company, in a burst of generosity, pays off the $1000 policy immediately. The design engineer solicits bids for reconstruction. The low bidder, a subsidiary of the oil company, bids a price of $1 per square yard of surface steel. Before the design engineer can start construction, he must convince the auditors that the cost will be less than the insurance payoff of $1000.

The mathematical formulation for his cost function may be expressed as

$$\$ = \pi R^2(\text{surface of top}) + 2\pi Rh(\text{surface of side}) \tag{1}$$

* From "Can Engineers Find Happiness Without Calculus?" *Hydrocarbon Processing*, Vol. 50, No. 8, August 1971. © Gulf Publishing Company, Houston, Texas.

subject to the constraint,

$$\pi R^2 h(\text{volume of tank}) \geq 3141.59(\text{required volume}) \tag{2}$$

Solution with the Calculus

We now proceed to solve in means of the calculus by forming the Lagrangian:

$$L = \pi R^2 + 2\pi RH - \lambda(\pi R^2 h - 3141.59) \tag{3}$$

Differentiating partially with respect to R, h, and λ and setting to zero, we have

$$\frac{\partial L}{\partial R} = 2\pi R + 2\pi h - 2\pi Rh\lambda = 0 \tag{4}$$

$$\frac{\partial L}{\partial h} = 2\pi R - \pi R^2 = 0 \tag{5}$$

$$\frac{\partial L}{\partial \lambda} = R^2 h - 1000\pi = 0 \tag{6}$$

Now (4), (5), and (6) may be rewritten as

$$R + h - Rh = 0 \tag{7}$$

$$\lambda = \frac{2}{R} \tag{8}$$

$$R^2 h = 1000 \tag{9}$$

By substitution of (8) in (7), we have

$$R + h - 2h = 0, \text{ or} \tag{10}$$
$$R = h \tag{11}$$

And then from (9) we have that

$$R = h = 10 \tag{12}$$

Now, by substitution of (12) into (1), we have that the total cost is

$$\$ = \pi(10)^2 + 2\pi(10)^2 = 300\pi = \$942.48. \tag{13}$$

Therefore the answer is "yes," we can afford it.

Solution with Geometric Programming

Geometric programming has the unnerving property that you may find the optimal solution before knowing the optimal values of the variables. Note that in the preceding example optimal values for the variables are necessary before optimal cost can be determined. Put another way, with geometric programming one can determine the cost of a design before designing it.

In order to formulate the above problem as a geometric programming problem, we first must cast all constraints into the form

$$f(x) \leq 1 \tag{14}$$

The volume constraint appears as

$$\pi R^2 h \geq 3141.59 \tag{15}$$

which we may rewrite as

$$1000\, R^{-2}h^{-1} \leq 1 \tag{16}$$

The mathematical formulation of the problem is, then,

Minimize:
$$\$ = \pi R^2 + 2\pi Rh \tag{17}$$

Subject to:
$$1000\, R^{-2}h^{-1} \leq 1 \tag{18}$$

We may write the *form* of the optimal solution at once by using the following rule:

Rule 1. The *form* of the optimal solution of *this* geometric programming problem is

$\$ = $ (coefficient of 1st term in cost function$/w_1)^{w_1}$
  times
  (coefficient of 2nd term in cost function$/w_2)^{w_2}$

  .

  .

  times
  (coefficient of last term in cost function$/w_{\text{last}})^{w_{\text{last}}}$
  times
  (coefficient of term in constraint)$^{w_{\text{last}+1}}$

From rule 1 and equations (17) and (18), we have

$$\$ = (\pi/w_1)^{w_1}(2\pi/w_2)^{w_2}(1000)^{w_3} \tag{19}$$

If we knew w_1, w_2, and w_3 we would now be able to write out the cost at once.

We now must generate constraints on w_1, w_2, and w_3 in order to solve (19). First, geometric programming requires that the sum of the w's *in the cost function* be 1, or in this case that

$$w_1 + w_2 = 1 \tag{20}$$

Rule 2. The equation for the ith variable is

(power of the ith variable in the first term in the cost function) $\times w_1$

plus

.

.

.

(power of the ith variable in the last term in the cost function) $\times w_{last}$

plus

.

.

.

(power of the ith variable in the constraint term) $\times w_{last+1}$

equals

zero

Rule 2 applied to R (the first variable) gives, from (17) and (18),

$$(2)w_1 + (1)w_2 - 2w_3 = 0 \tag{21}$$

Rule 2 applied to h (the second variable) gives, from (17) and (18),

$$(0)w_1 + (1)w_2 - w_3 = 0 \tag{22}$$

Now assembling equations (20), (21), and (22), we have

$$
\begin{aligned}
w_1 + w_2 \qquad\quad &= 1 \\
2w_1 + w_2 - 2w_3 &= 0 \\
w_2 - w_3 &= 0
\end{aligned} \tag{23}
$$

which is a set of *three* simultaneous *linear* equations in *three* unknowns, a simple problem in algebra. We have at once that

$$w_1 = \tfrac{1}{3} \qquad w_2 = \tfrac{2}{3} \qquad w_3 = \tfrac{2}{3} \tag{24}$$

By substitution in the form of the optimal solution (equation 19), we have

$$\$ = (\pi/(\tfrac{1}{3})^{1/3}(2\pi/(\tfrac{2}{3})^{2/3}(1000)^{2/3} = 300\pi = \$942.48 \tag{25}$$

It should be noted at this point that:

1. We have found the optimal cost *without* calculus.
2. We have found the optimal cost *before* finding optimal dimensions.
3. We had to solve a set of linear equations as opposed to a set of *nonlinear* equations before.

A moment's pause to consider the extensions of this approach to really grim chemical engineering problems is, at this point, recommended by the authors.

Now that we have determined that we can afford to build, we would like to determine the optimal dimensions. This leads us to:

Rule 3. At optimality, the optimal cost must equal

(the 1st *term* in the cost function/w_1)

which equals

(the 2nd *term* in the cost function/w_2)

which equals . . .

(the last term in the cost function/w_{last}).

From rule 3 and equation (17) we have

$$\$300\pi \text{(optimum cost)} = \pi R^2/\tfrac{1}{3} = 2\pi Rh/\tfrac{2}{3} \tag{26}$$

which may be written as

$$\$300\pi = 3\pi R^2 = 3\pi Rh \tag{27}$$

Note that by taking the first two terms we have at once that

$$R = 10 \tag{28}$$

and by taking the last two terms that

$$R = h \tag{29}$$

but this implies that

$$h = 10 \tag{30}$$

and the solution is complete

Something useful at no extra charge

Geometric programming has, however, delivered something else besides the answer. Lets look again at the *w*'s:

$$w_1 = \tfrac{1}{3} \qquad w_2 = \tfrac{2}{3} \tag{31}$$

It should be noted that the determination of the *w*'s has nothing whatever to do with the costs in the problem. *They express only the percentage contribution of that term to total cost no matter what the cost coefficients in the term are.* In short, the *w*'s have told us that the top of the tank will contribute one-third of the cost and the side will contribute two-thirds of the cost, *no matter what*.

The effect of this situation is that if costs must be cut, we have dictated that we shall save more by reducing the side surface rather than the top; that is, we should build a shorter tower. The extension to more meaningful design problems of this principle is, to say the least, exciting.

It should be explicitly understood that the formulation shown here is useful if and only if the following conditions hold:

1. The number of terms less the number of variables less one equals zero.
2. All coefficients on terms are positive.
3. The constraint has only one term.
4. All terms are polynomials.

The above conditions are not to imply that problems not conforming to them may not be solved; they can. Explicit applications to actual chemical engineering problems outside the stated conditions will appear in a forthcoming publication now in preparation by the authors.

EXAMPLE 2

Christmastree McCrude, the owner of the Everduster Oil Company has been given an ultimatum by his backers. They will not advance him next month's drilling money for his wildcat in the Atlas mountains unless he can show that: (1) he is changing bits at the right cycle to minimize operating costs, and (2) he can show that next month's costs should be less than $75,000. Now McCrude has found from bitter experience that the depth he can drill before having to change bits is approximated by the relationship $D = 400\sqrt{T}$, where D is cumulative feet and T is drilling time in days. Drilling costs are $2000 per day given a drilling rate of 10,000 feet per month. It takes, on the average, 8 hr to change a bit, at an average cost of $1000.
Can McCrude continue to operate at all, and if so, how?

Formulation

First the problem must be formulated as a cost to be minimized. If N = cycles per month and our drilling rate is 10,000 feet per month, we then have $N * D = 10,000$. But as we have, from above, that $D = 400\sqrt{T}$, we may substitute and get:

$$N = 10{,}000/400\sqrt{T} = 25/\sqrt{T} \tag{1}$$

Now, the cost in dollars per month may be written as

$$\$/\text{month} = \frac{N\,(\text{cycles})}{\text{month}} * \frac{T\,(\text{days})}{\text{cycle}} * \frac{2000(\$\ )}{\text{day}} + \frac{1000(\$\ )}{\text{cycle}} * \frac{N\,(\text{cycles})}{\text{month}} \tag{2}$$

By combining equations (1) and (2) we have for the monthly cost, C_m,

$$C_m = 50{,}000T^{+0.5} + 25{,}000T^{-0.5} \tag{3}$$

We must first take a derivative of equation (3) and set it equal to zero, giving

$$\frac{dC_m}{dT} = (0.5) * 50{,}000T^{-0.5} - (0.5) * 25{,}000T^{-1.5} = 0 \tag{4}$$

Solving for T, we obtain $T_{opt} = \frac{1}{2}$ day drilling each cycle. Upon examination of the second derivative at the point $T_{opt} = \frac{1}{2}$, we find that it is positive, and thus we have a minimum cost. We must now check to determine if this answer is feasible, so we have

$$N = 25/\sqrt{T} = 35.355 \text{ cycles/month} \tag{5}$$

which gives

$$\text{total days/cycle} = \underset{\text{drilling}}{\tfrac{1}{2}} + \underset{\text{bit changing}}{\tfrac{8}{24}} = \tfrac{5}{6} \text{ day/cycle} \tag{6}$$

We now have at once:

$\tfrac{5}{6}$ day/cycle $* 35.355$ cycles/month

$$= 29.463 \text{ days/month} < 30 \text{ days/month} \tag{7}$$

Therefore we know that the operating policy is feasible, and at last we may find out if we can afford to operate at all. Now, substituting $T_{opt} = \frac{1}{2}$ into the cost equation (3), we have

$$C_m = 50{,}000(\tfrac{1}{2})^{+0.5} + 25{,}000(\tfrac{1}{2})^{-0.5} = \$70{,}710.68 \tag{8}$$

So, at long last, the answer is *yes,* McCrude can continue to operate.

Solution using geometric programming

The above method seems quick enough, but geometric programming has the unnerving property that you may find the optimal cost before knowing the optimal operating policy. Note that in the preceding example, the optimal value for the policy was necessary in order to determine the optimal cost. In short: with geometric programming you can determine the *cost* of an optimum policy *before* knowing the policy.

Let us now do the preceding example as a geometric program with the following simple rules:

Rule 1. The form of the optimal solution of this geometric program is

$C_m^* = $ (coefficient of first cost function term$/w_1)^{w_1} *$ (coefficient of second cost function term$/w_2)^{w_2} * \cdots *$ (coefficient of last cost function term$/w_{\text{last}})^{w_{\text{last}}}$

From rule 1 and the equation for optimal cost, $C_m = 50{,}000T^{+0.5} + 25{,}000T^{-0.5}$, we have that

$$C_m{}^* = \left(\frac{50{,}000}{w_1}\right)^{w_1}\left(\frac{25{,}000}{w_2}\right)^{w_2} \tag{9}$$

Although this expression certainly *looks* more formidable than equation (3), note that if we knew w_1 and w_2, we would have $C_m{}^*$ at once. We must now create equations for w_1 and w_2 to solve equation (9). Geometric programming first required that the sum of the w's in the cost function be equal to 1, or in this case,

$$w_1 + w_2 = 1 \tag{10}$$

We now must formulate a rule to define an equation for each variable, which is as follows:

Rule 2. The equation for the variable i is

(power of ith variable in first cost function term) $* w_1 +$ (power of ith variable in second cost function term) $* w_2 + \cdots +$ (power of ith variable in last cost function term) $* w_{\text{last}} = 0$

From rule 2 and the equation for optimal cost, $C_m = 50{,}000T^{+0.5} + 25{,}000T^{-0.5}$, we have that

$$(+0.5)w_1 + (-0.5)w_2 = 0 \tag{11}$$

Now, rewriting equations (10) and (11) as

$$w_1 + w_2 = 1 \tag{12}$$
$$w_1 - w_2 = 0 \tag{13}$$

We have at once that $w_1 = w_2 = \frac{1}{2}$. Plugging these into the cost equation (9), we get

$$C_m{}^* = \left(\frac{50{,}000}{w_1}\right)^{w_1}\left(\frac{25{,}000}{w_2}\right)^{w_2} = \left(\frac{50{,}000}{\frac{1}{2}}\right)^{1/2}\left(\frac{25{,}000}{\frac{1}{2}}\right)^{1/2}$$
$$= \$70{,}710.68 \tag{14}$$

We now pause to note that:

1. Optimal cost was found *without* calculus.
2. Optimal cost was found before the optimal policy.

In short, we know that the optimum operating cycle will cost *before* we know what that cycle *is*. Thus, we can see that McCrude knows he can meet his backer's constraint on his costs; therefore he now wants to know what the optimal operating policy is. We therefore have the following rule:

Rule 3. At optimality, $C_m{}^* =$ (first cost function *term*/w_1) = (second cost function *term*/w_2) = $\cdots$ = (last cost function *term*/w_{last}).

From rule 3 and the cost equation, we have

$$C_m^* = \$70,710.68 = \frac{50,000T^{+0.5}}{\frac{1}{2}} = \frac{525,000T^{-0.5}}{\frac{1}{2}} \tag{15}$$

It can be seen that we may obtain the optimal value of T by taking: (a) the first and second terms of the above equation or (b) the first and last, or (c) the second and third; all giving the same answer, which is

$$T^* = \tfrac{1}{2} \text{ day/cycle} \tag{16}$$

and the solution is complete.

Sensitivity at no extra charge

You will recall that we promised that geometric programming would also deliver not just the answer first, but also the sensitivity of that answer to change in cost. Let us look again at the weights:

$$w_1 = w_2 = \tfrac{1}{2} \tag{17}$$

Each w is a measure of how much its term contributed to the total cost at the optimum solution. Or put another way, the w's express the percentage contribution of their term to total cost, *no matter how those costs may change*. In short, the w's tell us that, at optimum cost, the drilling expense and bit-changing expense *must be equal*. If these two expenses are *not* equal, then the operating policy is dead wrong. The real implication of this principle to more complex problems is simply that if you must cut costs, the w's will tell you *where,* and exactly *how much* the cut will affect total costs. On the other hand, if you should suddenly get more money to spend, the w's might tell you, with a more complex model, that it would be 10 percent more effective to move to a more expensive drilling mud than to do anything else. The application of this happy principle to design problems is equally straightforward; an example may be found in [2].

Conclusions

It is cheerfully admitted that the example given here is incomplete in many respects. In fact, the above formulation will work only on problems where:

1. The number of terms less the number of variables less one equals zero.
2. All coefficients on terms are positive.
3. All terms are polynomials.

After noting the above list the reader is certainly to be forgiven if he suspects that geometric programming seems to be useful only if (a) the phase of the moon is right, and (b) the day of the month is a prime number. The restrictions on when geometric programming is really useful can all be overcome in various ways, which are, unfortunately, beyond the scope of a Quick & Dirty manual. However this author contends that the most important use for geometric programming is that it can, quite often, give the design engineer or operations researcher bounds on optimal cost, even when "getting the optimum" answer" is very difficult with *any* method. To demonstrate this assertion of the usefulness of "bounding" with geometric programming, a Quick & Dirty for this method is supplied. This is followed by two examples; the first is an inventory model, the second, a model of a heat exchanger.

The two Quick & Dirtys supplied for formulation of nonlinear programming problems as geometric programs have differences that should be noted. The first Q & D is a "classical" statement of geometric programming, hopefully consistent with texts on the subject. The second Q & D is a much simpler statement of the first one for this author and other nonacademic readers.

CITED REFERENCES

[1] Duffin, R. J., Peterson, E. L., and Zener, C., *Geometric Programming,* Wiley, New York, 1967.
[2] Woolsey, R. E. D., Kochenburger, G. A., and Linck, K. R., "Can Engineers Find Happiness Without Calculus?", *Hydrocarbon Processing,* Aug. 1971, pp. 133–134.

Quick & Dirty GEOMETRIC PROGRAMMING FOR POSYNOMIALS[1]

Definition. A posynomial is a polynomial with no negative coefficients.

Geometric programming is a consequence of the geometric inequality that states that geometric averages are bounded above by their corresponding arithmetic averages, that is,

$$\prod_{n=1}^{N} x_n{}^{w_n} \leq \sum_{n=1}^{N} w_n x_n$$

where

$$\sum_{n=1}^{N} w_n = 1, \qquad w_n \geq 0$$

Given the posynomials $P_j(\bar{x}) = \displaystyle\prod_{i=1}^{N} x_i{}^{a_{ij}}$, consider the following problem.

Problem

Minimize:

$$f(\bar{x}) = \sum_{i=1}^{P} c_j P_j(\bar{x}) \qquad \text{where } c_j > 0$$

subject to:

$$\sum_{i=1}^{P(i)} c_{ik} P_{ik}(\bar{x}) \leq 1 \qquad i = 1, \ldots, M$$

where

$$P_{ik}(\bar{x}) = \prod_{n=1}^{N} \bar{x}_n{}^{a_{ik}} \quad \text{and} \quad c_{ik} > 0$$

Solution

Solve the system of *linear* equations ($w_i \geq 0$, $w_{ik} \geq 0$)

$$\sum_{=1}^{P} w_i = 1 \qquad \text{(normality)}$$

[1] Well, actually a Slow & Clean.

$$\sum_{j=1}^{P} a_{lj} w_j + \sum_{i=1}^{M} \sum_{k=1}^{P(i)} a_{ikl} w_{ik} = 0, \quad \mathcal{L} = 1, \ \ldots, N \qquad \text{(orthogonality)}$$

The answer is

$$f(\bar{x}^0) = \prod_{j=1}^{P} \left(\frac{c_i}{w_i}\right)^{w_i} \prod_{i=1}^{M} \left[\prod_{k=1}^{P(i)} \left(\frac{c_{kj}}{w_{kj}}\right)^{w_{kj}}\right] \left[\sum_{k=1}^{P(i)} w_{kj}\right]^{\sum_{k=1}^{P(k)} w_{ki}}$$

and the variables may be found from

$$c_j P_j(\bar{x}) = w_j f(\bar{x}^0) \qquad j = 1, \ \ldots, P$$

while

$$c_{ik} P_{ik}(\bar{x}) = \frac{w_{ik}}{w_i} \qquad k = 1, \ \ldots, P(i); \ i = 1, \ \ldots, M$$

Notes:

1. The problem with general polynomials can also be solved; see reference [2].
2. The difference between the number of weights (w_j and w_{ik}) and the number of terms plus one is the *degree of difficulty*—only 0 degree of difficulty problems are immediately solved.

References

Gue, R. L., and Thomas, M. E., *Mathematical Methods in Operations Research,* Macmillan, New York, 1968.
Wilde, D. J., and Beightler, C. S., *Foundations of Optimization,* Prentice-Hall, Englewood Cliffs, N.J., 1967.

Quick & Dirty GEOMETRIC PROGRAMMING RULES FOR POSYNOMIALS

1. The optimum value of the objective function is always of the form:

   $g_0(x)^* = $ (coefficient of 1st term/w_1)w_1 * (coefficient of 2nd term/w_2)w_2 * $\cdots$ * (coefficient of last term/w_{last})w_{last} * (Σw's in 1st constraint)$^{\Sigma w\text{'s in 1st constraint}}$ * $\cdots$ * (Σw's in last constraint)$^{\Sigma w\text{'s in last constraint}}$.

2. Equations generated for a geometric program are:

   Σw's in objective function $= 1$
   and for each primal variable x_j, with n variables and m terms,

   $$\sum_{i=1}^{i=m} [(w_i \text{ for each term}) * (\text{exponent on } x_j \text{ in that term})] = 0$$

   $$j = 1, 2, \ldots, n$$

3. Primal variables may be found by:

   $g_0(x)^* = $ (1st term in objective function/w_1) $=$ (2nd term in objective function/w_2) $= \cdots = $ (last term in objective function/w_{last})
   or for each constraint term,
   $w_{i\text{th term}} = (i\text{th term}) * (\text{sum of all } w\text{'s in that constraint})$

4. The degree of difficulty is given by:

   D.D. $=$ (no. of terms) $-$ (no. of variables) $- 1$

Quick & Dirty BOUNDING WITH POSYNOMIAL GEOMETRIC PROGRAMMING

For any posynomial geometric programming problem, it is always true that the sum of the pieces of the cost function must add up to 100 percent of the cost. Or, stated another way, the sum of the geometric programming w's in the objective function must sum to 1. In symbols:

$$\sum_{i=1}^{i=n} w_i = 1$$

where there are n terms in the objective function.

With zero degrees of difficulty we can, of course, find the numerical values of the w's at once. However, with higher degrees of difficulty we can still bound, very often, the w's in the objective function because from above we know that

$$1 \geq w_1 \geq 0 \quad 1 \geq w_2 \geq 0, \ldots, \quad 1 \geq w_n \geq 0$$

Example 1—Bounding Contributions to Cost

Thomopoulos and Lehman defined a formula for the EOQ in the following form:

$$\text{total cost} = K_1/Q + K_2Q + K_3Q^2$$
$$= \text{set-up cost} + \text{inventory holding cost} + \text{obsolescence cost}$$

Note that the above problem has three terms and one variable (Q), giving $3 - 1 - 1 = 1$ degree of difficulty. Forming the normality and orthogonality equations from geometric programming, we have

$$w_1 + w_2 + w_3 = 1$$

and

$$-w_1 + w_2 + 2w_3 = 0$$

1. Eliminating w_1 and solving for w_2 and w_3, we get $w_2 = (1 - 3w_3)/2$ and $w_3 = (1 - 2w_2)/3$. But from above we have $1 \geq w_2 \geq 0$ and $1 \geq w_3 \geq 0$, so we have at once that $w_3 \leq \frac{1}{3}$, and $w_2 \leq \frac{1}{2}$.
2. Eliminating w_2 and solving for w_1 and w_3, we get $w_1 = (1 + w_3)/2$ and $w_3 = 2w_1 - 1$. Again from above, using the fact that w_1 and w_3 are bounded above by 1 and below by 0, we have $w_1 \geq \frac{1}{2}$.
3. Eliminating w_3 and solving for w_1 and w_2, we get $w_2 = (2 - 3w_1)$ and $w_1 = (2 - w_2)/3$, which, operating as before, yield at once that $\frac{2}{3} \geq w_1 \geq \frac{1}{3}$.

Conclusion: For the above economic order quantity model, the necessary conditions for operating optimally are as follows:

1. Set-up cost must never be greater than 66.67 percent nor less than 50 percent of total cost.
2. Inventory holding cost must never be greater than 50 percent of total cost.
3. Obsolescence cost must never be more than 33.33 percent of total cost.

Reference

Thomopoulos, N. T., and Lehman, M., "Effects on Inventory Obsolescence and Uneven Demand on the EOQ Formula," *P & IM Journal*, Vol. 12, No. 4, 4th Qtr. 1971, pp. 27–40.

Example 2—Bounding Contributions to Cost

A very accurate model for the total cost of a heat exchanger is

Minimize

$$C_T(A,h_i,h_0) = C_A A + C_i h_i{}^{3.5} A + C_o h_0{}^{4.75} A$$

subject to

$$K_1 A^{-1} h_i{}^{-1} + K_2 A^{-1} h_0{}^{-1} + K_3 A^{-1} \leq 1$$

where

$$A = \text{surface area for heat transfer, ft}^2$$
$$C_i, C_0 C_A = \text{cost coefficients}$$
$$h_i, h_o = \text{heat transfer coefficients}$$

The constraint is a dimensionless form of the traditional heat exchanger design equation. The problem has six terms, three variables, and two degrees-of-difficulty.

The normality and orthogonality equations for this problem are

$w_1 + w_2 + w_3$ $= 1$ normality		(1)
$w_1 + w_2 + w_3 - w_4 - w_5 - w_6 = 0$ orthogonality for A		(2)
$3.5\, w_2 \quad - w_4 \quad = 0$ orthogonality for h_i		(3)
$4.75\, w_3 \quad - w_5 \quad = 0$ orthogonality for h_0		(4)

Combining equations (1) and (2) gives

$$w_4 + w_5 + w_6 = 1$$

Since the weights must always be positive (common sense, again), then

$$0 \leq w_4 \leq 1 \qquad 0 \leq w_5 \leq 1 \qquad 0 \leq w_6 \leq 1$$

Substituting equations (3) and (4) gives

$3.5w_2 = w_4 \leq 1$ or $w_2 \leq 1/3.5 = 0.2857$
$4.75w_3 = w_5 \leq 1$ or $w_3 \leq 1/4.75 = 0.2105$

Since $w_1 = 1 - (w_2 + w_3)$ and $w_2 + w_3 \leq 0.4962$, then $w_1 \geq 0.5038$. Thus, without solving the dual problem, we may write

$$0.5038 \leq w_1 \leq 1 \qquad 0 \leq w_2 \leq 0.2857 \qquad 0 \leq w_3 \leq 0.2105$$

The installed heat exchanger cost may thus never be less than 50.38 percent of the minimum total cost, the tube-side pumping cost may never exceed 28.57 percent of the minimum total cost, and the shell-side pumping cost may never exceed 21.05 percent of the minimum total cost.

An "Out-of-Kilter" Network Tutorial

Network flow algorithms have been developed to handle a special class of linear programming problems. These problems may each be described as a network whose links carry flow. Network algorithms take advantage of this special structure to produce an optimal solution much more quickly, with less storage required, and with virtually no round-off error in comparison with general linear programming codes. The objective here is to introduce the reader to the basic ideas involved in formulating a network problem, and to explain in a non-technical manner what the "out-of-kilter" network algorithm [1] *does*. This algorithm is very general and extremely efficient in solving network flow cost problems (as opposed to CPM-, PERT-, and GERT-type networks).

Network problems, as you might suspect, can be thought of intuitively as networks (but do not necessarily represent *physical* networks)—the points, places, or locations designated to be network "nodes", and the links or "arcs" that connect certain of these nodes. These arcs allow movement between the nodes they connect. Movement of flow along each network arc is restricted by a maximum capacity (ability to handle flow per unit time) and a minimum required flow (perhaps greater than zero). Also known is the cost (assumed constant) of transmitting each *unit* of flow from one node to another along an arc. The flow *is not* required to be fluid in the sense of a liquid, but must meet a physical restriction that one might normally expect of a flow. Roughly, flow cannot "stack up" at a node; total flow into a node must equal total flow out of that node. This property is called *conservation of flow*.

It is often surprising to discover the wide variety of practical problems that may be posed as the analog of flow in a capacitated cost network. Oil and gas pipelines, telephone lines, highway systems, electrical circuits, computer configurations, airline routes, the flow of work in an office, assembly lines, and, in general, most communication, transpor-

* From H. S. Swanson and R. E. D. Woolsey, "An Out-of-Kilter Network Tutorial," *Sigmap* 13, January 1973, pp. 34–40.

tation, and distribution systems form network structures. Problems as varied as determining the optimal number and location of oil drilling platforms in the ocean, routing river flow to avoid flooding, and making the optimal assignment of men to machines are examples of (not-so-obvious) network flow problems. If a problem is to be solved using a network approach, it must be possible to relate the variables of the problem to the flow in arcs of a visualized network and relate the costs or benefits accordingly.

In general, network problems may be characterized as falling into one of the three following categories:

1. Find the maximum flow from a designated node to a different designated node subject to the capacity restrictions on flow in each arc and conservation of flow at each node.
2. Find the maximum flow from a designated node to a different designated node *that minimizes the cost* incurred, subject to capacity restrictions on flow in each arc and conservation of flow at each node.
3. Find the flow that minimizes the cost of shipping k units (k is a known integer that might be less than the maximum flow) from a designated node to a different designated node, subject to capacity restrictions on flow in each arc and conservation of flow at each node.

The out-of-kilter algorithm can solve problems in each of the above categories (plus problems in some additional categories) by proper selection of costs, capacities, and network configuration (minimum cost circulation network flow problem).

In order to discuss the algorithm, a small amount of jargon is necessary. A *path* from node A to node B in a network is a set of sequential arcs that forms a route from A to B. Arcs (1, 2), (2, 3), (3, 4) form a path from node 1 to node 4 in the network of Figure 5. A *cycle* in a network is a path that ultimately leads back to the starting node. Arc (4, 1), in addition to the previously mentioned path, forms

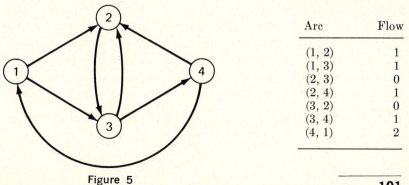

Arc	Flow
(1, 2)	1
(1, 3)	1
(2, 3)	0
(2, 4)	1
(3, 2)	0
(3, 4)	1
(4, 1)	2

Figure 5

a cycle. A *circulation* in a network is a set of flows on the arcs of the network that preserves conservation of flow at each node. The flows of the following table define a circulation for the network of Figure 5 (note that there are many other possible circulations).

The out-of-kilter algorithm operates in such a way as to maintain a circulation in the network while rerouting flows so as to minimize the sum of cost times flow and satisfy capacity restrictions on each arc. This generates an optimal solution to the minimum cost circulation network problem, if such a solution exists. The theoretical aspects of this process arise from the primal-dual theory of linear programming (complementary slackness) [1]. The brief discussion that follows is intended to give the reader an intuitive idea of how and why the algorithm works. A more detailed discussion may be found in earlier articles on this subject; see references [1], [2], and [3].

To find the optimal flow in a network, the algorithm is initialized with a circulation flow of 0 in each arc (conservation is preserved at each node). Note that such a circulation might not satisfy capacity constraints (the problem is dual feasible). In addition, a number must be assigned to each node (these node numbers are actually values of the dual variables, and they may be initialized at value 0). he "economic" or intuitive interpretation of each node number is the "value" or price of a unit of flow at that node. Examine an arc of the network, say from node x to node y. The cost C_{xy} of flow on arc (x, y) is known, so we can compute $D_{xy} = P_x + C_{xy} - P_y$, where $P_x(P_y)$ is the node number at node x (node y). Note that the economic interpretation of the number D_{xy} is then the value of flow at node x plus the cost of moving from node x to node y along arc (x, y) minus the value of flow at node y. Then, intuitively:

1. If $D_{xy} < 0$, the value of flow at node y is *greater* than the value of flow at node x plus the cost of getting the flow at node x to node y. This implies that the flow in arc (x, y) should be as great as possible, that is, equal to the upper bound on arc (x, y). $D_{xy} < 0 \rightarrow f_{xy} = u_{xy}$.
2. If $D_{xy} > 0$, then, similarly, the flow in arc (x, y) should be as little as possible (the cost of moving from node x to node y is greater than the increase in value of moving from node x to node y). The flow should equal the lower bound. $D_{xy} > 0 \rightarrow f_{xy} = 1_{xy}$.
3. If $D_{xy} = 0$, the increase in value of moving from node x to node y exactly matches the cost of doing so; thus the flow in arc (x, y) need only satisfy the capacity restrictions on arc (x, y). $D_{xy} = 0 \rightarrow 1_{xy} \leq f_{xy} \leq u_{xy}$.

If the flow in arc (x, y) is "appropriate" for the value of D_{xy}, then arc (x, y) is said to be "in kilter" (actually satisfies optimally conditions). Otherwise, an arc is said to be "out of kilter." If an arc (x, y) is out of kilter, the algorithm seeks to find a path from node y to node x that together with arc (x, y) forms a cycle along which the flow may be changed by a constant amount without disturbing conservation of flow at any node. Actually, a special kind of path must be found—one along which a change in flow would not worsen the "kilter condition" (cases 1–3 above) of any arc. In addition, the out-of-kilter algorithm has a routine to change flows once a cycle is found for an out-of-kilter arc, and a routine to change the node numbers (dual variables) when that becomes necessary. When each arc is in kilter the flow is optimal. To summarize, the algorithm proceeds as follows:

0. Start with any circulation and any set of node numbers.
1. Find an out-of-kilter arc, (s, t). If there is none, stop.
2. Determine if the flow in arc (s, t) is to be increased or decreased to bring (s, t) into kilter. If the flow should be increased, go to step 3. If the flow should be decreased, go to step 4.
3. Find a path from t to s along which the flow can be increased without causing any arc on the path to become more out of kilter. If a path is found, increase the flow along the path and also in (s, t). If (s, t) is in kilter, go to step 1. If (s, t) is still out of kilter, repeat step 3. If no path can be found, go to step 5.
4. Find a path from s to t along which the flow can be increased without causing any arc to become more out of kilter. If a path is found, increased the flow along the path and decrease the flow in (s, t). If (s, t) is in kilter, go to step 1. If (s, t) is still out of kilter, repeat step 4. If no path is found, go to step 5.
5. Change the node numbers. If (s, t) is in kilter, go to step 1. If (s, t) is still out of kilter, repeat step 2.

As an example of how to formulate a network problem, consider the frequently occurring "assignment problem." Essentially this problem consists of trying to match up n men with n machines (or machines with jobs or men with jobs) in such a way as to maximize the efficiency of work. In general there are some men who cannot operate certain machines, but each man must be assigned to one and only one machine (do not assign more than one man to each machine). The efficiency of each man on each (feasible) machine must be known. Usually the efficiency is measured by the average time required to perform a given task on a given machine (items/unit time, time to complete task, quality of output, etc). Note that assigning each man to the machine that he operates with the greatest efficiency might not be a solution to the problem, because several men might be "most efficient" on the same machine. Readers familiar with this problem will recognize that there are many variations. For example, there might be more men than machines, more machines then men, or one may wish to maximize the minimum efficiency of an assignment. Each of these problems may be solved by a simple adaption of the network formulation.

To solve the assignment problem described above, construct a network consisting of a node for each man (number these nodes 1 through n) and a node for each machine (numbered $n + 1$ through $2n$). The arcs of the network are determined by which men have the ability to operate which machines. In particular, if man i can operate machine j, then the network must have an arc from node i to node j. If $n = 3$, the network in Figure 6 might result. The network of Figure 6 shows that man 1 can operate each of machines 4, 5, or 6; man 2 can operate machines 5 or 6; man 3 can operate

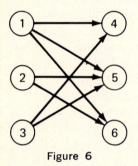

Figure 6

machines 4 or 5. In order to preserve conservation of flow at each node and to prepare the network of Figure 6 for solution by the out-of-kilter algorithm, some additions must be made to the network. Add node S, node T, and the connecting arcs as shown in Figure 7. This reduces the network to a "single source–single sink" network and will simplify that conservation of flow problem. Node S is called the "super source" node (it generates all the available flow), and node T is called the "super sink" node (it eventually absorbs all the available flow). As a final addition to the network, connect node T to node S by an arc (T, S), called the "circulation arc." The circulation arc connecting the super sink to the super source provides for conservation of flow between node T and node S.

Now, the upper bound, lower bound, and cost must be fixed for each arc in such a way as to ensure that the assignment problem will be solved by the out-of-kilter algorithm operating on the network of Figure 7. Recall that the algorithm will seek to minimize the sum of cost times flow in each arc while satisfying upper and lower bounds on flow in each arc and maintaining conservation of flow at each node. Consider the ordered triples of the table below as values of the upper bound (u), lower bound (l), and per unit cost (c) for the corresponding arc of the network shown in Figure 7. (A_{14} is the efficiency of man 1 working on machine 4, etc.)

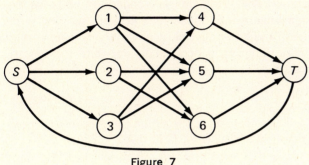

Figure 7

Arc	(u, l, c)
$(S, 1)$	$(1, 1, 0)$
$(S, 2)$	$(1, 1, 0)$
$(S, 3)$	$(1, 1, 0)$
$(1, 4)$	$(1, 0, -A_{14})$
$(1, 5)$	$(1, 0, -A_{15})$
$(1, 6)$	$(1, 0, -A_{16})$
$(2, 5)$	$(1, 0, -A_{25})$
$(2, 6)$	$(1, 0, -A_{26})$
$(3, 4)$	$(1, 0, -A_{34})$
$(3, 5)$	$(1, 0, -A_{35})$
$(4, T)$	$(1, 1, 0)$
$(5, T)$	$(1, 1, 0)$
$(6, T)$	$(1, 1, 0)$
(T, S)	$(3, 3, 0)$

For the first three arcs of the table, the upper and lower bounds each have value 1 to ensure that each man is assigned to *exactly* one machine. The following seven arcs have lower bounds of zero so as not to require which man is assigned to which machine. The "cost" on each of these arcs is the negative of the man–machine efficiency, because the out-of-kilter is a *minimizing* algorithm (maximizing efficiency is equivalent to minimizing the negative of efficiency, or inefficiency). The next three arcs have upper and lower bounds each equal to 1 in order to ensure that each machine is assigned *exactly* one man. The circulation arc ensures that three assignments are made (this is ensured regardless, due to conservation of flow requirements). Note that the only "costs" involved are the "inefficiency" measures, and these will be minimized.

Those arcs that have flow at optimality correspond to the optimal assignments to be made. Thus if there is flow in arc $(1, 6)$ at termination of the algorithm, man 1 should work on machine 6. As an added convenience, the flows will be in integer (counting) units, so that no fractional assignments will be made. The network solution to the assignment problem (and especially solutions to larger, more realistic problems) is usually obtained in one-half to one-third the time required by other codes.

CITED REFERENCES

[1]   Ford, L. R., and Fulkerson, D. R., *Flows in Networks,* Princeton University Press, Princeton, N.J., 1962.

[2]   Durbin, E. P., and Kroenke, D. M., "The Out-of-Kilter Algorithm: A Primer," Rand Corporation Memorandum, RM-5472-PR, Dec., 1967.

[3]   Fulkerson, D. R., "An Out-of-Kilter Method for Minimal-Cost Flow Problems," *J. Soc. Indust. Appl. Math.,* Vol. 9, 1961, pp. 18–27.

seven

Networks We Have Node and Loved

In this chapter, some actual problems are discussed and formulated as network problems, and the results are interpreted. This process was undertaken so as to make the product understandable to those who are not yet initiated into the mystical nature of network flow and graph theory.

A network can be thought of as a group of points, places, or locations designated as "nodes" of the network, together with another group of links or arcs that connect certain of these nodes. Arcs allow movement or flow between the nodes they connect. Network flow algorithms (an algorithm is a set of rules or steps that, if followed, produces a solution to a given kind of problem) have been developed to solve a special class of problems. These algorithms take advantage of the special node and arc structure of network problems to produce an optimal solution very quickly, with less storage required, and with virtually no round-off error in comparison with other methods (linear programming, dynamic programming) conventionally used in solving the same kinds of problems.

Others have taken on the task of creating and/or explaining network algorithms [1, 2, 3]. A particularly efficient and useful network algorithm is the out-of-kilter algorithm (OKA) due to D. R. Fulkerson [1, 2]. The OKA produces a solution to certain problems by finding a flow in the appropriate network that minimizes, over all arcs in the network, the sum of cost times flow. The purpose of this chapter, however, is to formulate and discuss some actual problems in terms of networks, and to interpret the network solutions to these problems. As a first example, let us consider the "bottleneck assignment problem"; Operations research types usually have neat-sounding names for their problems. To start at the beginning, let us describe the more commonly encountered "assignment problem." Given a group of workers, a group of machines to be operated by these workers, and

* By H. S. Swanson, R. E. D. Woolsey, and H. Hillis. Reprinted with permission from the March 1974 *Industrial Engineering.* Copyright © American Institute of Industrial Engineers, Inc., 25 Technology Park, Atlanta, Norcross, Georgia 30071.

a known efficiency for each worker operating each machine, the assignment problem is to assign exactly one worker to each machine (or workers to jobs, teachers to classes, etc.) so that the sum of the efficiencies resulting from the assignment is as large as possible. Note that merely assigning each worker to that machine on which he is most efficient is not necessarily a solution to the problem, because several workers may be most efficient on the same machine and the problem calls for exactly one worker for each machine. Thus it is likely that some workers will be assigned to machines other than the ones on which they are most efficient in order that the sum of the efficiencies be maximized. This problem can be formulated and solved as a network flow problem, and the optimal flow will indicate an assignment that maximizes the total efficiency. In particular, the network in Figure 8 models the assignment situation where three men

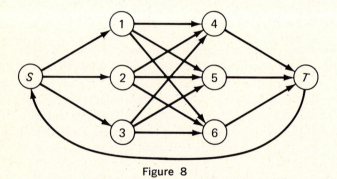

Figure 8

are to be assigned to three machines. Nodes 1, 2, and 3 represent the workers, and nodes 4, 5, and 6 represent the machines.

PROBLEM
BOTTLENECK ASSIGNMENT

Now, back to the bottleneck assignment problem, which differs slightly from the assignment problem just described in that the objective is to maximize the minimum efficiency resulting from the assignment. This objective is often realistic, for example, in series-type assembly lines with different work stations. In such a case, the worker with the minimum efficiency (the bottleneck) would determine the rate of output for the whole assembly line. It would be desirable, then, to maximize the minimum efficiency (maximize the bottleneck). This action determines an optimal assignment appropriate for this bottleneck situation, as opposed to finding the assignment that maximizes the sum of efficiencies. As you may have guessed, this problem has a network solution. In fact, this problem may be solved by sequentially solving several of the appropriate assignment problems. The algorithm is as follows:

1. Solve the (bottleneck assignment) problem as if it were an ordinary assignment problem; this is easily done by using the OKA. The OKA is a *minimizing* algorithm, so minimize the sum of inefficiencies (the negative of efficiency), which is equivalent to maximizing efficiency.
2. Look at the optimal solution from step 1. Determine from this solution the assignment with the greatest inefficiency (lowest efficiency). If there are ties, pick one arbitrarily.
3. Remove from the network used in step 1 the arcs that have inefficiencies (costs) greater than or equal to the inefficiency determined in step 2. (lowest efficiency – greatest inefficiency from step 1).
4. Go to step 1 with the new network determined by step 3.
5. Continue this process until it is impossible to make the desired number of assignments (as more and more arcs are deleted from the original network). This event is realized when OKA indicates "no feasible solution." The last *feasible* assignment made is then the optimal solution to the bottleneck assignment problem." The justification for this claim is that the OKA is forced to solve a sequence of assignment problems in which the *minimum efficiency* is constantly increasing (as more arcs are being deleted). This algorithm is illustrated by the following example:

Jobs

1	3	2	6	0
4	2	3	8	3
8	4	1	5	0
3	5	4	8	8
2	6	9	5	2

Men

The entry a_{ij} in the matrix represents the efficiency (number of units processed per hour) if man i is assigned to job j. The zero entries (a_{15}, a_{35}) indicate that both man 1 and man 3 are unqualified for job 5.

Solving the bottleneck problem as if it were an ordinary assignment problem (12 nodes, 36 arcs), the OKA produces the following assignment:

man 1 → job 2   with efficiency of 3
man 2 → job 4   with efficiency of 8
man 3 → job 1   with efficiency of 8
man 4 → job 5   with efficiency of 8
man 5 → job 3   with efficiency of 9

The sum of the efficiencies is 36; the lowest efficiency is 3. Thus, delete those entries in the matrix (and corresponding arcs in the network) with efficiencies less than or equal to 3. Now there are 12 nodes and 24 arcs comprising the network. Solving this assignment network with the OKA produces the following solution:

man 1 → job 4   with efficiency of 6
man 2 → job 1   with efficiency of 4
man 3 → job 2   with efficiency of 4
man 4 → job 5   with efficiency of 8
man 5 → job 3   with efficiency of 9

The sum of the efficiencies has now decreased to 31, but the smallest efficiency has increased to 4. To continue, delete those arcs of the assignment network with efficiencies less than or equal to 4. There are now 12 nodes and 21 arcs. The OKA now indicates that there is no feasible solution to this new network. Therefore, the above is optimal for the bottleneck assignment problem. There is a $33\frac{1}{3}$ percent increase in output with this solution over the original assignment, even though the *sum* of the efficiencies is smaller (the bottleneck is larger).

As a second example, consider the problem of determining the minimum number of workers necessary to accomplish a fixed schedule of partially overlapping tasks. A different setting for the same problem is to determine the fewest number of machines needed to perform a schedule of tasks with known set-up times, or to determine the minimum number of airplanes needed to service a known flight schedule [1]. The OKA has been used to solve this very problem in connection with determining the minimum number of buses required to service a regional transportation authority's proposed route and schedule [4]. We shall explain the network formulation as we proceed with the following example (due to Dr. Paul Jensen, Department of Industrial Engineering, the University of Texas at Austin).

Ten tasks are to be performed. Their start and end times are shown in the table below. The array shows the time it takes (in minutes) to go from one task to any other (set-up time). We are asked to find the minimal number of workers to perform the tasks.

Task	Start	End	1	2	3	4	5	6	7	8	9	10
1	1:00 P.M.	1:30 P.M.	—	60	10	230	180	20	15	40	120	30
2	6:00 P.M.	8:00 P.M.	10	—	40	75	40	5	30	60	5	15
3	10:30 P.M.	11:00 P.M.	70	30	—	0	70	30	20	5	120	70
4	4:00 P.M.	5:00 P.M.	0	50	75	—	20	15	10	20	60	10
5	4:00 P.M.	7:00 P.M.	20	240	150	70	—	15	5	240	90	65
6	12:00 NOON	1:00 P.M.	200	15	20	75	120	—	30	30	15	45
7	2:00 P.M.	5:00 P.M.	15	30	60	45	30	15	—	10	5	0
8	11:00 P.M.	12:00 MIDNIGHT	20	35	15	120	75	30	45	—	20	15
9	8:10 P.M.	9:00 P.M.	25	60	15	10	100	70	80	60	—	120
10	1:45 P.M.	3:00 P.M.	60	60	30	30	120	40	50	60	70	—

From this data it is possible to determine which tasks are "related" to which other tasks; related is used here in the sense that a given job can be completed and a new job can be set up before that new job is scheduled to start. For example, job 1 is related to each of jobs 2, 3, 7, 8, and 9, but is not related to jobs 4, 5, 6, or 10 (end of job 1 is at 1:30 P.M.; set-up time for job 4 is 230 min equals 3 hr 50 min; adding those times it is seen that the 4:00 P.M. start time of job 4 precludes job 1 and job 4 being related). In this manner it is seen that:

job 1 is related to jobs 2, 3, 7, 8, 9
job 2 is related to jobs 3, 8, 9
job 3 is not related to any job
job 4 is related to jobs 2, 3, 8, 9
job 5 is related to jobs 3, 8
job 6 is related to jobs 2, 3, 4, 5, 7, 8, 9, 10
job 7 is related to jobs 2, 3, 8, 9
job 8 is not related to any job
job 9 is related to jobs 3, 8
job 10 is related to jobs 2, 3, 4, 8, 9

Note that the fewest number of individuals required to perform these tasks is equal to the maximal number of (unrelated) tasks, no two of which can be performed by the same individual. To solve this problem with the OKA, devise an assignment network that assigns certain tasks to certain other tasks (these assigned tasks are grouped so that they may be performed by the same individual). In addition to the source and sink nodes, there are to be two "columns" of nodes, with as many nodes in each column as there are tasks. The arcs for this network are determined by whether or not two given nodes are related. Thus, the node corresponding to task 1 in the first column of nodes is connected to those nodes in the second column corresponding to tasks 2, 3, 7, 8, and 9. Nodes corresponding to tasks 3 and 8 need not appear in the first column of nodes (but will appear in the second column), because these tasks are not related to any other tasks (but other tasks are related to them).

The upper bound on the flow in the return or circulation (super sink to super source) arc is equal to the number of tasks minus the number of tasks not related to any tasks. In our example, this is 8. The upper bound on flow in each other arc is 1. The lower bound on flow in each arc is 0 (zero).

The objective is to find the maximum flow in this capacitated network. This is accomplished by setting the unit cost of flow in the return arc to a negative number (say, -10), and setting the unit cost of flow in each other arc equal to 0 (zero). The maximum flow (optimal solution) for this network determines the minimal number of workers necessary to accomplish the schedule of tasks. In particular, arcs that have a positive flow indicate which tasks should be grouped so that they can be performed by a single individual. The number of such groups determines the minimal number of individuals required. The following assignment arcs have positive flow at optimality:

task 1   → task 7
task 4   → task 2
task 5   → task 3
task 6   → task 10
task 7   → task 9
task 9   → task 8
task 10 → task 4

Recall that arcs exist in the network only if nodes are related. Thus the solution is to be interpreted as follows: Task 1 is related to task 7, which is related to task 9, which is related to task 8:

task 1 → task 7 → task 9 → task 8

These four tasks are connected (each is related to the next), and may be done sequentially by a single individual. This "string" of tasks is broken when task 8 is not assigned to any other task. There are two additional strings of tasks:

task 6 → task 10 → task 4 → task 2
task 5 → task 3

Thus, these three groups or strings of tasks each require a separate individual to perform them; no fewer than three individuals can accomplish these ten tasks within the given constraints on start, end, and set-up times.

As a third example, consider the frequently occurring "transportation problem": Minimize the total cost of supplying the known demand for a commodity at each of a given number of outlets, using a given number of storage locations each with a known availability of the commodity. The (constant) per unit cost of transporting the commodity between each storage location and each outlet is assumed to be known. In addition to the standard distribution-type transportation problems, both the "cut and fill" road construction problem and the allocation of school buses from garages to schools fit into the transportation format. The OKA efficiently produces an optimal solution to such problems, and the network structure is identical to that of the assignment network (see Figure 9): one column of nodes corresponding to storage locations and another column of nodes corresponding to outlets. The only non-zero network costs occur on the arcs connecting locations to outlets. These arcs each have lower bounds of zero and upper bounds large enough to be nonrestrictive. The arcs from the super source node to location nodes each have lower bounds of zero, upper bounds equal to the availability of the commodity at the storage location (so that availability will not be exceeded), and a unit cost of zero. The arcs from outlet nodes to super sink node each have lower and upper bounds equal to the demand at the outlet, (so that demand will be met at each outlet) and a zero unit cost. The circulation arc has lower and upper bounds equal to the sum of the demands and a zero unit cost. The OKA operating on this network will minimize the total cost of supplying each demand without exceeding any supply. The solution will be integer valued, and the arcs with positive flow indicate how the supply from each storage location should be allocated to the outlets.

Finally, consider how the OKA might be used to solve two additional network problems: The "max flow" problem and the "shortest path" problem. The max flow problem might occur, for example, in simulating the operation of a pipeline system. Each arc of the network on which the OKA operates to solve the max flow problem has a lower bound of zero and a known upper bound (dictated by the particular problem). Assign a unit cost of zero to each of these arcs. The circulation arc must have a lower bound of zero, an upper bound sufficiently large to be nonrestrictive (sum of the capacities of the other arcs will suffice), and a negative unit cost. The negative cost encourages flow in the circulation arc (OKA minimizes the sum of cost time flow), and conservation of flow ensures that this flow is drawn through the network. Eventually, the capacities of the network arcs will limit flow in this circulation arc. This produces the maximum flow in the network.

The shortest path problem occurs in routing-type problems in which the objective is to find how to connect two given locations by a path over which the sum of the distances traveled is as small as possible.

The network represents all possible links connecting the two locations. Each link should have a lower bound of zero, an upper bound of 1, and a cost equal to the distance of that link (arc). Connect the two locations by a circulation arc, and fix the lower and upper bounds of this arc at 1. Assign a zero cost to this arc. In order to satisfy the lower and upper bounds (both equal to 1), the OKA will find the shortest path through the network. The arcs with positive flow indicate the shortest path connecting the two locations of interest.

(PLEASE TURN TO PAGES 115–121 FOR THE PROGRAM LISTING.)

CITED REFERENCES

[1] Ford, L. R., and Fulkerson, D. R., *Flows in Networks,* Princeton University Press, Princeton, N.J., 1962.
[2] Phillips, D. T., and Jensen, P. A., "Network Flow Optimization with the Out-Of-Kilter Algorithm, Part I—Theory," *Research Management,* Feb. 1971.
[3] Swanson, H. S., and Woolsey, R. E. D., "An Out-Of-Kilter Network Tutorial," *SIGMAP Newsletter,* No. 13, Jan. 1973, pp. 34–40.
[4] Saha, J. L., "An Algorithm for Bus Scheduling Problems," *Operational Research Quarterly,* Vol. 21, No. 4, Dec. 1970, pp. 463–475.

```
      DIMENSION COST(100)
      DIMENSION I(100),J(100),HI(100),LO(100),FLOW(100),PI(100)
      IMPLICIT INTEGER(A-Z)
      LOGICAL INFES
  100 FORMAT(2I)
  105 FORMAT(16I)
  110 FORMAT(8I)
  115 FORMAT( '1NUMBER OF NODES = ',I5,/,' NUMBER OF ARCS = ',I5,///,5X,
     1'M',5X,'I',5X,'J',6X,'COST',10X,'HI',11X,'LO',//,(3(2X,I4),
     13(3X,I10)))
    1 FORMAT(' ENTER THE NUMBER OF NODES AND ARCS'/)
    2 FORMAT(' ENTER SEQUENCE OF ARCS   (8 ARCS PER LINE
     1IS MAXIMUM)'/)
    3 FORMAT(' ENTER THE PER UNIT COST FOR EACH ARC'/)
    4 FORMAT(' ENTER THE UPPER BOUND OF EACH ARC'/)
    6 FORMAT(' ENTER THE LOWER BOUND OF EACH ARC'/)
      WRITE(3,1)
      READ(5,100) NODES,ARCS
      WRITE(3,2)
      READ(5,105)  (I(M),J(M),M=1,ARCS)
      WRITE(3,3)
      READ(5,110)  (COST(M),M=1,ARCS)
      WRITE(3,4)
      READ(5,110)  (HI(M),M=1,ARCS)
      WRITE(3,6)
      READ(5,110)  (LO(M),M=1,ARCS)
      DO 5 M=1,ARCS
    5 FLOW(M)=0
      DO 10 M=1,NODES
   10 PI(M)=0
 6666 CONTINUE
      CALL NETFLO(NODES,ARCS,I,J,COST,HI,LO,FLOW,PI,INFES,IBT,NBT)
      IF(.NOT.INFES) WRITE(6,120)
      WRITE(6,115)NODES,ARCS,(M,I(M),J(M),COST(M),HI(M),LO(M),M=1,ARCS)
      WRITE(6,125) (M,FLOW(M),M=1,ARCS)
      WRITE(6,130) (M,PI(M),M=1,NODES)
      WRITE(6,500) IBT,NBT
  120 FORMAT(///, ' SOLUTION INFEASIBLE')
  125 FORMAT(///,' ARC   FLOW(ARC)', /,(1X,I4,2X,I10))
  130 FORMAT(///,' NODE    PI(NODE)',/,(1X,I4,2X,I10))
  500 FORMAT(/,5X,' THE NUMBER OF BREAKTHROUGHS IS ',I6,//,5X,' THE NUMB
     1ER OF NONBREAKTHROUGHS IS ',I6,//)
 3838 CONTINUE
      END
      SUBROUTINE NETFLO(NODES,ARCS,I,J,COST,HI,LO,FLOW,PI,INFES,IBT,NBT)
      DIMENSIONI(100),J(100),COST(100),HI(100),LO(100),NB(100),
     1FLOW(100),PI(100),NA(100)
      LOGICAL INFES
      IMPLICIT INTEGER(A-Z)
      CHECK FEASIBILITY OF FORMULATION
           INFES=.TRUE.
      DO 10 A=1,ARCS
   10 IF(LO(A).GT.HI(A)) GO TO 39
      SET INF TO MAX AVAILABLE INTEGER
   16     INF=999999
          AOK=0
      IBT=0
      NBT=0
          *****IBT IS A COUNTER ON NUMBER OF BREAKTHROUGHS ****
      **** NBT IS A COUNTER ON NUMBER OF NONBREAKTHROUGHS ****
```

115

```
C     FIND OUT OF KILTER ARC
20    DO 21 A=1,ARCS
      IA=I(A)
      JA = J(A)
        C=COST(A)+PI( IA )-PI( JA )
        IF((FLOW(A).LT.LO(A)).OR.(C.LT.0.AND.FLOW(A).LT.HI(A))) GO TC 22
21    IF((FLOW(A).GT.HI(A)).OR.(C.GT.0.AND.FLOW(A).GT.LO(A))) GO TC 23
C     NO REMAINING OUT OF KILTER ARCS
      GO TO 38
22        SRC=J(A)
          SNK=I(A)
          E=+1
      GO TO 24
23        SRC=I(A)
          SNK=J(A)
          E=-1
      GO TO 24
C     ATTEMPT TO BRING OUT OF KILTER ARCS INTO KILTER
24    IF((A.EQ.AOK).AND.(NA(SRC).NE.0)) GO TO 25
          AOK=A
      DO 26 N=1,NODES
          NA(N)= 0
          NB(N)=0
          NA(SRC)=IABS(SNK)*E
26        NB(SRC)=IABS(AOK)*E
25        COK=C
27        LAB=0
      DO 30 A=1,ARCS
      JA=J(A)
      IA=I(A)
      IF((NA(IA).EQ.0.AND.NA(JA).EQ.0).OR.(NA(IA).NE.0..AND.NA(JA).NE.0)
     1)GO TO 30
      C= COST(A)+PI(IA) - PI(JA)
      IF(NA(IA).EQ.0) GO TO 28
      IF(FLOW(A).GE.HI(A).OR.(FLOW(A).GE.LO(A).AND.C.GT.0))GO TO 30
      NA(JA) = I(A)
      NB(JA) = A
      GO TO 29
28    IF(FLOW(A).LE.LO(A).OR.(FLOW(A).LE.HI(A).AND.C.LT.0))GO TO 30
      IA = I(A)
      NA(IA) = -J(A)
      NB(IA) = -A
29    LAB = 1
C NODE LABELED, TEST FOR BREAKTHRU
      IF(NA(SNK).NE.0) GO TO 33
30    CONTINUE
C NO BREAKTHRU
      IF(LAB.NE.0) GO TO 27
      NBT=NBT+1
C DETERMINE CHANGE TO PI VECTOR
      DEL = INF
      DO 31 A=1,ARCS
      JA=J(A)

      IA=I(A)
      IF((NA(IA).EQ.0.AND.NA(JA).EQ.0).OR.(NA(IA).NE.0.AND.NA(JA).NE.0))
     1GO TO 31
      C=COST(A)+PI(IA)-PI(JA)
      IF(NA(JA).EQ.0.AND.FLOW(A).LT.HI(A)) DEL= MIN0(DEL,C)
      IF(NA(JA).NE.0.AND.FLOW(A).GT.LO(A)) DEL= MIN0(DEL,-C)
```

116

```
   31 CONTINUE
      IF(DEL.EQ.INF.AND.(FLOW(AOK).EQ.HI(AOK).OR.FLOW(AOK).EQ.LO(ACK)))
     1DEL=IABS(COK)
      IF(DEL.EQ.INF) GO TO 39
C EXIT, NO FEASIBLE FLOW PATTERN
C CHANGE PI VECTOR BY COMPUTED DEL
      DO 32 N=1,NODES
   32 IF(NA(N).EQ.0) PI(N)=PI(N)+DEL
C FIND ANOTHER OUT-OF-KILTER ARC
      GO TO 20
C BREAKTHRU, COMPUTE INCREMENTAL FLOW
   33 EPS=INF
      IBT=IBT+1
      NI=SRC
   34 NJ=IABS(NA(NI))
      A=IABS(NB(NI))
      C=COST(A)-ISIGN(IABS(PI(NI)-PI(NJ)),NB(NI))
      IF(NB(NI).LT.0) GO TO 35
      IF(C.GT.0.AND.FLOW(A).LT.LO(A)) EPS=MIN0(EPS,LO(A)-FLOW(A))
      IF(C.LE.0.AND.FLOW(A).LT.HI(A)) EPS=MIN0(EPS,HI(A)-FLOW(A))
      GO TO 36
   35 IF(C.LT.0.AND.FLOW(A).GT.HI(A)) EPS=MIN0(EPS,FLOW(A)-HI(A))
      IF(C.GE.0.AND.FLOW(A).GT.LO(A)) EPS=MIN0(EPS,FLOW(A)-LO(A))
   36 NI=NJ
      IF(NI.NE.SRC) GO TO 34
C CHANGE FLOW VECTOR BY COMPUTED EPS
   37 NJ=IABS(NA(NI))
      A=IABS(NB(NI))
      FLOW(A)=FLOW(A)+ISIGN(EPS,NB(NI))
      NI=NJ
      IF(NI.NE.SRC) GO TO 37
C FIND ANOTHER OUT OF KILTER ARC
      AOK=0
      GO TO 20
   39 INFES = .FALSE.
   38 CONTINUE
      RETURN
      END
```

```
1,2,1,1
1,3,1,1
1,4,1,1
1,5,1,1
1,6,1,1
2,7,1,0,-1
2,8,1,0,-3
2,9,1,0,-2
2,10,1,0,-6
2,11,1,0,0
3,7,1,0,-4
3,8,1,0,-2
3,9,1,0,-3
3,10,1,0,-8
3,11,1,0,-3
4,7,1,0,-8
4,8,1,0,-4
4,9,1,0,-1
4,10,1,0,-5
4,11,1,0,0
5,7,1,0,-3
5,8,1,0,-5
5,9,1,0,-4
5,10,1,0,-8
5,11,1,0,-8
6,7,1,0,-2
6,8,1,0,-6
6,9,1,0,-9
6,10,1,0,-5
6,11,1,0,-2
7,12,1,0,0
8,12,1,
9,12,1
10,12,1,
11,12,1,
12,1,5,5,
0,0,
```

* THE CONVENTION USED FOR INPUT DATA IS:
from node, to node, upper bound, lower bound, cost
The absence of a number in the sequence denotes zero

SOLUTION FOR BOTTLENECK ASSIGNMENT PROBLEM
ITTERATION #1

ARC NO.	I	J	UB	LB	COST	FLOW
1	1	2	1	1	0	1
2	1	3	1	1	0	1
3	1	4	1	1	0	1
4	1	5	1	1	0	1
5	1	6	1	1	0	1
6	2	7	1	0	-1	0
7	2	8	1	0	-3	1
8	2	9	1	0	-2	0
9	2	10	1	0	-6	0
10	2	11	1	0	0	0
11	3	7	1	0	-4	0
12	3	8	1	0	-2	0
13	3	9	1	0	-3	0
14	3	10	1	0	-8	1
15	3	11	1	0	-3	0
16	4	7	1	0	-8	1
17	4	8	1	0	-4	0
18	4	9	1	0	-1	0
19	4	10	1	0	-5	0
20	4	11	1	0	0	0
21	5	7	1	0	-3	0
22	5	8	1	0	-5	0
23	5	9	1	0	-4	0
24	5	10	1	0	-8	0
25	5	11	1	0	-8	1
26	6	7	1	0	-2	0
27	6	8	1	0	-6	0
28	6	9	1	0	-9	1
29	6	10	1	0	-5	0
30	6	11	1	0	-2	0
31	7	12	1	0	0	1
32	8	12	1	0	0	1
33	9	12	1	0	0	1
34	10	12	1	0	0	1
35	11	12	1	0	0	1
36	12	1	5	5	0	5

TOTAL COST   -36

NODE	PI
1	19
2	13
3	15
4	16
5	17
6	16
7	11
8	10
9	11
10	7
11	12
12	19

INPUT DATA

BOTTLENECK ASSIGNMENT PROBLEM

ITTERATION #2

```
1,2,1,1
1,3,1,1
1,4,1,1
1,5,1,1
1,6,1,1
2,10,1,0,-6
3,7,1,0,-4
3,10,1,0,-8
4,7,1,0,-8
4,8,1,0,-4
4,10,1,0,-5
5,8,1,0,-5
5,9,1,0,-4
5,10,1,0,-8
5,11,1,-,-8
6,8,1,0,-6
6,9,1,0,-9
6,10,1,0,-5
7,12,1,0,0
8,12,1,
9,12,1
10,12,1,
11,12,1,
12,1,5,5,
0,0,
```

SOLUTION FOR BOTTLENECK ASSIGNMENT PROBLEM
ITTERATION #2

ARC NO.	I	J	UB	LB	COST	FLOW
1	1	2	1	1	0	1
2	1	3	1	1	0	1
3	1	4	1	1	0	1
4	1	5	1	1	0	1
5	1	6	1	1	0	1
6	2	10	1	0	-6	1
7	3	7	1	0	-4	1
8	3	10	1	0	-8	0
9	4	7	1	0	-8	0
10	4	8	1	0	-4	1
11	4	10	1	0	-5	0
12	5	8	1	0	-5	0
13	5	9	1	0	-4	0
14	5	10	1	0	-8	0
15	5	11	1	0	-8	1
16	6	8	1	0	-6	0
17	6	9	1	0	-9	1
18	6	10	1	0	-5	0
19	7	12	1	0	0	1
20	8	12	1	0	0	1
21	9	12	1	0	0	1
22	10	12	1	0	0	1
23	11	12	1	0	0	1
24	12	1	5	5	0	5

NODE	PI
1	26
2	18
3	20
4	24
5	26
6	26
7	16
8	20
9	22
10	12
11	26
12	26

eight

Economic Analysis

The traditional methods of economic analysis are straightforward, understandable, and useful as decision-making tools. Surprisingly, these same methods are foreign or unknown to many who could benefit from their use. Terms such as *capitalized cost, discounted cash flow, double rate declining balance depreciation,* and others are sometimes used but are not understood. Because we have found methods of economic evaluation to be especially useful and relevant, we wish to include mention of them in this Q & D manual. This subject matter, however, would expand without bound if we were to attempt to present it in a self-contained and complete manner. Instead, we wish only to briefly describe the classical methods of economic analysis (*present worth, equivalent annual cost,* and *rate of return*); to briefly present the notion that the *value* of money changes with time (If you don't believe this concept, will you lend me $1000 today and let me repay you $1000 ten years from now?); to list the factors that properly "adjust" the value of money with respect to time (these factors are used in the methods of economic analysis); and to include some sample problems that are susceptible to methods of economic analysis. This is not an attempt to educate, but to expose the uninitiated to economic analysis. We suggest some good texts for those who are interested in pursuing the subject, and wish that we could also include a chapter on managerial accounting.

DEFINITIONS

Creativity = process of generating better alternatives according to acceptable criteria.

Economic decision making = selecting the best of competing alternatives according to economic criteria.

Investment = spending or saving money with the expectation of profit.

Interest = money paid for the use of money.

Opportunity cost of capital = the potential profit from alternative investments foregone by accepting an opportunity to invest.

Time value of money: the *value* of an amount of money *at a particular time* is whatever the money is *worth* at that time, given an interest rate or cost of capital.

Nominal interest rate = interest rate stated as a yearly rate, but compounded more frequently than yearly.

Effective interest rate = interest rate stated as a yearly rate and compounded yearly.

Example

Consider the following two machines. Both can do the required work. Based on their respective streams of present and future expenditures, which machine represents the better economic alternative?

machine 1

$2000	$100	$100		$100	$100
	1 YR	2 YR		9 YR	10 YR

machine 2

$1000	$200	$200		$200	$200
	1 YR	2 YR		9 YR	10 YR

If i = 10 percent, then the time value today of:

$2000	today is	$2000.00	$1000	today is	$1000.00
100	1 year hence is	90.91	200	1 year hence is	181.82
100	2 years hence is	82.64	200	2 years hence is	165.28
100	3 years hence is	75.13	200	3 years hence is	150.26
100	4 years hence is	68.30	200	4 years hence is	136.60
100	5 years hence is	62.09	200	5 years hence is	124.18
100	6 years hence is	56.45	200	6 years hence is	112.90
100	7 years hence is	51.32	200	7 years hence is	102.64
100	8 years hence is	46.65	200	8 years hence is	93.30
100	9 years hence is	42.41	200	9 years hence is	84.82
100	10 years hence is	38.55	200	10 years hence is	77.10
$3000		$2614.45	$3000		$2228.90

Note that both machines require the identical *dollar* amount of out-of-pocket costs ($3000). However, since these costs are incurred over a period of time, the *values* of the costs differ. In terms of the value of the future cost commitment (at the present time), machine 2 is superior to machine 1 (present value of cost for machine 2 is less than that for machine 1). In the following pages we show how to determine the *equivalent value* of streams of money occurring over time.

P = investment in equipment; the total first cost

L = salvage value at the end of the economic life

n = the economic life in years on the basis that the rate of return i in annual cost problems is for a 1-year period.

I = series of equal end-of-period incomes

D = a series of end-of-period disbursements

i = the minimum required rate of return

AC = equivalent annual cost

PW = present worth

Rule 0. Not to decide is to decide (do nothing is one economic alternative).

Rule 1. Each dollar spent should return itself and at least the cost of capital before there is any notion of profit.

Rule 2. The value of money increases (in value) over time; thus, in order to compare (add or subtract) sums of money dispersed or collected over time, one must compute or know the equivalent value of each sum of money at a particular time.

Methods

There are three traditional methods used in economic analysis (comparison of economic alternatives):

1. *Present worth or discounting.* Rule: Compute the *value* of costs and incomes at the present time and choose the alternative with the best present worth.

$$PW = P + D \, \text{USPWF}_{i-n} - I \, \text{USPWF}_{i-n} - L \, \text{SPPWF}_{i-n}$$

2. *Annual cost/annual worth.* Rule: Convert the cost and income patterns of alternatives into *equivalent* (in value of money sense) uniform series computed with the minimum required rate of return. Choose the project with the least "equivalent annual cost."

$$AC = (P - L) \, \text{CRF}_{i-n} + Li + D - I$$

3. *Rate of return.* Gross income is used for basically two purposes: (a) to repay all costs, and (b) to pay a rate of return on capital. Thus the rate of return on an investment is that interest rate which makes costs *equivalent* (in a *value* of money sense) to income. *Rule:* Equate the equivalent annual cost to the equivalent annual income of a project; solve for that interest rate which

makes this expression an equality; choose the project with the largest rate of return.

$$(P - L) \text{CRF}_{i-n} + Li + D = I \quad \text{(solve for } i)$$

Capitalized-cost comparison-a present-worth comparison for a period assumed to be infinite. (See special-purpose time-value factors.)

Cash flow = profit + depreication—often used when including depreciation and taxes in economic evaluation.

Interest compounding periods and periodic payment periods are equal; payments come at the end of compounding periods.

1. Given the value P of an amount of money at a given time, to find the *value* of P at a later time (n interest periods later), multiply P by "single-payment compound amount factor,"

$$\text{SPCAF}_{i-n} = (1 + i)^n$$

2. Given the value S of an amount of money at a given (future) time, find the *value* of S at a previous time (n interest periods previous) by multiplying S by "single-payment present-worth factor,"

$$\text{SPPWF}_{i-n} = \frac{1}{(1 + i)^n}$$

3. Given a uniform series of end-of-interest-period payments R, to find the value S of n such payments, multiply R by "uniform-series compound amount factor,"

$$\text{USCAF}_{i-n} = \left[\frac{(1 + i)^n - 1}{i} \right]$$

The value of S coincides with the last payment, R.

4. To find the uniform series of n end-of-interest-period payments that will accumulate in value to a given future sum, S, multiply S by "sinking fund deposit factor,"

$$\text{SFDF}_{i-n} = \left[\frac{i}{(1 + i)^n - 1} \right]$$

5. To find the value P of a future uniform series of payments R at the end of n interest periods, multiply R by "uniform series

present worth factor,"

$$\text{USPWF}_{i-n} = \left[\frac{(1+i)^n - 1}{i(1+i)^n}\right]$$

The value of P precedes the first payment R by one period.

6. To find the future uniform series of n end-of-interest-period payments R that will exactly recover a present sum P with interest i, multiply P by "capital recovery factor,"

$$\text{CRF}_{i-n} = \left[\frac{i(1+i)^n}{(1+i)^n - 1}\right]$$

Lists of these factors are tabulated in many texts [1, 2].

Special-purpose time-value factors

Limiting values of factors (as $n \to \infty$):

$\text{SPCAF}_{i-\infty} = \infty$	$\text{USPWF}_{i-\infty} = \dfrac{1}{1}$
$\text{SPPWF}_{i-\infty} = 0$	$\text{CRF}_{i-\infty} = i$
$\text{USCAF}_{i-\infty} = \infty$	$\text{SFDF}_{i-\infty} = 0$

Values of factors (with $i = 0\%$):

$\text{SPCAF}_{0-n} = 1$	$\text{SPPWF}_{0-n} = 1$
$\text{USCAF}_{0-n} = n$	$\text{USPWF}_{0-n} = n$
$\text{SFDF}_{0-n} = \dfrac{1}{n}$	$\text{CRF}_{0-n} = \dfrac{1}{n}$

PROBLEMS FOR ECONOMIC ANALYSIS

1. A family plans to build a house for $20,000 including land. They estimate that they will own it for 15 years, at which time they can sell for $20,000 as a result of appreciation of the land. They estimate the following costs of annual operation: fuel, $250; repairs, $100; lawn maintenance and snow removal, $40; insurance, $75; water, $40; property tax, 4 percent of full value; and, at the end of every 3 years, painting and overhaul, $300. They plan to finance this from bank deposits earning 4 percent compounded quarterly. Make an AC computation.

2. An investment plan is expected to pay the following: $5000 at the end of the first year, and subsequent annual income payments decreasing $200 each year. Compute the annual worth of this plan if an investor's minimum required rate of return is 5 percent and the incomes continue for 10 years.

3. A sportsman plans to purchase an outboard cruiser for $2500 and to keep it 5 years before replacing it. He believes that he can sell it at that time for $800. His disbursements for gas, oil, repair, storage, license, and dock privileges will be $700 the first year and will increase $50 a year thereafter. Find his equivalent annual cost of ownership if his minimum required rate of return in his ventures is 10 percent.

4. A bulldozer costs $14,000 new and has a service life of 10 years. If its purchaser expects to use it only 2 years and then sell it for $9000, what is his *AC* if the minimum rate of return is 15 percent?

5. A 36-inch pipeline can be installed for $98,000. Its operating costs include the cost of pumping and maintenance and amount to $22,000 each year. A 30-inch line can be installed for $73,000, but the operating cost will be $31,000. Either line is expected to serve for 20 years with 10 percent salvage when replaced at that date. Compare the two alternatives if the company's minimum required rate of return is 20 percent.

6. A third-class railroad car costs $1000 and has an annual operating cost of $13,000. A first-class car costs $70,000 and costs $18,000 a year to operate. Both are expected to be obsolete in 5 years. Salvage value of the third-class car is $10,000; on the first-class car it is $15,000. The first-class car averages $15,000 more per year in revenue. If these can be used as alternatives on a given line, which should be selected if the minimum required rate of return for the railroad is 15 percent?

7. Plan A requires an initial investment of $2000 and has an economic life of 2 years. Plan B costs $4500 and is expected to last 5 years. If the salvage value is zero in both cases and interest is 15 percent, which alternative is least expensive?

8. The purchasing agent of a cargo manufacturing concern is trying to decide whether to buy high carbon steel or carbide-tipped cutting tools for the metal shop's lathes. The carbide tools cost $2000 and have an estimated life of 3 years. The steel tools cost $1400 but last only 2 years. Salvage values are zero. Company's minimum required rate of return is 20 percent. Which?

9. A salesman wants to sell you a $3000 car. He says the payments will be $150 a month for 2 years or $130 a month for 35 months. Which deal should you take? What is the nominal interest rate in each case?

10. The purchase of a machine requires an initial expense of $10,000. The machine will last 5 years with $4000 salvage. Income from the machine is $3000 per year and operating costs are $2000. What is the rate of return on this alternative?

11. You are buying a house that costs $50,000. You make a 10 percent down payment. You pay the balance with a 25-year loan at 8 percent. If your payments are made at the end of each year and are equal, how much are your annual payments?

12. You purchase a new car and are shown the following calculations:

Amount of purchase	$4000.00
Monthly payment	$200.00
Number of monthly payments	24
Total payments 200 × 24	$4800.00
Interest charge 4800 − 4000	$800.00
Interest charge per year 800/2	$400.00
Interest rate 400/4000 × 100 percent	10%

Is 10 percent really the effective interest rate you are paying? What is wrong with the analysis? Show how you would determine the effective interest rate. (*Hint:* Find the nominal interest rate first.)

CITED REFERENCES

[1] Taylor, G. A., *Managerial and Engineering Economy,* Van Nostrand, Reinhold, New York, 1964.
[2] Stermole, F. J., *Economic Evaluations and Investment Decision Methods,* Colorado School of Mines Press, Golden, Colorado, 1972.

PERT-CPM

PERT and CPM, acronyms for "program evaluation and review technique" and "critical path method," respectively, are network techniques used to aid in the planning, scheduling, monitoring, and control of activities that are related to each other. For example, CPM is frequently used in the construction industry to help organize and schedule those activities that together constitute a given construction project. PERT was first used to help coordinate the activities in the development of the Polaris missile system. PERT and CPM differ from each other in that activity times are handled differently by these two closely related techniques. In using CPM, one assumes that the activity times are known with certainty (deterministic activity times); PERT allows for uncertainty and statistical variation in activity times (stochastic activity times). Nevertheless, PERT and CPM are closely related (CPM may be a special case of PERT), and a variety of projects are subject to analysis by either technique [1]:

1. Construction projects.
2. Planning and launching a new product.
3. A turnaround in an oil refinery (or other maintenance projects).
4. Installing and debugging a computer system.
5. Scheduling ship construction and repairs.
6. Manufacture and assembly of large job-lot operations.
7. Missile countdown procedures.
8. End-of-the month closing of accounting records.
9. Research and development projects.

Two characteristics are common to projects subjected to PERT/CPM analysis [1]:

1. Each project consists of a well-defined, finite collection of jobs, or activities, which when completed mark the end of the project.

* From H. S. Swanson and R. E. D. Woolsey, "A PERT-CPM Tutorial," *Sigmap* 16, April 1974, pp. 54-62.

2. Some activities are related to other activities of the same project:
   a. Each *activity* has a known *event* that initiates or marks the beginning of that activity and another event that signals the completion of that activity. This distinct starting and stopping relates the activities in time.
   b. There are some activities whose initiation depends upon the completion of other activities. This is a technological relatedness (for example, on a manned space flight, the crew ought to be aboard and strapped in before the craft is launched).

We shall depict *activities* and *events* and show the relationship of activities of a project by the use of a graph or network. Activities correspond to network arcs and events to network nodes. Note that an arc (activity) begins at a node (initial event) and ends at a different node (terminal event).

From a list of all activities together with their beginning and end events, the time order of activities is determined. Then for each activity, predecessor and successor relations are identified. The network is drawn in such a way as to incorporate these dependencies. Moving from left to right along any path of the network, an activity can be initiated only after *each* predecessor activity has been completed. The art of constructing PERT/CPM networks is discussed in reference [1].

It has been said that after listing the activities of a project (this is part of the planning function) and determining how these activities are related and dependent (scheduling function), 98 percent of the benefit of PERT/CPM has been achieved. Without quibbling about percentages, we now wish to finish our short discussion by indicating the monitoring and control advantages derived from using the PERT/CPM method. To do so, we shall show how the "forward-backward" algorithm is used to find the *critical path* in a network. The critical path is a sequence of activities that are critical to the completion of the project in that if any activity on this path is delayed, the completion of the project is delayed by a like amount of time. We illustrate with a CPM network, because deterministic systems are usually more simple than stochastic ones (PERT). We shall then show how the forward–backward algorithm can be adjusted to handle PERT networks.

Consider the CPM network in Figure 9. The number on each arc is the time needed to complete the activity corresponding to that arc. The nodes are numbered, and an arc is identified by its begin node number and end node number. For example, the arc from node 2 to node 5 is denoted (2, 5).

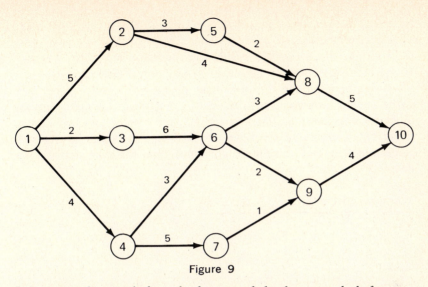

Figure 9

Let us put the cart before the horse and do the example before explaining how to do it. CPM is simple enough for you to catch on quickly. We shall state the rules after you understand what to do. Suppose that we designate the start time of the project as time $t = 0$ [activities (1, 2), (1, 3), and (1, 4) begin simultaneously (because no activities precede them)]. Then the earliest we can initiate activities of the project is $t = 0$, and the earliest possible finish time for activity (1, 2) is $t = 5$; the early finish time for activity (1, 3) is $t = 2$; the early finish time for activity (1, 4) is $t = 4$. Because activity (1, 2) must be completed before either activity (2, 5) or activity (2, 8) can be started, the early start time for those two activities is $t = 5$, and their early finish times are $t = 8$ and $t = 9$, respectively. Computing early start and early finish for each activity, we have:

Activity	Early Start	Early Finish
(1, 2)	0	5
(1, 3)	0	2
(1, 4)	0	4
(2, 5)	5	8
(2, 8)	5	9
(3, 6)	2	8
(4, 6)	4	7
(4, 7)	4	9
(5, 8)	8	10
(6, 8)	8	11
(6, 9)	8	10
(7, 9)	9	10
(8, 10)	11	16
(9, 10)	10	14

Note that the early start time for activities $(6, 8)$ and $(6, 9)$ is $t = 8$. This occurs because *all* predecessor activities [activities $(3, 6)$ and $(4, 6)$] must be *completed* before the successor activities [activities $(6, 8)$ and $(6, 9)$] can be initiated.

If we are to complete the project at time $t = 16$ [activity $(8, 10)$ is the last to be completed], we realize that the latest possible start times for activities $(8, 10)$ and $(9, 10)$ are $t = 11$ and $t = 12$, respectively. Continuing to move "backwards" through the network computing late start time and late finish time for each activity, we have:

Activity	Late Start	Late Finish
$(8, 10)$	11	16
$(9, 10)$	12	16
$(7, 9)$	11	12
$(6, 8)$	8	11
$(5, 8)$	9	11
$(2, 8)$	7	11
$(6, 9)$	10	12
$(3, 6)$	2	8
$(4, 6)$	5	8
$(4, 7)$	6	11
$(1, 4)$	1	5
$(1, 3)$	0	2
$(1, 2)$	1	6

This completes the forward–backward algorithm. The critical path consists of those activities (x, y) for which early start $(x, y) =$ late start (x, y). The critical path in the example network contains activities $(1, 3)$, $(3, 6)$, $(6, 8)$, and $(8, 10)$. This is the longest" path through the network.

In summary:

1. Forward pass: Compute early start and early finish for each activity:
   a. $ES = 0$ for each "beginning" activity.
   b. $EF = ES +$ duration of activity.
   c. ES of successor activities $=$ maximum of EF time for all predecessor activities.
   d. Early finish time for entire project is the largest early finish time of all activities.
2. Backward pass: Compute late start and late finish for each activity:
   a. $LF =$ project completion time for each "ending activity."
   b. $LS = LF -$ duration of activity.

    c.   *LF* of predecessor activities = minimum of *LS* times of all successor activities.

Now, back to the horse. The idea here is to make two passes through the network. The forward pass moves from left to right through the network, and is used to determine the earliest completion time for the entire project. This is accomplished by determining the early start time (*ES*) and the early finish time (*EF*) for each activity in the network. The early start time for an activity (x, y) is the earliest time that activity can be initiated. The early finish time for an activity (x, y) is the early start time for (x, y) plus the time required to accomplish activity (x, y). Thus, $EF(x, y) = ES(x, y) + t(x, y)$. If exactly one activity terminates at a node (see node 4 in example), the early start time for each activity beginning at this node is equal to the early finish time of the activity terminating there. Recall that before an activity can begin, all of its immediate predecessors must have been completed. Therefore, if more than one activity terminates at a single node (see node 6 in example), the early start time for any activity initiating from this node is the largest of the early finish times of all activities terminating there. The leftmost, or start node, has no predecessor, and the beginning activities have an early start time of zero. Continue to compute early start and early finish for each successor activity until all activities in the project have been considered. The early finish time for the activity "ending" the project is the earliest completion time for the project.

The second or backward pass of the algorithm starts at the "end" of the network and moves "backwards" from right to left, utilizing the information from the forward pass to determine the critical path. This is accomplished by computing the late start time (*LS*) and the late finish time (*LF*) for each activity. The late start time for an activity (x, y) is the latest time that activity can begin without delaying the completion of the entire project. The late finish time for an activity (x, y) is the late start time for (x, y) plus the time required to accomplish activity (x, y). Thus $LS(x, y) = LF(x, y) - t(x, y)$. The rightmost or end node has no successor, and each ending activity has a late finish time equal to the earliest completion time for the entire project as determined by the forward pass. This late finish time minus the duration time of each ending activity determines the late start time for each ending activity. If exactly one activity initiates from a node (see node 9 in example), the late finish time for any activity terminating there is equal to the late start time of the activity initiating from that node. If more than one activity initiates from a node (see node 6 in example), the late finish time for any activity terminating there is equal to the *smallest* of the late start times of all activities initiating from this node. Continue to compute late finish and late start for each prodecessor activity until all activities in the project have been considered.

Each activity whose *late start equals* its *early start* lies on the *critical path* of activities. The difference between early start and late start for an activity is called the total slack for that activity. Each activity on the critical path has zero total slack. However, project activities with positive total slack allow schedulers some flexibility in fixing start times. This is critical for example, when several activities would require a resource (say, bulldozers) simultaneously. Shifting the start time of some activities (with positive total slack) requiring the resource helps to smooth work schedules and relieve bottlenecks while preventing delay in project completion time (see reference [1], Chap. 7).

PERT differs from CPM in that PERT activity times are stochastic. What this means in practice is that we need to "hedge" on the activity times for some projects. This is done by assigning three completion times to each PERT activity: an optimistic time estimate, t_o (if everything goes right); a pessimistic time estimate, t_p (if everything goes wrong); and an expected, average, or "best guess" time estimate, t_m (if things go as they usually do). These three estimates are used to compute an "expected time duration," t_e, which is to be used for the estimate of the corresponding activity in the forward–backward algorithm:

$$t_e = \frac{t_o + 4t_m + t_p}{6}$$

The "best guess" estimate is weighted more heavily than the other two, less likely estimates. This computation approximates the average of the BETA statistical frequency distribution function (justifications are given in reference [1]). For example, if for some activity, $t_o = 5$ days, $t_m = 8$ days, and $t_p = 17$ days, $t_e = \frac{54}{6} = 9$ days as an "expected duration" of the activity. An estimate of the standard deviation, S_t, of the distribution of the duration of this activity is given by

$$S_t = \frac{t_p - t_o}{6}$$

an estimate of the variance, V_t, of the distribution is obtained by squaring $S_t : V_t = S_t^2$. Do you now see how magical stochastic networks are? PERT differs from CPM in using these *three* estimates of activity times, approximating a distribution function, and acknowledging uncertainty; PERT *does not* remove or lessen uncertainty. To use the forward–backward algorithm to find the "expected longest path" in a PERT network, (1) obtain the necessary three estimates for each activity; (2) compute t_e, S_t, and V_t for each activity; (3) determine time and technological dependencies as before; (4) use t_e in place of the single CPM time estimate; (5) proceed as before with the forward–backward algorithm. The sum of the values of V_t on the "expected critical path" is an estimate of uncertainty of the path.

CITED REFERENCES

[1] Wiest, J. D., and Levy, F. K., *A Management Guide to PERT/ CPM,* Prentice-Hall, Englewood Cliffs, N.J., 1969.

ten

Odds and Ends

General Discussion

Discussion of the Individual Q & D's

Q & D for the Minimal Spanning Tree
Q & D To Minimize the Cost of a Testing Sequence
Q & D for Finding Optimal Discount Prices
Q & D for Optimum Cash Replenishment with Lumpy Demand
Q & D for Balancing Workloads
Q & D for Warehouse Location (Grange's Method)
Q & D for Weighting Objectives and Selecting Alternatives

This chapter is simply what its title indicates, a group of odds and ends of Quick & Dirty methods that, somehow, do not fit anywhere else. As in the first chapter, there is a brief discussion of all the individual Quick & Dirtys, which is then followed by the Quick & Dirty methods and conversational lists.

Q & D FOR THE MINIMAL SPANNING TREE

This is one of the best-known methods in the operations research literature, and is usually referred to as the "greedy algorithm." The reason for this name is simply that being the greedy one at each step turns out to be the optimal procedure. In the example, the Q & D refers to the digging of the necessary ditches to connect up a group of oil wells in such a way that the total ditching length (and therefore cost) is a minimum. The reader will notice at once that all the possible connections are not present in the example. (Students will also point this out to the teacher.) In an actual situation of this type, all the connections would not be present for at least two reasons. The first reason might be that there is a vertical drop between one well and an (apparently) nearby one. It is patently not cost effective to ditch down the side of a cliff. The second reason is that there may be a rancher between the two wells who does not wish the ditch to cross his property. When given this answer the student often asks why the agency or company in question cannot condemn the property and go on through. Because this author is himself a rancher, it is pointed out to the student that if you sue me in my home county, *you lose*. As one of my nearby neighbors once put it, "They'll never win because you cain't impanel a jury in this county that ain't my kin." Another objection to this method often arises because all connections are straight line. Again, it must be explained that if you pump oil over a mountain, bring it down the other side, and put in a right angle turn, you may encounter some problems with moments of inertia, to say nothing of cavitation. It must be realized that a slug of oil 3 miles long and traveling 20–30 mph exerts a nontrivial force.

Q & D TO MINIMIZE THE COST OF A TESTING SEQUENCE

This method is one of the Q & D's that provokes the usual reaction of "Of course, what else would you do!" However, it is interesting to consider that this problem was first presented in the literature by Mitten in 1960. The most important assumption for this method is that the tests are *independent*. It can be seen that an algorithm can be constructed when some of the tests are *dependent* by using Bayes' methods of probability.

Q & D FOR FINDING
OPTIMAL DISCOUNT PRICES

The author has used this method many times as a homework assignment that will be graded by the owner of a nearby bookstore. Following the Q & D is the result of one such homework, done by Mr. S. Dugal of the University of Waterloo. The form designed was selected by the owner of the Book Barn in Waterloo, Ontario, for shop use. A nomogram for feasible ranges of book prices and expected times to dispose of slow-moving inventory can easily be constructed for any given markup and turnover rate, pasted on the wall, and used. All that is required is a straightedge for reading off the lower bound on the discount price.

Q & D FOR OPTIMUM CASH REPLENISHMENT
WITH LUMPY DEMAND

We assume that a local operation with varying cash demand must forecast demand from a central office and receive replenishments accordingly. Given that the cash manager is able to forecast his cash demands for some time in advance, he wants to optimize his replenishments to minimize the sum of replenishment and cash-holding costs. This problem may be considered as a restatement of the inventory problem with conditions of varying forecasted demand treated earlier in Chapter 2. Again, the method of Silver and Meal is used for a heuristic solution to this problem. Two examples follow the Quick & Dirty, and a conversational, time-shared program for doing the examples is demonstrated following the examples.

Q & D FOR BALANCING WORKLOADS

Say that we have a group of service departments with existing workloads. Suddenly there is an influx of a batch of jobs to be distributed in some "balanced" manner across the departments. This is the classic "loading" problem, and what is presented here is one of the better heuristic methods to distribute such an incoming workload "equally." It is not difficult to construct cases for which this method gives a bad result, so it should be used with care.

Q & D FOR WAREHOUSE LOCATION (GRANGE'S METHOD)

The method presented here assumes that the fixed costs of constructing a warehouse are virtually the same no matter which location is chosen. The usual warehouse location problem assumes the contrary, with the result that it usually requires formulation as a mixed-integer programming problem. Also, the user should consider the fact that forecasts for transportation cost for a warehouse not yet built are, at best, shaky; therefore, using an optimizing code on such a problem could perhaps be considered a case of blatant overkill.

Q & D FOR WEIGHTING OBJECTIVES AND SELECTING ALTERNATIVES

This procedure, although simple-minded, is perhaps the most useful in this book because of the wide variety of problems to which it can be applied. For some time now this author has assigned students in his class to "optimize" their career choices with this method. The most interesting thing that emerges from this kind of exercise is that the student suddenly finds that some objective he had not rated very high in his own mind is overriding many of the others that he *thought* were more important.

A good example of this was shown when a student found that all his best offers of employment in terms of money, prestige, and chances for advancement were in the Cleveland area. When he went there, he found that the river going through the middle of town had been declared a fire hazard. He then decided that perhaps he had not ranked environmental influences highly enough. He is now living and working in Morrison, Colorado.

Another interesting use for this method was one in which a new office was to be constructed for a Canadian corporation, located in a city situated between the two present offices. The problem arose because there was considerable difference of opinion as to which groups should be moved from their present offices to the new office. The authors suggested that this Q & D be distributed to the executives involved. The executives would then be instructed to define the "objectives" of the new office and weigh these objectives as outlined in the Q & D. An "alternative" in this case would be the movement of a certain group to the new office. The alternatives could then be evaluated by each executive by the subjective method of the Q & D. A meeting of the concerned executives would then take place to see if there was a sufficient intersection for some easy decisions. Of course, if the decision had already been made by the president of the company as to who would go where, the above procedure would still give him some good information as to possible pitfalls he might have overlooked.

Quick & Dirty THE MINIMAL SPANNING TREE

Assume that we have a batch of locations we wish to connect with pipe or cable in such a way that total length of connection is a minimum and such that every location is connected.

Method

1. Select any location arbitrarily and then connect it to the nearest location.
2. Identify the unconnected location that is closest to a connected location and then connect these two. Repeat this until all locations are connected.

Example

The Quicksand Oil Company wishes to dig ditches to connect all wells in a given field with control cable. Because ditching in West Texas is quite expensive, the company wishes to dig the cheapest possible ditches (in terms of length) as possible. A map of the allowed ditches is shown in Figure 10. The optimal solution is shown in Figure 11.

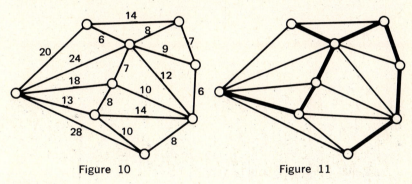

Figure 10   Figure 11

Reference

Hillier, F. S., and Lieberman, G. J., *Introduction to Operations Research,* Holden-Day, San Francisco, 1967, p. 223.

CONVERSATIONAL LIST FOR THE Q & D FOR THE MINIMAL SPANNING TREE (PROGRAM 10.1)

```
MINIMAL SPANNING TREE

ENTER ARCS AS FOLLOWS:

STARTING NODE, ENDING NODE, DISTANCE

STOP INPUT BY TYPING:0,0,0

ARC   1:1,2,4
ARC   2:1,3,7
ARC   3:1,4,9
ARC   4:2,3,4
ARC   5:2,4,5
ARC   6:3,5,7
ARC   7:4,5,1
ARC   8:0,0,0

DONE

THE M. S. T. CONSISTS OF THE FOLLOWING ARCS:

ARC   1( 1, 2)
ARC   4( 2, 3)
ARC   5( 2, 4)
ARC   7( 4, 5)

DO YOU WISH TO DO ANOTHER PROBLEM?:NO
```

Quick & Dirty TO MINIMIZE THE COST OF A TESTING SEQUENCE

Say that an item is to be subjected to a group of independent tests. Each test has a known cost per item of doing the test. Also, each test has a certain probability (from past history) that an item will fail the test. We wish to sequence the tests in such a way that the cost of the test sequence is minimized.

Method

1. Order the tests from left to right in order of the increasing ratio: (cost/probability of failure).
2. Stop; this is the optimal solution.

Example

Consider a drill that must be tested by quality control with data as follows:

Test	Probability of Failure	Cost of Test per Item	Cost/ Probability	Order of Tests
Drop	0.30	$0.10	0.33	2
Heat	0.05	$0.14	2.80	5
Vibration	0.10	$0.20	2.00	4
Short	0.40	$0.06	0.15	1
Visual defects	0.15	$0.066	0.44	3

Reference

Mitten, L. G., "An Analytic Solution to the Least Cost Testing Sequence Problem," *Journal of Industrial Engineering,* Vol. XI, No. 1, Jan.–Feb. 1960, p. 17.

Quick & Dirty FOR FINDING OPTIMAL DISCOUNT PRICES

We assume that a retailer has accumulated some slow-moving inventory. He wants to discount the items in hope of a quick sale. The cash proceeds from these sales will be immediately put back into the fast-moving inventory. What is the optimum discount price to charge to ensure that the immediate cash proceeds will earn back the loss within the time it would have taken to move the "dogs" at their present price. Levary and Gidean showed that no reduction in profits occurs if

$$R_{max} = B - C = CPTt$$

where

R_{max} = maximum reduction of price
B = present selling price
C = cash proceeds if sold at discounted price
P = profit margin
T = number of times stock turns over during a year (average turnover)
t = number of years from now until expected mean date of sale if no reduction in price is allowed

Now the above formula may be rewritten as

$$C = \frac{B}{1 + PTt}$$

Example

Let us consider an item with a present price of $10. The markup or profit margin is 33.33 percent, the average turnover is five times a year and, at the present rate of sale, it will take 3 years to clean out the inventory of this item. From the formula for C we have

$$C = \frac{10}{1 + (\frac{1}{3})(5)(3)} = \$1.66$$

We therefore know that if we do not discount the item *below* this price, we shall not reduce profits. To show that this is so, let us return to the first formula. We may see at once that if the discount price *were* $1.66, our immediate loss would be $B - C$ or ($10 − $1.66) = $8.34. But if we take the $1.66 and put it into the fast-moving inventory at a markup of 33.33 percent, the profit on one sale would be CP = (cash proceeds times profit margin) = $(1.66)(\frac{1}{3})$ = $.55. But because we are going to sell this item on the average five times a year, we have $CPT = \$2.78$ as our profit for the year. However, it was going to take us 3 years to move the inventory, and the 3 years return would be $CPTt = \$8.34$, which gives

$$R_{max} = B - C = \$8.34 = CPTt = (\$1.66)(\tfrac{1}{3})(5)(3) = \$8.34$$

We therefore have an immediate lower bound on a discounted price.

Reference

Levary, G., "A Pocket-Sized Case Study in Operations Research Concerning Inventory Markdown," *Operations Research,* Vol. 4, No. 6, Dec. 1956, pp. 738–740.

Quick & Dirty FORM FOR FINDING OPTIMAL DISCOUNT PRICES FOR BOOKS

Should you have some poor-selling books you wish to get rid of, the following is a simple way to find the *discount price* at which you can sell these books as soon as possible and not lose any money.
Use the following steps to obtain the discount price:

Number of slow-moving books	A ____
Number of slow-moving books you can sell in 1 year at the present price	B ____
Divide box A by box B	C ____
The average turnover of all your stock in 1 year	D ____
Multiply box C by box D	E ____
The average markup on all your stock	F ____
Multiply box E by box F	G ____
Add 1 to box G	H ____
Your present selling price for the slow-moving books	I ____
Divide box I by box H	J ____

Box J is your *Discount price.*

Example

Number of slow-moving books	A 6
Number of slow-moving books you can sell in 1 year at the present price	B 2
Divide box A by box B	C 3
The average turnover of all your stock in 1 year	D 5
Multiply box C by box D	E 15
The average markup on all your stock	F $33\frac{1}{3}$%
Multiply box E by box F	G 5
Add 1 to box G	H 6
Your present selling price for the slow-moving books	I $10
Divide box I by box H	J $1.66

Box J is your *discount price.*

Quick & Dirty FOR OPTIMUM CASH REPLENISHMENT WITH LUMPY DEMAND

Area concentration banking can create a situation in which the local cash manager does not have spending authority for his accounts receivable but must requisition cash account replenishments from a central office. Given the demands for cash several periods in the future, the cash manager wants to know how to plan his cash balance to minimize the sum of replenishment costs plus cash-holding costs. The procedure for developing this policy is as follows.

Method

1. Calculate

$$M = \frac{2(\text{fixed transaction cost of obtaining a cash replenishment})}{(\text{opportunity interest cost of holding cash})}$$

2. Set $T = 0$. The current period is 1. last $T = 0$. last demand $= 0$.

3. For the current period calculate $G = (\text{period} - \text{last } T)^2$ (demand in the current period). If G is bigger than M, go to step 4. If G is less than or equal to M, repeat step 3 with the next period as the current period.

4. Calculate T, the time this replenishment will last.

$$T = \sqrt{\frac{M}{\text{demand in the current period}}} + \text{last } T$$

5. If the difference of the number of the last period looked at in step 3 minus T is greater than 1, round T *up* to the next whole number of periods.

6. Calculate the current total demand that is needed through T periods. First, find the largest whole number of periods in T (e.g., if $T = 3.87$, the largest whole number of periods in T is 3). The total demand through T periods is

   current total demand = demand in period 1 + demand in period 2 + $\cdots$ + demand in period that is the largest whole number in T + (the fraction that remains in T) (demand in the period that is the next whole number above T)

7. Calculate the replenishment Q that will last through T periods.

   Q = current total demand − last total demand

8. Set last T = current T and last total demand = current total demand. Go to step 3.

146

Example 1

Suppose that the fixed transaction cost of obtaining a cash replenishment is $75.00, and the interest opportunity cost of holding cash is 5.4 percent. Demand forecasted for periods 1 through 4 is

Period	1	2	3	4
Demand	$2143	$1568	$3216	$2575

1. $M = 2(75) \div (0.054) = 2777.78$.
2. $T = 0$, current period $= 1$, last $T = 0$, and last demand $= 0$.
3. $G = (1 - 0)^2(2143) = 2143 > 2777.78$? No; set current period $= 2$.
   $G = (2 - 0)^2(1568) = 6272 > 2777.78$? Yes; go to step 4.
4. $T = \sqrt{2777.78/1568} + 0 = 1.33$ periods.
5. Last period $- T = 2 - 1.33 = 0.67 > 1$? No.
6. Current total demand $=$ demand in period $1 + 0.33$(demand in period 2)
   $= 2143 + 0.33(1568) = \$2662.00$.
7. $Q = 2662.00 - 0 = \$2662.00$.
8. last $T = 1.33$ periods; last demand $= \$2662.00$.
3. $G = (2 - 1.33)^2(1568) = 7.04 > 2777.78$? No.
   $G = (3 - 1.33)^2(3216) = 8969.10 > 2777.78$? Yes; go to step 4.
4. $T = \sqrt{2777.78/3216} + 1.33 = 2.26$ periods.
5. Last period $- T = 3 - 2.26 = 0.74 > 1$? No.
6. Current total demand $= 2143 + 1568 + 0.26(3216) = \$4547.16$.
7. $Q = 4547.16 - 2662.00 = \$1885.16$.

Example 2

Same data as Example 1, but now fixed transaction cost of cash replenishment is $57.00.

1. $M = 2(57) \div (0.054) = 2111.11$.
2. $T = 0$, current period $= 1$, last $T = 0$, and last demand $= 0$.
3. $G = (1 - 0)^2(2143) = 2143 > 2111.11$? Yes; go to step 4.
4. $T = \sqrt{2111.11/2143} + 0 = 0.99$ periods.
5. Last period $- T = 1 - 0.99 = 0.01 > 1$? No.
6. Current total demand $= 2143(0.99) = \$2127.00$.
7. $Q = 2127 - 0 = \$2127.00$.
8. Last $T = 0.99$ periods; last demand $= \$2127.00$.
3. $G = (1 - 0.99)^2(2143) = 0.2143 > 2111.11$? No.
   $G = (2 - 0.99)^2(1568) = 1591.51 > 2111.11$? No.
   $G = (3 - 0.99)^2(3216) = 12992.96 > 2111.11$? Yes; go to step 4.
4. $T = \sqrt{2111.11/3216} + 0.99 = 1.80$.
5. Last period $- T = 3 - 1.80 = 1.2 > 1$? Yes; round up T to 2.00.
6. Current total demand $= 2143 + 1568 = \$3711.00$.
7. $Q = 3711.00 - 2127.00 = \$1584.00$.

CONVERSATIONAL LIST FOR THE Q & D FOR OPTIMUM CASH REPLENISHMENT WITH LUMPY DEMAND (PROGRAM 10.2)

OPTIMUM CASH MANAGEMENT

DO YOU WANT THE TUTORIAL:YES

THIS PROGRAM WILL CALCULATE THE OPTIMUM CASH BALANCE REPLENISHMENT UNDER CONDITIONS OF TIME-VARYING DEMAND.

YOU WILL BE ASKED TO PROVIDE THE FOLLOWING INFORMATION:

1) THE OPPORTUNITY COST OF HOLDING CASH, THAT IS, WHAT INTEREST RATE YOUR CASH COULD EARN YOU INVESTED ELSEWHERE,
2) THE FIXED TRANSACTION COST OF OBTAINING A CASH BALANCE REPLENISHMENT,
3) THE NUMBER OF TIME PERIODS IN ADVANCE FOR WHICH YOU HAVE THE CASH BALANCE DEMAND INFORMATION,
4) THE FORECASTED DEMAND FOR CASH IN EACH PERIOD,
AND 5) WHETHER OR NOT ALL CASH NEEDED IN A PERIOD MUST BE AVAILABLE AT THE START OF THE PERIOD.

ENTER THE OPPORTUNITY COST OF HOLDING CASH (DECIMAL FRACTION):0.054

ENTER THE FIXED TRANSACTION COST OF OBTAINING A CASH REPLENISHMENT:75

ENTER THE NUMBER OF TIME PERIODS FOR WHICH YOU HAVE FORECASTED DATA:4

ENTER CASH BALANCE DEMANDS FOR PERIODS 1 THROUGH 4,
SEPARATED BY COMMAS:2143,1568,3216,2575

MUST ALL CASH NEEDED IN A PERIOD BE AVAILABLE
AT THE START OF THE PERIOD:NO

OPTIMUM CASH REPLENISHMENT IS $ 2662.00.

THIS WILL RUN OUT 1.33 TIME PERIODS FROM THE STARTING DATE.

DO YOU WISH TO CALCULATE THE NEXT CASH REPLENISHMENT:YES

OPTIMUM CASH REPLENISHMENT IS $ 1886.34.

THIS WILL RUN OUT 2.26 TIME PERIODS FROM THE STARTING DATE.

DO YOU WISH TO CALCULATE THE NEXT CASH REPLENISHMENT:YES

OPTIMUM CASH REPLENISHMENT IS $ 3148.57.

THIS WILL RUN OUT 3.30 TIME PERIODS FROM THE STARTING DATE.

DO YOU WANT TO LOOK AT ANOTHER FORECAST:YES

ENTER THE OPPORTUNITY COST OF HOLDING CASH (DECIMAL FRACTION):0.024

ENTER THE FIXED TRANSACTION COST OF OBTAINING A CASH REPLENISHMENT:85

ENTER THE NUMBER OF TIME PERIODS FOR WHICH YOU HAVE FORECASTED DATA:4

ENTER CASH BALANCE DEMANDS FOR PERIODS 1 THROUGH 4,
SEPARATED BY COMMAS:2143,1568,3216,2575

MUST ALL CASH NEEDED IN A PERIOD BE AVAILABLE
AT THE START OF THE PERIOD:YES

OPTIMUM CASH REPLENISHMENT IS $ 3711.00.

THIS WILL RUN OUT 2.00 TIME PERIODS FROM THE STARTING DATE.

DO YOU WISH TO CALCULATE THE NEXT CASH REPLENISHMENT:YES

OPTIMUM CASH REPLENISHMENT IS $ 5791.00.

THIS WILL RUN OUT 4.00 TIME PERIODS FROM THE STARTING DATE.
DO YOU WANT TO LOOK AT ANOTHER FORECAST:NO

Quick & Dirty FOR BALANCING WORKLOADS

Assume that you have a group of M facilities with existing workloads, L_j. Further assume that you have a group of N incoming jobs of size w_i. We wish to distribute the workload across the facilities in such a way as to balance the total workload as equally as possible.

Method

1. Find the average final workload, L^*, as follows:
   $L^* =$ (sum of existing workloads + sum of incoming jobs)/
   (no. of facilities $= M$)
2. For each facility j, find its excess capacity, c_j, as follows:
   $c_j = L^* - L_j$
3. List the incoming jobs (the w_i), in descending order of size.
4. Put the w_i at the top of its list in the c_j that is just big enough to hold it. Cross off the w_i just placed and go to step 4. If no c_j can hold it, go to step 5.
5. Put the w_i in the facility with the largest remaining excess capacity. Cross off the w_i and also that facility from the list of c_j. go to step 4.

Example

Say that we have four facilities with workloads at present of $L_1 = 150$, $L_2 = 170$, $L_3 = 220$, and $L_4 = 240$. We have incoming jobs to be distributed as follows: w_1 through w_8 are 100, 80, 70, 70, 40, 30, 20, 10. Following the above method, we have:

1. $L^* = (150 + 170 + 220 + 240 + 100 + 80 + 70 + 70 + 40 + 30 + 20 + 10)/4 = 300$.
2. $c_1 = 300 - 150 = 150$, $c_2 = 300 - 170 = 130$, $c_3 = 300 - 220 = 80$, $c_4 = 300 - 240 = 60$.
3. w_1 through w_8 are 100, 80, 70, 70, 40, 30, 20, 10.
4. Forming a table of the c_j in descending order, we have from left to right using step 4,

c_4 60	60	60	60	60 − 40 = 20	20 − 20 = 0	0
c_3 80	80 − 80 = 0	0	0	0	0	0
c_2 130 − 100 = 30	30	30	30	30 − 30 = 0	0	0
c_1 150	150	150 − 70 = 80 − 70 = 10	10	10	10 − 10 = 0

We therefore conclude that a good solution is to allocate jobs of 70, 70, and 10 to facility 1, jobs of 100 and 30 to facility 2, one job of 80 to facility 2, and jobs of 40 and 20 to facility 1.

Reference

Greenberg, I., "Application of the Loading Algorithm to Balance Workloads," *AIIE Transactions,* Vol. 4, No. 4, Dec. 1972, pp. 337–339.

Quick & Dirty FOR WAREHOUSE LOCATION (GRANGE'S METHOD)

Consider the following problem. No more than three warehouses are to be built from among five possible locations to supply five customers. Up to three locations must be chosen on which to build warehouses; and furthermore, each customer may be supplied from only one warehouse. Warehouse locations must be chosen to minimize the total annual shipping costs from all warehouses to all customers. The annual shipping costs are given below:

| Customers | Warehouse sites | | | | |
	A	B	C	D	E
1	75	675	1,275	1,800	1,675
2	1,710	342	1,368	2,565	1,822
3	2,448	1,224	306	1,683	1,945
4	2,740	1,644	548	685	850
5	19,320	12,880	8,050	805	922

Method

1. Circle the lowest cost in each row. This is the way customers would be supplied if all sites had warehouses. If any column has no circled costs, drop this site from further consideration. If the number of columns with at least one circled cost is less than or equal to the maximum number of warehouses that may be built, stop. If not, go to step 2.

| Customers | Warehouse sites | | | | |
	A	B	C	D	E
1	(75)	675	1,275	1,800	1,675
2	1,710	(342)	1,368	2,565	1,822
3	2,448	1,224	(306)	1,683	1,945
4	2,740	1,644	(548)	685	850
5	19,320	12,880	8,050	(805)	922

Number of columns with circled costs = 4 > 3 = maximum number of warehouses that may be built; go to step 2.

2. For each warehouse site column not yet eliminated, find the rows with circled costs. In those rows, find the smallest *uncircled* cost (among the remaining site columns). Compute the cost of eliminating the site by subtracting from each circled cost the smallest uncircled cost, and then adding these differences together for the site column. This elimination cost would be the total added cost of supplying all customers from all the other remaining sites. (For site C, the elimination cost is $(1224 - 306) + (685 - 548) = 1053$.) After computing the elimination start costs for each remaining site, drop the warehouse site with the smallest elimination cost. If the number of warehouse sites remaining equals the maximum number of warehouses that may be picked, stop. Each customer will be supplied from the cheapest remaining site. If too many sites remain, repeat step 2.

		Warehouse sites			
Customers	A	B	C	D	
1	75	675	1,275	1,800	←Customer 1 is
2	1,710	342	1,368	2,565	supplied by
3	2,448	1,224	306	1,683	site B in the
4	2,740	1,644	548	685	final solution.
5	19,320	12,880	8,050	805	
Elimination cost	600	1,026	1,053	7,245	

Three warehouses remain; stop.

An important assumption in this method is that the fixed cost of building a warehouse at all sites is about the same, and the variable cost of building warehouses of different sizes is also about the same at each site. A typical problem might be the distribution of heavy equipment parts in which the annual shipping costs account for most of the costs of distribution.

By continuing the elimination step, the best combinations of fewer warehouses may be found. If insufficient funds exist to build all the warehouses immediately, the best order of construction may be thus obtained. In the example, the next site to be dropped would be C; the order of construction would therefore be D, B, and C.

CONVERSATIONAL LIST FOR THE Q & D FOR WAREHOUSE LOCATION (PROGRAM 10.3)

```
WAREHOUSE LOCATION FOR MINIMUM SHIPPING COST

DO YOU WANT THE TUTORIAL:YES

THIS PROGRAM LOCATES A NUMBER OF WAREHOUSES TO MINIMIZE SHIPPING COSTS
TO CUSTOMERS.  THE PROGRAM REQUIRES THE FOLLOWING INPUT DATA:

     1) MAXIMUM NUMBER OF WAREHOUSES THAT MAY BE BUILT,
     2) TOTAL NUMBER OF POSSIBLE SITES FOR WAREHOUSES (MUST EQUAL OR
        EXCEED THE NUMBER OF WAREHOUSES THAT MAY BE BUILT),
     3) NUMBER OF CUSTOMERS TO BE SERVICED (ONLY ONE WAREHOUSE MAY
        SERVE EACH CUSTOMER),
     4) ANNUAL COST OF SUPPLYING EACH CUSTOMER FROM EACH POSSIBLE
        WAREHOUSE SITE; COSTS ARE DETERMINED ON THE BASIS OF CUSTOMER
        ORDER VOLUMES (TONS/YEAR), DISTANCES (MILES), AND FREIGHT RATES
        ($/TON-MILE).


WHAT IS THE MAXIMUM NUMBER OF WAREHOUSES THAT MAY BE BUILT:3

HOW MANY POSSIBLE WAREHOUSE SITES ARE THERE:4

HOW MANY CUSTOMERS MUST BE SERVED:5

LIST THE ANNUAL SHIPPING COSTS TO EACH CUSTOMER
FROM WAREHOUSE SITE  1, SEPARATED BY COMMAS:
75,1710,2448,2740,19320

LIST THE ANNUAL SHIPPING COSTS TO EACH CUSTOMER
FROM WAREHOUSE SITE  2, SEPARATED BY COMMAS:
675,342,1224,1644,12880

LIST THE ANNUAL SHIPPING COSTS TO EACH CUSTOMER
FROM WAREHOUSE SITE  3, SEPARATED BY COMMAS:
1275,1368,306,548,8050

LIST THE ANNUAL SHIPPING COSTS TO EACH CUSTOMER
FROM WAREHOUSE SITE  4, SEPARATED BY COMMAS:
1800,2565,1683,685,805

BUILD WAREHOUSES ON THE FOLLOWING SITES:


     4

     2

     3


IF INSUFFICIENT FUNDS ARE AVAILABLE TO BUILD ALL THE WAREHOUSES
IMMEDIATELY, BUILD THEM IN THE ORDER GIVEN ABOVE.


SUPPLY CUSTOMER  1 FROM WAREHOUSE  2 AT ANNUAL COST OF $    675.00
SUPPLY CUSTOMER  2 FROM WAREHOUSE  2 AT ANNUAL COST OF $    342.00
SUPPLY CUSTOMER  3 FROM WAREHOUSE  3 AT ANNUAL COST OF $    306.00
SUPPLY CUSTOMER  4 FROM WAREHOUSE  3 AT ANNUAL COST OF $    548.00
SUPPLY CUSTOMER  5 FROM WAREHOUSE  4 AT ANNUAL COST OF $    805.00
TOTAL ANNUAL COST OF SHIPPING FROM ALL WAREHOUSES
TO ALL CUSTOMERS IS $        2676.00
```

Quick & Dirty FOR WEIGHTING OBJECTIVES AND SELECTING ALTERNATIVES

Assume that we have a group of objectives that we wish to satisfy to some level, which we shall call $O_1, O_2, \ldots, O_n$. Further, assume that we have defined a group of alternatives or strategies that satisfy some or all of the objectives. These are called $A_1, A_2, \ldots, A_m$. We desire to find the alternative that will maximize our satisfaction over the given group of objectives.

Method

1. First put the objectives in order of importance.
2. Now assign the first objective a satisfaction level of 100 youdels.
3. Now, keeping in mind that the first objective got 100 youdels, determine how many youdels the second objective would give.
4. Following the above process, assign the appropriate youdel value to each objective; these are called the "weights" for each objective and are symbolized by w_j.
5. Now sum the youdel values for all the objectives. In symbols:

$$\text{total youdels} = \sum_{j=1}^{j=n} w_j$$

6. Now, for each objective find the percent satisfaction (symbolized by p_j), for each objective by the following formula:

$$p_j = w_j/(\text{total youdels}) \quad \text{for } j = 1, 2, \ldots, n.$$

7. Now form a table of objectives and alternatives as shown below:

	O_1	O_2	O_1	$\cdots$	O_n
A_1	a_{11}	a_{12}	a_{11}	$\cdots$	a_{1n}
A_2	a_{21}	a_{22}	a_{23}	$\cdots$	a_{2n}
.					
.					
.					
A_m	a_{m1}	a_{m2}	a_{m1}	$\cdots$	a_{mn}

where the a_{ij} is the amount that alternative i *satisfies* objective j on a 0–10 basis

8. To determine which alternative best satisfies the objectives, for each alternative calculate the payoff as follows:

$$\sum_{j=1}^{j=n} p_j * a_{ij} \quad \text{for each } i = 1, 2, \ldots, m$$

9. Choose the alternative that gives the biggest payoff.

eleven
Esotericae-Academic Quick & Dirtys

General Discussion

The Q & D's in this chapter are included because they have rather straightforward descriptions and can be met in *much* more rigorous form elsewhere. We have attempted to present them in somewhat less intimidating form for the casual reader (or user), with the usual necessary sacrifice of assured optimality.

Q & D FOR DETERMINING MAXIMUM FLOW THROUGH A CAPACITATED NETWORK

This method is usually presented as the "labeling" method for determining the maximum flow through a capacitated network. The best reference for this is Ford and Fulkerson's book, *Flows in Networks* (Princeton University Press, 1962), and the reader who wishes to do it *right* is referred to that work. The Q & D is followed by a demonstration program of a problem. The program will, as before, be found in the appendix.

Q & D FOR FINDING THE SHORTEST PATH FROM NODE 1 TO ALL OTHERS

This "shortest-path" method is often confused by students with the "minimal spanning tree" method in Chapter 10. It *is* true that it is not difficult to construct networks where the shortest path from some given node and the minimal spanning tree are identical. It should be carefully pointed out that the two methods do very different things and have rather different applications. Again, a demonstration run of a program is provided.

THE SLIPPERY ALGORITHM

One of the most-studied problems in the integer programming literature is the problem of optimizing a linear objective function subject to one constraint, where the variables are required to be zero or one. The method presented here is sufficiently gross to have been rejected by virtually every respectable journal in the profession. It has only one virtue; it does very well on the few hundred problems we have fed it.

Quick & Dirty FOR DETERMINING MAXIMUM FLOW THROUGH A CAPACITATED NETWORK

Given a capacitated network such as the one shown in Figure 12.

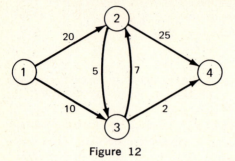

Figure 12

Method

1. Form the capacity matrix as illustrated below:

		To node			
		1	2	3	4
From node	1	×	20	10	0
	2	0	×	5	25
	3	0	7	×	2

2. Start at the source node 1 in the matrix. Go to the right, stopping at the last square with nonzero capacity.
3. Go down until a × is encountered.
4. a. If there is a nonzero square to the right, go to the last one and go to step 3 if the square is *not* in the last column. If the square *is* in the last column, go to step 6.
   b. If there is no nonzero square to the right, go to a nonzero left-most square, if one exists, and go to step 5.
   c. If there is no nonzero square on the left, nor one on the right, back up to the last nonzero square where you turned up (or down) to the present ×, set that square to zero, and go to step 2. If, by setting a square to zero, all of the entries in the source node row are set to zero, *stop*. The optimal solution has been found.
5. Go up until an × is encountered, and go to step 4.
6. Find the smallest number along the traced path, considering only those numbers that appear in (a) the ending square, or (b) a square in which the path makes a right-angle turn.

7. Increase the flow by the above number in those arcs defined by the above path. Subtract the number from each square as defined in step 6. Go to step 2. If this subtraction results in all zero in the last column, *stop*. The optimal solution has been found.

The optimal flows in the given matrix determined by this procedure are illustrated in Figure 13.

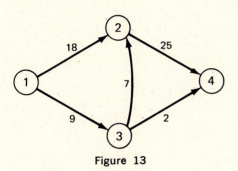

Figure 13

Reference

Acton, F. S., *Numerical Methods That Work,* Harper & Row, New York, 1970, pp. 524–528.

CONVERSATIONAL LIST FOR THE MAX-FLOW MIN-CUT NETWORK (PROGRAM 11.1).

```
MAX-FLOW MIN-CUT

ENTER ARC DATA AS:  SOURCE, SINK, CAPACITY; END WITH 0,0,0
1,2,3
1,3,1
2,3,1
2,4,4
3,2,1
3,4,1
0,0,0
```

NET AT START

FROM NODE	TO NODE	CAPACITY	FLOW
1	2	3	0
1	3	1	0
2	3	1	0
2	4	4	0
3	2	1	0
3	4	1	0

NET AT BREAKTHROUGH

FROM NODE	TO NODE	CAPACITY	FLOW
1	2	3	3
1	3	1	0
2	3	1	0
2	4	4	3
3	2	1	0
3	4	1	0

NET AT BREAKTHROUGH

FROM NODE	TO NODE	CAPACITY	FLOW
1	2	3	3
1	3	1	1
2	3	1	0
2	4	4	3
3	2	1	0
3	4	1	1

NET AT OPTIMUM

FROM NODE	TO NODE	CAPACITY	FLOW
1	2	3	3
1	3	1	1
2	3	1	0
2	4	4	3
3	2	1	0
3	4	1	1

⏱ Quick & Dirty FOR FINDING THE SHORTEST PATH
FROM NODE 1 TO ALL OTHERS

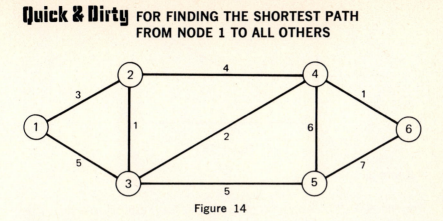

Figure 14

Assume a network of distances as shown in Figure 14. In order to determine the distance from node 1 to all other nodes we calculate a table as shown below, where

$f_{k,i}$ = distance from node 1 to node i that is minimum at step k

and where $f_{1,j} = d_{1,j}$ for the first step, given that:

$d_{i,j}$ = distance from node i to node j if the arc exists, and
$d_{i,j} = \infty$ when the arc does *not* exist.

Calculating $f_{1,j}$ by the above rule, we have the first column in the table below. The following $f_{k,j}$ are then calculated by the rule:

$$f_{k,j} = \underset{i}{\text{minimum}} \ \{f_{k-1,i} + d_{i,j}\}$$

	f_{1i}	f_{2i}	f_{3i}	f_{4i}	f_{5i}	f_{6i}
f_{k1}	0	0	0	0	0	0
f_{k2}	3	3	3	3	3	3
f_{k3}	5	4	4	4	4	4
f_{k4}	∞	7	6	6	6	6
f_{k5}	∞	10	9	9	9	9
f_{k6}	∞	∞	8	7	7	7

After $k^* =$ (no. nodes − 1) steps, stop. The last column has the minimum distances from node 1 to all others. To determine if a given arc is in the final minimum distance tree, see if $d_{i,j} = f_{k*,j} - f_{k*,i}$. If so, the arc is in the tree. From this calculation, the final tree is shown in Figure 15.

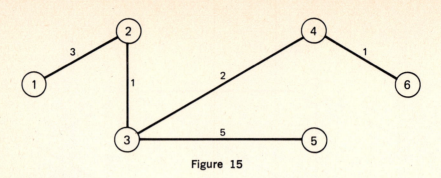

Figure 15

Reference

Dreyfus, S. E., "An Appraisal of Some Shortest Path Algorithms," The Rand Corporation, RM-5433-PR, Oct. 1967.

CONVERSATIONAL LIST FOR THE SHORTEST PATH PROGRAM (PROGRAM 11.2)

```
SHORTEST PATH FROM NODE ONE TO ALL OTHERS

ENTER ARCS AS:  STARTING NODE, ENDING NODE, DISTANCE

STOP INPUT BY TYPING: 0,0,0
ARC  1:1,2,3
ARC  2:1,3,5
ARC  3:2,3,1
ARC  4:2,4,4
ARC  5:3,4,2
ARC  6:3,5,5
ARC  7:4,5,6
ARC  8:4,6,1
ARC  9:5,6,7
ARC 10:0,0,0


STATUS OF NETWORK AT ITERATION  1

FROM NODE       TO NODE       DISTANCE
    1              2            3.00
    1              3            5.00

STATUS OF NETWORK AT ITERATION  2

FROM NODE       TO NODE       DISTANCE
    1              2            3.00
    1              3            4.00
    1              4            7.00
    1              5           10.00

STATUS OF NETWORK AT ITERATION  3

FROM NODE       TO NODE       DISTANCE
    1              2            3.00
    1              3            4.00
    1              4            6.00
    1              5            9.00
    1              6            8.00
```

STATUS OF NETWORK AT ITERATION   4

FROM NODE	TO NODE	DISTANCE
1	2	3.00
1	3	4.00
1	4	6.00
1	5	9.00
1	6	7.00

STATUS OF NETWORK AT ITERATION   5

FROM NODE	TO NODE	DISTANCE
1	2	3.00
1	3	4.00
1	4	6.00
1	5	9.00
1	6	7.00

STATUS OF NETWORK AT OPTIMUM

FROM NODE	TO NODE	DISTANCE
1	2	3.00
1	3	4.00
1	4	6.00
1	5	9.00
1	6	7.00

THE SHORTEST PATH FROM NODE 1 CONSISTS OF:

ARC(1, 2)
ARC(2, 3)
ARC(3, 4)
ARC(3, 5)
ARC(4, 6)

DO ANOTHER?:NO

Quick & Dirty THE SLIPPERY ALGORITHM

The "slippery algorithm" is used to solve the frequently occurring "knapsack problem" (select a group of projects that are collectively constrained by a single resource; the decision is *do* or *not do* (1 or 0) for each project):

$$\text{MAX } z = \sum_{j=1}^{N} c_j x_j \qquad x_j = 0 \text{ or } 1, j = 1, \ldots, N$$

$$\text{S.T.} \sum_{j=1}^{N} b_j x_j \leq B \qquad c_j, b_j, B > 0, j = 1, \ldots, N$$

Method

1. Compute the "efficiency," E_j, of each variable, x_j, where $E_j = c_j/b_j$ (payoff per unit of consumed resource).
2. Renumber (index) the variables in order of decreasing efficiency.
3. Determine the most efficient variable, x_j, with value of 0, and set this variable equal to $1(x_j = 1)$.
4. Determine the amount of resource remaining, B' (project x_j consumes b_j units of resource).
5. a. If $B' > b_{j+1}$, go to step 3 (there is sufficient remaining resource to do the "next" project).
   b. If $B' = b_{j+1}$, set $x_{j+1} = 1$ and stop; the resource has been exactly consumed. An *optimal solution* is $x_1 = x_2 = \ldots, x_j = x_{j+1} = 1$; $x_{j+2} = x_{j+3} = \cdots = x_N = 0$.
   c. If $B' < b_{j+1}$, go to step 6.
6. Decide whether this solution is "good enough" (it may or may not be optimal) $x_1 = x_2 = \cdots = x_j = 1$; $x_{j+1} = x_{j+2} = \cdots = x_n = 0$; $z = c_1 + c_2 + \cdots + c_j$. To do so, compute an upper bound on the optimal value, $z*$, of the objective function: $z* \leq z' = c_1 + c_2 + \cdots + c_j + (E_{j+1})(B')$.
   a. If $z' - z$ is "small," the present solution is "close to" the optimal solution (the smaller, the closer). The solution might be optimal even though $z' - z > 0$.
   b. If $z' - z$ is not "small enough," or if one wishes to try to improve the present solution, go to step 7.
7. Try one or more of the following "slipping" schemes:
   a. Consider the remaining variables "out of order": See if one or more "less efficient" variables can be set equal to 1, subject to the amount of remaining resource. Compare new value of z to z'.
   b. See if one or more variables with value of 1 can be "slipped" back to 0 so that some less efficient variable(s) can be set to 1 with a net improvement in z without violating the constraint. Compare new value of z to z'.

8. If nothing else works, go to your boss for an increased allocation of resource (try to increase B) and return to step 1.

Examples

$$\text{Maximize } z = 20x_1 + 18x_2 + 17x_3 + 15x_4 + 15x_5 + 10x_6 + 5x_7 + 3x_8 + x_9 + x_{10}$$

S.T. $\quad 30x_1 + 25x_2 + 20x_3 + 18x_4 + 17x_5 + 11x_6 + 5x_7 + 2x_8 + x_9 + x_{10} \leq 55$ (65)

$E_j \quad\quad 0.667 \quad 0.720 \quad 0.850 \quad 0.833 \quad 0.882 \quad 0.909 \quad 1.00 \quad 1.50 \quad 1.00 \quad 1.00$

The two examples differ only in the amount of resource available; Example 1, $B = 55$; Example 2, $B = 65$.

To avoid extra notation, we choose *not* to reorder variables (step 2).

Variable	Value of z	Remaining Resource $B = 55$	Variable	Value of z	Remaining Resource $B = 65$
$x_8 = 1$	3	53	$x_8 = 1$	3	63
$x_7 = 1$	8	48	$x_7 = 1$	8	58
$x_9 = 1$	9	47	$x_9 = 1$	9	57
$x_{10} = 1$	10	46	$x_{10} = 1$	10	56
$x_6 = 1$	20	35	$x_6 = 1$	20	45
$x_5 = 1$	35	18	$x_5 = 1$	35	28
x_3 cannot go; $z' = 35 + 18\,(.85) = 50.3$			$x_3 = 1$	52	8
$x_4 = 1$	50	0	x_4 cannot go; $z' = 52 + 8(.833) = 58.66$		
z and z' are close enough; stop			slip x_6 and x_4		
			$x_6 = 0$	42	19
			$x_4 = 1$	57	1
			z and z' are close enough; stop		

twelve

Some Final Instructions for Using this Book and Surviving as a Professional

The perceptive reader has, by this time, recognized this book for the hodge-podge of methods, models, and opinions that it really is. Any organization found in this book is solely the fault of the editorial staff of Harper & Row, and certainly not due to the perpetrators as being beyond their collective ability. The authors offer in mitigation that the profession of operations research/management science presents the spectacle of similar organization to the outsider. On this basis the authors can say that we are just conforming to the prevailing standards of our profession. Candor compels the authors, as usual, to point out that we have an ax to grind, and if we can grind it and-simultaneously enrich others, to say nothing of ourselves, so much the better. Our bias has been, is, and will be applicational success as the only proper measure for the profession.

We contend that many O.R./M.S. groups were hosed off wholesale because they were staffed by people who worshipped the wrong totems. The totem of "publishing papers in academic journals" is a good one only if the reward structure in which you have the fortune to be embedded will pay you for it. If that is what you have been trained to do and *want* to do, look around. If you are not at a university, might we suggest that you, being a drain on the corporate purse, may be at the wrong place? Further, good sense says that the optimum policy is to leave before they find you out. By so doing you will (a) be more secure, (b) excite the envy of your co-workers, and (c) have it said of you by the accountants that you were smarter than they gave you credit for. Of course, we shall have to admit that you can also find a position with the government, in which you are equally sure of not being found out so long as you don't rise too far.

At this point the authors proffer the celebrated H. Halbrecht 80/20 rule for survival as a professional. It has been observed by this gentleman that in O.R./M.S. work it is usual that the first 20 percent of the effort and/or money and/or time spent on a project usually results in 80 percent of the customer's satisfaction with the work. After this point has been reached, the customer usually wants to stop any further work because of some stupid reason such as: "That's all I really need." The O.R. man is usually shocked that the customer would want anything less than the "optimum" solution and remonstrates with him vigorously that he be allowed to continue on to 100 percent.

At this point we must recall that the customer is being asked to pony up another 80 percent of the funding, *when he thinks that he has what he came for.* Now, the O.R. man is convinced that the customer does not have what he needs. But we have to face the fact that the customer is usually going to be a better judge of that than the man still trying to sell him something. We now pause to inquire as to why the O.R. man wants to continue and get the "closed-form" solution when he already has a happy customer on his hands. We contend that the reason is a faulty education. The O.R. man has been educated to think that he has not done anything worthy of professional respect until he can prove that his method "converges in a finite number of steps." But in order to prove convergence he will need more funding: funding that the customer, strangly, is often unwilling to provide. We see here a perfect example of a man attempting to serve two masters. The ultimate futility of such attempts has been noted earlier and with greater insight by a teacher in Palestine and will not be repeated here. We would further contend that there is quite a bit of "good" O.R./M.S. done, but good here means effective and/or useful and does not mean publishable. As one of us has said before [1], really useful studies often are not published because the company will not allow publication because the method results in a competitive advantage to the company. It can be responsibly argued that few good applications have come out of the government sector because of the red tape involved in getting them out to the public. In short, the structure you are in not only does not reward you but, indeed, might take steps to punish you if you published a useful result in O.R./M.S. But isn't there *some* reward? American industry in particular is well known to reward useful employees with more money and/or appropriate status symbols. I recall, vividly, how simple this reward system can be from a visit to my production scheduling class by a production manager of a local firm. He described the problems they were having trying to get a very complex materials requirements plan on the computer and running. Finally one student was inspired to ask the following question: "Well, you certainly have one hell of a problem; tell me, what do you get if you get it running?" At first the production manager didn't understand the question. When he did, his answer was short and to the point: "I get to keep my job."

The above story brings us back to proper use of this manual. Bluntly, the purpose is to serve as a guidebook to "keeping the job" (assuming, of course, you are so fortunate as to *find* one.) Again the authors must warn against indiscriminate use of the Q & D's without some thoughtful consideration about the problem situation. As a good example, consider the chapter on production scheduling techniques. The authors cannot state strongly enough that treating the methods in this book as a "bag of tricks" is a sure road to ruin. Often there exist implicit assumptions behind each and every technique. The authors have attempted to list them whenever possible, as a guide for the unwary. Often, however, the authors have assumed that "any fool can plainly see" that certain methods require carefully delimited situations. To be more specific, consider the method for minimizing the number of late jobs in Chapter Two. Working a few examples will quickly demonstrate that the "push-down, pop-up" innate cussedness of Mother Nature is at work again. By "push-down, pop-up" we mean simply that if you push down one problem, you often find that another has popped up to take its place. With this method, it is easy to see that usually the jobs selected to be late are really going to get it in the ear. What this can mean politically is eventual elimination of your position, unless you *really* understand (a) who the boss *really* is, and (b) how your performance is *actually* measured. Therefore we must conclude that an awareness of the political, behavioral, and sociological circumstances are not only useful but damned necessary for the reader's continued survival as a practitioner.

Again, looking at the same chapter, we notice that there are many different ways we can optimize the schedule of a group of jobs on just one process. In the light of this author's experience, the practitioner should try to come up with a heuristic to fit his own particular situation by combining some of the Q & D's presented here. The reader who can, at once, pick out one particular Q & D as "the answer" is well advised to look again. The Q & D's are guideposts; they are not panaceas. The teacher who uses this book should avail himself of the opportunities to enable the student to see why some of the methods work. After teaching, for example, the Q & D for minimizing total flow time on two machines (Johnson's rule), the teacher should then require the class to suggest reasons why the short jobs on the first machine tend to be placed first. An immediate justification is that it seems reasonable to put the shortest job on the first machine first because that will minimize initial idle time on the second machine. Following from this, we can then suggest that it seems very unlikely that total idle time on the second machine will be a minimum if the *initial* idle on that machine is not a minimum. The teacher can then start at the other end of the schedule and, using the same reasoning, work his way in until he runs into the schedule coming from the other direction. It can then be seen that Johnson's rule can be used again and again at a basis for other Q & D's that follow.

The chapter on inventory control methods omits any discussion of the growing importance of materials requirements planning procedures in inventory control. This was done because it was felt that such strongly computer-dependent methods had no place in a manual of this type. Therefore, with humble apologies to Ollie Wight, I can do no more than refer interested readers to his many publications on the subject. The student whose interest is production and inventory control should be prepared for a considerable shock if he obtains a job in this particular field. From this author's experience, he will rapidly find that good forms design is, as a rule, more important than any mathematical model or computer program he can devise. This author has learned, through bitter experience, that any new system of production and inventory control had better use a form that looks just like the old form and, whenever possible, uses the same information. As an example of this, the author recalls an occasion where a PERT cost system was implemented in a very painless fashion in a large machine tool company. The new forms looked just like the old forms, with two more boxes for more information. The next stage was when the foremen received the reports typed on IBM typewriters. It was some time before the foremen realized that the reports were now being typed by a computer, (using an IBM typewriter that looked just like what they had seen before). By the time they discovered that they were dealing with a computer program, they were accustomed to using the system.

One other real danger in teaching students to generate their own Q & D's we call the chiseled-on-stone syndrome. What happens is that (a) a Q & D is requested and delivered to fit a specific, well-defined situation, then (b) the situation changes, and (c) the Q & D is still used. This author recalls visiting a nameless manufacturing facility that, years before, had requested a Q & D for reordering parts. The Q & D was in the form of a nomogram that required only that a straightedge be laid across two lines, with the answer to be read off of the remaining line. This author was, at first, very satisfied to find the Q & D glued to the wall with considerable evidence of constant use, plus the usual graffiti. Satisfaction increased when an expediter ran up, grabbed the straightedge hanging from the wall nearby, applied it to the Q & D, read off an answer, and returned to the bowels of the shop. Satisfaction went away when it was discovered shortly afterward that the company (a) was not making the same thing any more, and (b) was using totally different machines. This author made some excuse to catch an earlier plane before the local bean counter found out that he was the latter day Moses who had left that particular stone tablet behind.

For some years now it has been the author's private joke that the textbooks for his operations research introductory course were Peter and Hull, *The Peter Principle;* Townsend, *Up the Organization;* Parkinson, *In-Laws-and-Outlaws*. This author would then suggest to his class that for outside reading, any standard text on operations research would do just fine. The point of this book list was that at the start of the semester, the student would think that the teacher had got the required texts and the outside readings backwards. Hopefully, however, by the end of the semester the students would agree with the teacher that the presentation was correct. Bluntly put, this author contends that, from his experience, 90 percent of the problem faced by the practitioner is *not* technical. Example after example of the right method yielding the optimum solution but not being used because the O.R. people were unable to sell it have become a commonplace in our profession. There is a common feeling among academic products of operations research that "the methods are so good that they sell themselves." For this reason corporate O.R. groups usually sit and wait expectantly for a knock on the door. Some corporate O.R. groups (now nonexistent) waited until the bean counters caught up with them and fired them. Earlier, in an article on this very subject [2], this author pointed out that "even prostitutes solicit."

Another suggestion for the budding professional is that he take a bean counter to lunch and make a friend of him. The accountant can be the greatest ally for which an up-and-coming O.R. man can hope. The O.R. man, in theory, knows what to do with data when he gets it, but he usually does not know (a) where it comes from, (b) how it is collected, and (c) how much he can trust it. With a good cost accountant at his elbow, the O.R. man can achieve wonders by the intersection of mutual interests and abilities. This subject was also discussed in depth by this author in [3].

Reading the professional journals of O.R./M.S., one *does* get the impression that nobody ever makes a mistake. The student is encouraged to balance this opinion by reading some other references of this author [3, 4, 5, 6]. The most common error is model overkill. That is, the practitioner has done with more when he could easily have done with less (usually for less money). See also references [7] and [8].

Required reading for graduate students in the M.S./O.R. profession should certainly include *The Prince* and *The Discourses* of Niccolo Machiavelli. This author has had the gratifying feeling of having students return and tell him of how cases, particularly in the *Discourses,* have actually appeared in their work experience. Finally, this author suggests that all graduate students be required to read and discuss Walter Goerlitz' *History of the German General Staff.* In this author's experience, it is very difficult for students to see clearly the difference between suggesting policy alternatives and giving the decision maker an *answer.* Goerlitz cogently argues that this same difficulty was what brought about the downfall of the greatest staff organization, with the possible exception of the Roman Curia, that the world has ever seen. Also, this book drives home the point that if a person wants the glory of decision making, he has no place in a staff position such as O.R./M.S. The difference between line and staff is that staff suggests, and line *decides* and accepts the responsibility for the decision. From the above we can restate the "iron law" of consulting:

If I make the decision and I am right, you will never remember.
If I make the decision and I am wrong, you will never *forget.*

This author has defined so many "laws" that the reader is commended to the references mentioned above. However, if we had to choose one to guide the practitioner, other than the obvious one of not charging for his work if the customer is in any way dissatisfied, the authors would choose this one:

People Would Rather Live with a Problem They Cannot Solve than Accept a Solution They Cannot Understand

CITED REFERENCES

[1] R. E. D. Woolsey, "Operations Research and Management Science Today," *Operations Research,* Vol. 20, No. 3, 1972, pp. 729–737.

[2] R. E. D. Woolsey, "Some Reflections on Surviving as an Internal Consultant, Azerbaijan and Two Thieves," *Interfaces,* Vol. 5, No. 1, 1974, pp. 48–52.

[3] R. E. D. Woolsey, "A Candle to St. Jude, or Four Real World Applications of Integer Programming," *Interfaces,* Vol. 2, No. 2, 1972, pp. 20–27.

[4] R. E. D. Woolsey, "A Novena to St. Jude, or Four Edifying Case Studies in Mathematical Programming," *Interfaces,* Vol. 4, No. 1, 1973, pp. 32–39.

[5] R. E. D. Woolsey, "O Tempora O Mores, O. C. Jackson Grayson, Jr." *Interfaces,* Vol. 4, No. 3, 1974, pp. 76–78.

[6] R. E. D. Woolsey, "The Measure of M.S./O.R. Applications, or Let's Hear It for the Bean Counters," *Interfaces,* Vol. 5, No. 2, 1975.

[7] R. E. D. Woolsey and David A. Gulley, "You Can *Too* Use Operations Research," *Health Services Research,* Vol. 8, No. 2, pp. 97–101.

[8] R. E. D. Woolsey, "Homage to W. A. C. Bennette and the Canadian Operational Research Society," *Interfaces,* Vol. 4, No. 4, 1974, pp. 43–46.

[9] A. Charnes and W. W. Cooper, *Management Models and Industrial Applications of Linear Programming,* Vol. I and II, John Wiley & Sons, New York, 1961.

Program Appendix

The programs that follow have been written in FORTRAN-IV for the Digital Equipment Corporation's PDP-10 computer. They were originally written for the Digital Equipment PDP-8 or PDP-11 minicomputer in the FOCAL language, but were converted to FORTRAN to facilitate use.

The programs used in this manual represent no particular breakthroughs in programming. They are presented mainly to show how a number of the techniques discussed in the manual may be easily implemented in a *conversational* mode on a computer. For this reason, the programs are deliberately programmed in a modular format to facilitate understanding of what is going on and to ease any expansion to other methods with a minimum of reprogramming. Further, it is certainly not expected by the authors that any of the programs will be used with no modification in an industrial situation. They should be treated as signposts rather than a road, and certainly not a freeway.

The authors gratefully acknowledge that the necessary reprogramming and improvement in format of the programs are totally due to our colleague in O.R., Dr. Franklin E. Grange II of Standard Oil of Indiana.

PROGRAM 1.1   APICS SHOP SCHEDULING

```
C ** MAIN PROGRAM **
      COMMON/JOBS/NJ,P(20),IO(20),W(20)/PROC/NP
      DATA YES,XNO/'Y','N'/
    1 FORMAT(' APICS SHOP SCHEDULING'/)
    2 FORMAT(' HOW MANY PROCESSES ARE THERE?:'$)
    3 FORMAT(' ONE PROCESS SCHEDULING'/)
    4 FORMAT(I3,' PROCESS SCHEDULING TO MINIMIZE TOTAL TIME THRU SHOP'/,
    5 FORMAT(' HOW MANY JOBS ARE THERE?:'$)
    6 FORMAT(' CHOOSE ONE OF THE FOLLOWING TO OPTIMIZE:'////' 1.   MINIMIZ
     1E SUM OF COMPLETION TIMES'//' 2.   MINIMIZE WEIGHTED SUM OF COMPLET
     2ION TIMES'//' 3.   MINIMIZE MAXIMUM TARDINESS'//' 4.   MAXIMIZE MINI
     3MUM LATENESS'//' 5.   MINIMIZE NUMBER OF LATE JOBS'/)
    7 FORMAT(' INPUT A 1, 2, 3, 4, OR 5 AS WANTED:'$)
    8 FORMAT(G)
    9 FORMAT(/' OPTIMIZE THIS JOB ANOTHER WAY?:'$)
   10 FORMAT(/' DO MORE SCHEDULING?:'$)
   11 FORMAT(' ALL JOBS PROCESSED IN SAME ORDER THRU THE SHOP?:'$)
   12 FORMAT(A1)
C ** GENERAL INPUT **
      WRITE(4,1)
   50 WRITE(4,2)
      P(1)=0.
      W(1)=0.
      READ(4,8) NP
      IF(NP.GT.1) GO TO 51
C ** 1 PROCESS **
      WRITE(4,3)
      WRITE(4,5)
      READ(4,8) NJ
      WRITE(4,6)
   52 WRITE(4,7)
      READ(4,8) NM
      IF(NM.EQ.1) CALL TRICK1
      IF(NM.EQ.2) CALL TRICK2
      IF(NM.EQ.3) CALL TRICK3
      IF(NM.EQ.4) CALL TRICK4
      IF(NM.EQ.5) CALL TRICK5
C ** RERUN OPTIONS **
      WRITE(4,9)
      READ(4,12) ANSWER
      IF(ANSWER.EQ.YES) GO TO 52
   53 WRITE(4,10)
      READ(4,12) ANSWER
      IF(ANSWER.EQ.YES) GO TO 50
      STOP
C ** 2+ PROCESSES **
   51 WRITE(4,4) NP
      WRITE(4,5)
      READ(4,8) NJ
      ANSWER=YES
      IF(NP.EQ.2) WRITE(4,11)
      IF(NP.EQ.2) READ(4,12) ANSWER
      IF(ANSWER.EQ.YES) CALL TRICK6
      IF(ANSWER.EQ.XNO) CALL TRICK7
      GO TO 53
      END
```

```fortran
C ** MINIMIZE SUM OF COMPLETION TIMES **
      SUBROUTINE TRICK1
      COMMON/JOBS/NJ,P(20),IO(20),W(20)
    1 FORMAT(' INPUT PROCESSING TIMES FOR EACH JOB, SEPARATED BY COMMAS'
     1/' AND ENDING WITH A CARRIAGE RETURN'/)
    2 FORMAT(20G)
    3 FORMAT(' OPTIMUM SEQUENCE TO'//' 1.  MINIMIZE SUM OF COMPLETION TI
     1MES'/(I3))
      IF(P(1).GT.0) GO TO 4
      WRITE(4,1)
      READ(4,2) (P(I),I=1,NJ)
    4 CALL SORT(NJ,P,IO)
      WRITE(4,3) (IO(I),I=1,NJ)
      RETURN
      END
C ** MINIMIZE WEIGHTED SUM OF COMPLETION TIMES **
      SUBROUTINE TRICK2
      COMMON/JOBS/NJ,P(20),IO(20),W(20)
      DIMENSION WT(20)
    1 FORMAT(' INPUT PROCESSING TIMES FOR EACH JOB, SEPARATED BY COMMAS'
     1/' AND ENDING WITH A CARRIAGE RETURN'/)
    2 FORMAT(' INPUT WEIGHTS ON JOBS, SEPARATED BY COMMAS'/' AND ENDING
     1 WITH A CARRIAGE RETURN'/)
    3 FORMAT(' OPTIMUM SEQUENCE TO'//' 2.  MINIMIZE WEIGHTED SUM OF COM
     1PLETION TIMES'/(I3))
    4 FORMAT(20G)
      IF(P(1).GT.0) GO TO 6
      WRITE(4,1)
      READ(4,4) (P(I),I=1,NJ)
    6 WRITE(4,2)
      READ(4,4) (WT(I),I=1,NJ)
      DO 5 I=1,NJ
    5 P(I)=P(I)/WT(I)
      CALL SORT(NJ,P,IO)
      WRITE(4,3) (IO(I),I=1,NJ)
      DO 7 I=1,NJ
    7 P(I)=P(I)*WT(I)
      RETURN
      END
C ** MINIMIZE MAXIMUM TARDINESS **
      SUBROUTINE TRICK3
      COMMON/JOBS/NJ,P(20),IO(20),W(20)
    1 FORMAT(' INPUT DUE DATES FROM NOW FOR EACH JOB, SEPARATED BY COMMA
     1S'/' AND ENDING WITH A CARRIAGE RETURN'/)
    2 FORMAT(' OPTIMUM SEQUENCE TO'//' 3.  MINIMIZE MAXIMUM TARDINESS'/(
     1I3))
    3 FORMAT(20G)
      IF(W(1).GT.0) GO TO 4
      WRITE(4,1)
      READ(4,3) (W(I),I=1,NJ)
    4 CALL SORT(NJ,W,IO)
      WRITE(4,2) (IO(I),I=1,NJ)
      RETURN
      END
```

```
C ** MAXIMIZE MINIMUM LATENESS **
      SUBROUTINE TRICK4
      COMMON/JOBS/NJ,P(20),IO(20),W(20)
    1 FORMAT(' INPUT PROCESSING TIMES FOR EACH JOB, SEPARATED BY COMMAS'
     1/' AND ENDING WITH A CARRIAGE RETURN'/)
    2 FORMAT(' INPUT DUE DATES FROM NOW FOR EACH JOB, SEPARATED BY COMMA
     1S'/' AND ENDING WITH A CARRIAGE RETURN'/)
    3 FORMAT(' OPTIMUM SEQUENCE TO'//' 4.  MAXIMIZE MINIMUM LATENESS'/(I
     13))
    4 FORMAT(20G)
      IF(P(1).GT.0) GO TO 6
      WRITE(4,1)
      READ(4,4) (P(I),I=1,NJ)
    6 IF(W(1).GT.0) GO TO 7
      WRITE(4,2)
      READ(4,4) (W(I),I=1,NJ)
    7 DO 5 I=1,NJ
    5 P(I)=W(I)-P(I)
      CALL SORT(NJ,P,IO)
      WRITE(4,3) (IO(I),I=1,NJ)
      DO 8 I=1,NJ
    8 P(I)=W(I)-P(I)
      RETURN
      END
C ** MINIMIZE NUMBER OF LATE JOBS **
      SUBROUTINE TRICK5
      COMMON/JOBS/NJ,P(20),IO(20),W(20)
    1 FORMAT(' INPUT PROCESSING TIMES FOR EACH JOB, SEPARATED BY COMMAS'
     1/' AND ENDING WITH A CARRIAGE RETURN'/)
    2 FORMAT(' INPUT DUE DATES FROM NOW FOR EACH JOB, SEPARATED BY COMMA
     1S'/' AND ENDING WITH A CARRIAGE RETURN'/)
    3 FORMAT(' LATE JOB IS ',I2)
    4 FORMAT(/' OPTIMUM SEQUENCE TO'//' 5.  MINIMIZE NUMBER OF LATE JOBS
     1'/(I3))
    5 FORMAT(/I3,' JOBS ON TIME, ',I2,' JOBS LATE')
    6 FORMAT(20G)
      IF(P(1).GT.0) GO TO 12
      WRITE(4,1)
      READ(4,6) (P(I),I=1,NJ)
   12 IF(W(1).GT.0) GO TO 13
      WRITE(4,2)
      READ(4,6) (W(I),I=1,NJ)
   13 CALL SORT(NJ,W,IO)
C ** FIND LATE JOBS, IF ANY **
      NN=NJ-1
      N=NJ
    7 T=0
      DO 8 I=1,N
      J=IO(I)
      T=T+P(J)
      IF(T.GT.W(J)) GO TO 9
    8 CONTINUE
      WRITE(4,4) (IO(I),I=1,NJ)
      NN=NJ-N
      WRITE(4,5) N,NN
      RETURN
C ** REJECT LONGEST JOB **
    9 LATEST=1
      DO 10 J=1,I
      K=IO(J)
      IF(P(LATEST).LT.P(K)) LATEST=J
   10 CONTINUE
      J=LATEST
      LATEST=IO(J)
      N=N-1
      WRITE(4,3) LATEST
      DO 11 K=J,NN
   11 IO(K)=IO(K+1)
      IO(NJ)=LATEST
      GO TO 7
      END
```

```
C ** SORTING SUBROUTINE **
      SUBROUTINE SORT(N,X,I)
      DIMENSION X(20),I(20)
      K=1
      I(K)=1
    2 K=K+1
      IF(K.GT.N) RETURN
      KK=K
      I(K)=K
    3 KK=KK-1
      IF(KK.EQ.0) GO TO 2
      KKK=I(KK)
      IF(X(KKK).LE.X(K)) GO TO 2
      I(KK+1)=KKK
      I(KK)=K
      GO TO 3
      END
C ** MINIMIZE TOTAL TIME FOR ORDERED JOBS ON 2 MACHINES **
      SUBROUTINE TRICK7
      DIMENSION IA(20),IB(20),IAB(20),IBA(20),JAB(20),JBA(20),PAB(2,20),
     1PBA(2,20)
      COMMON/JOBS/NJ
    1 FORMAT(' PLEASE ENTER PROCESSING TIMES FOR EACH JOB ON PROCESS'/'
     1 1 AND 2 SEPARATED BY COMMAS'//' ENTER ORDER AS:  1,2 OR 2,1 OR 1,
     20 OR 0,2'/)
    2 FORMAT(' JOB ',I2,':'$)
    3 FORMAT('+ORDER?:'$)
    4 FORMAT(/' OPTIMAL ORDER ON MACHINE ',I1,' IS:'/(10(2X,I2)/))
    5 FORMAT(2G)
      KA=0
      KB=0
      KAB=0
      KBA=0
      WRITE(4,1)
C ** INPUT JOB DATA AND CLASSIFY **
      DO 6 I=1,NJ
      WRITE(4,2) I
      READ(4,5) A,B
      WRITE(4,3)
      READ(4,5) J,K
      IF(J.EQ.1.AND.K.EQ.0) GO TO 7
      IF(J.EQ.1.AND.K.EQ.2) GO TO 8
      IF(J.EQ.2.AND.K.EQ.1) GO TO 9
      KB=KB+1
      IB(KB)=I
      GO TO 6
    7 KA=KA+1
      IA(KA)=I
      GO TO 6
    8 KAB=KAB+1
      IAB(KAB)=I
      PAB(1,KAB)=A
      PAB(2,KAB)=B
      GO TO 6
    9 KBA=KBA+1
      IBA(KBA)=I
      PBA(1,KBA)=B
      PBA(2,KBA)=A
    6 CONTINUE
      CALL JONSON(KAB,JAB,IAB,PAB)
      CALL JONSON(KBA,JBA,IBA,PBA)
      K=1
      WRITE(4,4) K,(JAB(I),I=1,KAB),(IA(I),I=1,KA),(JBA(I),I=1,KBA)
      K=2
      WRITE(4,4) K,(JBA(I),I=1,KBA),(IB(I),I=1,KB),(JAB(I),I=1,KAB)
      RETURN
      END
```

```
C ** JOHNSON'S METHOD **
      SUBROUTINE JONSON(NJ,IO,JO,PAB)
      DIMENSION IO(20),PAB(2,20),ICHK(20),JO(20)
      K=NJ
      J=1
      DO 1 I=1,NJ
    1 ICHK(I)=0
    2 M=0
      DO 3 I=1,NJ
      IF(ICHK(I).EQ.1) GO TO 3
      IF(M) 4,4,5
    5 IF(PAB(1,I).GT.X.AND.PAB(2,I).GT.X) GO TO 3
    4 M=I
      X=AMIN1(PAB(1,I),PAB(2,I))
      L=1
      IF(X.EQ.PAB(2,I)) L=2
    3 CONTINUE
      IF(M.EQ.0) RETURN
      ICHK(M)=1
      IF(L-1) 6,6,7
    6 IO(J)=JO(M)
      J=J+1
      GO TO 2
    7 IO(K)=JO(M)
      K=K-1
      GO TO 2
      END
C ** GUPTA'S METHOD WITH SWITCH TO JOHNSON'S **
      SUBROUTINE TRICK6
      COMMON/JOBS/NJ,V(20),IO(20)/PROC/NP
      DIMENSION P(20,10),PAB(2,20),JO(20)
    1 FORMAT(' PLEASE ENTER PROCESSING TIME FOR EACH JOB ON PROCESS'/
     1' 1 THRU ',I2,' SEPARATED BY COMMAS'/)
    2 FORMAT('+JOB ',I2,':'$)
    3 FORMAT(10G)
    4 FORMAT(' OPTIMUM SEQUENCE TO'//' MINIMIZE TOTAL PROCESSING TIME '
     1:'/(I3))
      WRITE(4,1) NP
      IF(NP.EQ.2) GO TO 7
      NP1=NP-1
      DO 5 I=1,NJ
      WRITE(4,2) I
      READ(4,3) (P(I,J),J=1,NP)
      V(I)=999999.
      DO 6 J=1,NP1
    6 V(I)=AMIN1(V(I),(P(I,J)+P(I,J+1)))
      IF(P(I,1).LT.P(I,NP)) V(I)=-V(I)
    5 V(I)=1./V(I)
      CALL SORT(NJ,V,IO)
    9 WRITE(4,4) (IO(I),I=1,NJ)
      RETURN
    7 DO 8 I=1,NJ
      WRITE(4,2) I
      JO(I)=I
    8 READ(4,3) PAB(1,I),PAB(2,I)
      CALL JONSON(NJ,IO,JO,PAB)
      GO TO 9
      END
```

PROGRAM 2.1 ECONOMIC ORDER QUANTITY, CONSTANT DEMAND, NO SHORTAGES ALLOWED

```
  DATA YES/'Y'/
1 FORMAT(' INVENTORY MODEL, NO SHORTAGES ALLOWED'//' PLEASE INPUT
 1 HOLDING COST PER ITEM PER DAY'/' AS A DECIMAL FRACTION PERCENTAGE
 2 OF ITEM SELLING PRICE:'$)
2 FORMAT(' PLEASE INPUT SETUP COST PER PRODUCTION RUN:'$)
3 FORMAT(' HOW MANY ITEMS ARE NEEDED:'$)
4 FORMAT(' OVER HOW MANY DAYS:'$)
5 FORMAT(' OPTIMAL INTERVAL BETWEEN PRODUCTION RUNS IS ',I4,' DAYS
 1.'//' OPTIMAL ORDER QUANTITY IS ',I8,' UNITS.'//' COST OF THIS P
 2RODUCTION SCHEDULE IS $',F10.2//' DO ANOTHER?:'$)
6 FORMAT(' THANK YOU AND GOODBYE')
7 FORMAT(G)
8 FORMAT(A1)
9 WRITE(4,1)
  READ(4,7) C1
  WRITE(4,2)
  READ(4,7) CS
  WRITE(4,3)
  READ(4,7) R
  WRITE(4,4)
  READ(4,7) T
  ITSTAR=SQRT(2.*CS*T/C1/R)
  IQSTAR=SQRT(2.*CS*R/C1/T)
  TEC=SQRT(2.*C1*T*CS*R)
  WRITE(4,5)   ITSTAR,IQSTAR,TEC
  READ(4,8) ANSWER
  IF(ANSWER.EQ.YES) GO TO 9
  WRITE(4,6)
  STOP
  END
```

PROGRAM 2.2 ECONOMIC ORDER QUANTITY, CONSTANT DEMAND, SHORTAGES ALLOWED

```
    DATA YES/'Y'/
 1  FORMAT(' INVENTORY MODEL WITH SHORTAGES'//' PLEASE INPUT HOLDING
 1  COST PER ITEM PER DAY'/' AS A DECIMAL FRACTION PERCENTAGE OF ITEM
 2  SELLING PRICE:'$)
 3  FORMAT(' PLEASE INPUT SETUP COST PER PRODUCTION RUN:'$)
 4  FORMAT(' HOW MANY ITEMS ARE NEEDED:'$)
 5  FORMAT(' OVER HOW MANY DAYS:'$)
 6  FORMAT(' PLEASE INPUT SHORTAGE COST PER ITEM PER DAY (IN $):'$)
 7  FORMAT(' OPTIMAL INTERVAL BETWEEN PRODUCTION RUNS IS ',I7,' DAYS
 1  .'//' OPTIMAL ORDER QUANTITY IS ',I7,' UNITS.'//' SHORTAGE AT END
 2  OF PRODUCTION CYCLE IS',I7,' UNITS.'//' COST OF THIS PRODUCTION S
 3  CHEDULE IS $',F10.2)
 8  FORMAT(/' DO ANOTHER?:'$)
 9  FORMAT(' THANK YOU AND GOODBYE')
12  FORMAT(G)
10  WRITE(4,1)
    READ(4,12) C1
    WRITE(4,3)
    READ(4,12) CS
    WRITE(4,4)
    READ(4,12) R
    WRITE(4,5)
    READ(4,12) T
    WRITE(4,6)
    READ(4,12) C2
    ITS=SQRT(((2.*T*CS)*(C1+C2))/(R*C1*C2))
    IQ = SQRT((2.*R*CS*(C1+C2))/(T*C1*C2))
    IS = IQ - SQRT((2*R*CS*C2)/(C1*T*(C1+C2)))
    TC=SQRT((2.*R*T*C1*CS*C2)/(C1+C2))
    WRITE(4,7) ITS,IQ,IS,TC
    WRITE(4,8)
    READ(4,12) V
    IF(V.EQ.YES) GO TO 10
    WRITE(4,9)
    STOP
    END
```

PROGRAM 2.3 ECONOMIC ORDER QUANTITY, UNCERTAIN DEMAND, SHORTAGES ALLOWED, DISCRETE UNITS

```
      DIMENSION  P(99)
      DATA NO/'N'/
      INTEGER ANSWER
    1 FORMAT(' INVENTORY FOR SPARE PARTS WITH HISTORY'///' PLEASE INPUT
     1 COST OF SPARE PURCHASED WITH ASSEMBLY:'$)
    2 FORMAT(' PLEASE INPUT SHORTAGE COST:'$)
    3 FORMAT(' PLEASE INPUT HISTORICAL DATA CONSISTING OF THE NUMBER OF'
     1/' ASSEMBLIES REQUIRING THE NUMBER OF REPLACEMENT PARTS INDICATED.
     2'/' BEGIN WITH ZERO REPLACEMENTS; DATA FOR 1, 2, 3, AND SO FORTH'/
     3' MUST FOLLOW.'//' DATA ENDS WHEN ZERO FOUND IN 2ND COLUMN.'//6X,
     4'*****HISTORY TABLE*****'/' # PARTS REPLACED',5X,'# ASSEMBLIES'/
     58X,'0',18X,':'$)
    4 FORMAT('+',6X,I2,18X,':'$)
    5 FORMAT(' OPTIMAL STOCK LEVEL IS ',I5/)
    6 FORMAT(' DO YOU WISH TO DETERMINE THE RANGE OF SHORTAGE COST'/
     1' FOR WHICH A GIVEN STOCK LEVEL HOLDS TRUE:'$)
    7 FORMAT(' WHAT IS THE GIVEN STOCK LEVEL:'$)
    8 FORMAT(' STOCK ',I3,' UNITS WHEN THE SHORTAGE COST IS GREATER THAN
     1 $',F10.2/' BUT LESS THAN $',F10.2/)
    9 FORMAT(G)
   10 FORMAT(A1)
      WRITE(4,1)
      READ(4,9) C1
      WRITE(4,2)
      READ(4,9) C2
      WRITE(4,3)
      READ(4,9) P0
      I=0
      SUM=P0
   11 I=I+1
      WRITE(4,4)  I
      READ(4,9) P(I)
      SUM=SUM+P(I)
      IF(P(I)) 12,12,11
   12 I=I-1
      P0=P0/SUM
      P(1)=P0+P(1)/SUM
      II=1
      IF((C2/(C1+C2)).GE.P0.AND.(C2/(C2+C1)).LE.P(1))WRITE(4,5) II
      DO 13  II=2,I
      P(II)=P(II-1)+P(II)/SUM
   13 IF((C2/(C1+C2)).GE.P(II-1).AND.(C2/(C2+C1)).LE.P(II))WRITE(4,5)II
   14 WRITE(4,6)
      READ(4,10) ANSWER
      IF(ANSWER.EQ.NO) STOP
      WRITE(4,7)
      READ(4,9) L
      A=P(L)/(1-P(L))*C1
      IF(L) 15,15,16
   15 B=P0/(1-P0)*C1
      GO TO 17
   16 B=P(L-1)/(1-P(L-1))*C1
   17 WRITE(4,8) L,B,A
      GO TO 14
      END
```

PROGRAM 2.4 ECONOMIC ORDER QUANTITY, TIME-VARYING DEMAND (SILVER AND MEAL METHOD)

```
      DIMENSION D(52)
      DATA YES/'Y'/
1     FORMAT(44H SILVER AND MEAL EOQ FOR TIME-VARYING DEMAND//26H DO YOU
     1 WANT THE TUTORIAL:$)
2     FORMAT(A1)
3     FORMAT(55H THIS PROGRAM WILL CALCULATE THE EOQ FOR ONE ITEM UNDER/
     135H CONDITIONS OF TIME-VARYING DEMAND.//54H YOU WILL BE ASKED TO E
     2NTER THE FOLLOWING INFORMATION://26H (1) THE COST OF THE ITEM,/54H
     3 (2) THE CARRYING CHARGE PER PERIOD OF TIME, EXPRESSED/40H AS A DE
     4CIMAL FRACTION OF THE ITEM COST,/33H (3) THE SET-UP OR ORDERING CO
     5ST,/85H (4) THE NUMBER OF TIME PERIODS IN ADVANCE FOR WHICH YOU HA
     6VE THE DEMAND INFORMATION,/42H (5) THE FORECASTED DEMAND IN EACH P
     7ERIOD,/70H AND (6) WHETHER OR NOT ALL STOCK NEEDED IN A PERIOD MUS
     8T BE AVAILABLE/29H AT THE START OF EACH PERIOD.//)
4     FORMAT(28H ENTER THE COST OF THE ITEM:$)
5     FORMAT(46H ENTER THE CARRYING CHARGE (DECIMAL FRACTION):$)
6     FORMAT(35H ENTER THE SET-UP OR ORDERING COST:$)
7     FORMAT(33H ENTER THE NUMBER OF TIME PERIODS/36H FOR WHICH YOU HAVE
     1 FORECASTED DATA:$)
8     FORMAT(36H ENTER DEMAND FOR PERIODS 1 THROUGH ,I2,22H, SEPARATED B
     1Y COMMAS:/)
9     FORMAT(47H MUST ALL STOCK NEEDED IN A PERIOD BE AVAILABLE/28H AT T
     1HE START OF THE PERIOD:$)
10    FORMAT(16H OPTIMUM EOQ IS ,I7,8H PIECES.//18H THIS WILL RUN OUT,F7
     1.2,37H TIME PERIODS FROM THE STARTING DATE.)
101   FORMAT(//49H DO YOU WISH TO CALCULATE THE NEXT REPLENISHMENT:$)
11    FORMAT(13(/),37H DO YOU WANT TO LOOK AT ANOTHER ITEM:$)
12    FORMAT(G)
13    FORMAT(50G)
22    FORMAT(46H NEXT REPLENISHMENT WILL OCCUR SOMETIME AFTER ,I2,22H PE
     1RIODS HAVE ELAPSED.//40H MORE DATA IS NECESSARY IN THE FORECAST.)
      WRITE(4,1)
      READ(4,2) V
      IF(V.EQ.YES) WRITE(4,3)
181   WRITE(4,4)
      READ(4,12) C
      WRITE(4,5)
      READ(4,12) XI
      WRITE(4,6)
      READ(4,12) S
      WRITE(4,7)
      READ(4,12) N
      WRITE(4,8) N
      READ(4,13) (D(J), J=1,N)
      WRITE(4,9)
      READ(4,2) V
      IF(V.EQ.YES) GO TO 14
      EOQSUM=0
      K=1
      T=0
      XM=2*S/C/XI
18    TOLD=T
      EOQOLD=EOQSUM
15    DO 16 J=K,N
      X=(J-T)**2*D(J)
16    IF(X.GT.XM) GO TO 17
```

```
17      IF(X.LE.XM) GO TO 173
        T=TOLD + SQRT(XM/D(J))
        CHECK=FLOAT((J-1))
        IF(T.LT.CHECK) T=CHECK
        K=J
        EOQ=0
        I=INT(T)
        IF(I.EQ.0) GO TO 170
        DO 171 J=1,I
171     EOQ=EOQ + D(J)
        EOQSUM=EOQ + (T-I)*D(I+1)
        EOQ=EOQ + (T-I)*D(I+1) - EOQOLD
        GO TO 172
170     EOQ=T*D(1) - EOQOLD
        EOQSUM=T*D(1)
172     IEOQ=INT(EOQ)
        WRITE(4,10) IEOQ, T
        IF(K.EQ.N) GO TO 182
        WRITE(4,101)
        READ(4,2) V
        IF(V.EQ.YES) GO TO 18
182     WRITE(4,11)
        READ(4,2) V
        IF(V.EQ.YES) GO TO 181
        STOP
173     WRITE(4,22) N
        GO TO 182
        STOP
14      XM=S/C/XI
        K=0
21      G=XM
        IEOQ=0
        DO 20 J=K+1,N
        IEOQ=IEOQ+D(J)
        X=(J-K)**2*D(J+1)
        IF(X.GT.G) GO TO 19
20      G = G+(J-K)*D(J+1)
19      T=J
        WRITE(4,10) IEOQ, T
        K=J
        IF(K+1.GE.N) GO TO 182
        WRITE(4,101)
        READ(4,2) V
        IF(V.EQ.YES) GO TO 21
        GO TO 182
        END
```

PROGRAM 2.5 NON-STOCKING CRITERION

```
      DATA YES,XMFG,ORDR/'Y','M','O'/
    1 FORMAT(' THIS PROGRAM DETERMINES IF A GIVEN ITEM SHOULD BE'/'
    1 STOCKED OR NOT STOCKED'//' PLEASE INPUT THE FOLLOWING DATA'//'
    2 HOLDING COST PER ITEM PER YEAR?:'$)
    2 FORMAT(' SELLING PRICE PER ITEM?:'$)
    3 FORMAT(' PRODUCTION COST PER ITEM?:'$)
    4 FORMAT(' YEARLY DEMAND?:'$)
    5 FORMAT(' AVERAGE ORDER SIZE?:'$)
    6 FORMAT(' ESTIMATE PER CENT OF SALES LOST IF ITEM NOT STOCKED?:'$)
    7 FORMAT(' IF ITEM IS MANUFACTURED, ENTER M; IF ORDERED, ENTER O:'$)
    8 FORMAT(' ENTER ORDERING COST PER ORDER?:'$)
    9 FORMAT(' ENTER SETUP COST PER PRODUCTION RUN?:'$)
   10 FORMAT(' ANNUAL PRODUCTION RATE?:'$)
   11 FORMAT(' ITEM SHOULD BE STOCKED'//' DO NOT STOCK IT IF ANNUAL
    1 DEMAND FALLS BELOW ',I5,' ITEMS'//' DO AGAIN?:'$)
   12 FORMAT(' ITEM SHOULD NOT BE STOCKED'//' STOCK IT IF ANNUAL DEMAND
    1 IS AT LEAST ',I5,' ITEMS'//' DO AGAIN?:'$)
   13 FORMAT(G)
   14 FORMAT(A1)
   15 WRITE(4,1)
      READ(4,13) CHOLD
      WRITE(4,2)
      READ(4,13) PRICE
      WRITE(4,3)
      READ(4,13) CPROD
      WRITE(4,4)
      READ(4,13) DEMAND
      WRITE(4,5)
      READ(4,13) AVGORD
      WRITE(4,6)
      READ(4,13) PCTLOS
      WRITE(4,7)
      READ(4,14) QUERY
      IF(QUERY.EQ.ORDR) GO TO 16
      WRITE(4,9)
      READ(4,13) CSETUP
      WRITE(4,10)
      READ(4,13) RATE
      GO TO 17
   16 WRITE(4,8)
      READ(4,13) CSETUP
   17 Q = (PCTLOS/100.*(PRICE-CPROD)+CSETUP/AVGORD*(1.-PCTLOS/100.))**2
      IF(QUERY.EQ.XMFG) Q=Q+2.*CSETUP*CHOLD/RATE
      Q=2.*CSETUP*CHOLD/Q
      IQ=Q
      IF(Q.GT.DEMAND)  WRITE(4,12) IQ
      IF(Q.LE.DEMAND)  WRITE(4,11) IQ
      READ(4,14) QUERY
      IF(QUERY.EQ.YES) GO TO 15
      STOP
      END
```

PROGRAM 3.1 SWANSON AND WOOLSEY CAPITAL BUDGETING METHOD

```
      DIMENSION C(20),B(20),A(20,20),G(20),IY(20),ISORT(20)
      DATA YES/'Y'/
 1    FORMAT(' SWANSON & WOOLSEYS CAPITAL BUDGETING QUICK & DIRTY'//
     1' DO YOU WANT THE TUTORIAL:'$)
 2    FORMAT(' THIS PROGRAM ASSUMES THAT YOU HAVE A GROUP OF PROJECTS
     1 THAT'/' ARE CONSTRAINED BY A GROUP OF SCARCE RESOURCES, SUCH AS
     2 MEN,'/' MONEY, OR MATERIALS.  YOU DESIRE TO CHOOSE FROM THESE
     3 PROJECTS'/' IN SUCH A WAY AS TO MAXIMIZE YOUR PAYOFF.  YOU WILL
     4 BE ASKED'/' TO INPUT THE NUMBER OF PROJECTS, THE NUMBER OF
     5 RESOURCES, THE'/' PAYOFF ASSOCIATED WITH EACH PROJECT, THE AMOUNT
     6 OF EACH RESOURCE'/' AVAILABLE, AND THE AMOUNT OF EACH RESOURCE
     7 THAT EACH PROJECT'/' REQUIRES.'/)
 3    FORMAT(' HOW MANY PROJECTS ARE THERE?:'$)
 4    FORMAT(' HOW MANY DIFFERENT RESOURCES ARE THERE?:'$)
 5    FORMAT(' LIST THE PAYOFF VALUES FOR THE PROJECTS, SEPARATED BY
     1 COMMAS'/)
 6    FORMAT(' WHAT IS THE AVAILABILITY OF RESOURCE ',I2,':'$)
 7    FORMAT(' LIST THE AMOUNT OF RESOURCE ',I2,' NEEDED FOR THE
     1 PROJECTS SEPARATED'/' BY COMMAS'/)
 8    FORMAT(' PROJECT OUT')
 9    FORMAT(/' OPTIMUM FOUND, PAYOFF=',F10.2//' DO THE FOLLOWING PROJEC
     1TS'/)
 24   FORMAT(' PROJECT ',I2)
 10   FORMAT(20G)
 11   FORMAT(A1)
 20   FORMAT(' NO SOLUTION POSSIBLE')
      WRITE(4,1)
      READ(4,11) ANSWER
      IF(ANSWER.EQ.YES) WRITE(4,2)
      WRITE(4,3)
      READ(4,10) N
      WRITE(4,4)
      READ(4,10) M
      WRITE(4,5)
      READ(4,10) (C(J), J=1,N)
      DO 12 I=1,M
      WRITE(4,6) I
      READ(4,10) B(I)
      WRITE(4,7) I
      READ(4,10) (A(I,J), J=1,N)
      DO 13 J=1,N
 13   B(I)=B(I)-A(I,J)
      B(I)=-B(I)
 12   IF(B(I).LT.0.) B(I)=0.
      DO 14 J=1,N
      X=0
      DO 15 I=1,M
 15   X=X+B(I)*A(I,J)
      IY(J)=1
 14   G(J)=C(J)/X
      ISORT(1)=1
      DO 16 J=2,N
      ISORT(J)=J
      K=J
 17   K=K-1
      KK=ISORT(K)
      IF(G(KK)-G(J))16,16,18
 18   ISORT(K+1)=KK
      ISORT(K)=J
      IF(K.GT.1) GO TO 17
```

```
16 CONTINUE
   DO 21 J=1,N
   DO 22 I=1,M
   IF(B(I).GT.0.) GO TO 23
22 CONTINUE
   JJJ=J-1
   DO 25 JJ=1,JJJ
   JK=ISORT(JJ)
   DO 26 I=1,M
   IF((B(I)+A(I,JK)).GT.0) GO TO 25
26 CONTINUE
   DO 27 I=1,M
27 B(I)=B(I)+A(I,JK)
   IY(JK)=1
25 CONTINUE
   PAYOFF=0
   DO 28  JJ=1,N
28 PAYOFF=PAYOFF+C(JJ)*IY(JJ)
   WRITE(4,9) PAYOFF
   DO 29  JJ=1,N
29 IF(IY(JJ).EQ.1) WRITE(4,24) JJ
   STOP
23 JJ=ISORT(J)
   WRITE(4,8)
   IY(JJ)=0
   DO 21 I=1,M
21 B(I)=B(I)-A(I,JJ)
   WRITE(4,20)
   STOP
   END
```

PROGRAM 3.2 $$$EXECUTIVE$$$ CAPITAL BUDGETING METHOD

```
       DIMENSION A(20,20),B(20),C(20),X(20),S(20),G(20),Y(20),SAVEY(20),C
      1HANGE(20),CHANG(20)
2      FORMAT(50G)
21     FORMAT(24X,'$$$ EXECUTIVE $$$'//' DO YOU WANT THE TUTORIAL:'$)
22     FORMAT(A1)
23     FORMAT(' THIS PROGRAM ASSUMES THAT YOU HAVE A GROUP OF PROJECTS (U
      1P TO 20) THAT'/' ARE CONSTRAINED BY A GROUP OF SCARCE RESOURCES, S
      1UCH AS MEN, MONEY, OR'/' MATERIALS.  YOU DESIRE TO CHOOSE FROM THE
      1SE PROJECTS IN SUCH A WAY AS'/' TO MAXIMIZE YOUR NET PRESENT VALUE
      1 OF FUTURE CASH FLOWS (PAYOFFS).'////' YOU WILL BE ASKED TO INPUT T
      1HE NUMBER OF PROJECTS, THE NUMBER OF'/' RESOURCES, THE NET PRESENT
      1 VALUE OF FUTURE CASH FLOWS (PAYOFF) ASSOCI-'/' ATED WITH EACH PRO
      1JECT, THE AMOUNT OF EACH RESOURCE AVAILABLE, AND THE'/' AMOUNT OF
      1 EACH RESOURCE THAT EACH PROJECT REQUIRES.'//)
24     FORMAT(' HOW MANY PROJECTS ARE THERE:'$)
25     FORMAT(/' HOW MANY DIFFERENT RESOURCES ARE THERE:'$)
26     FORMAT(/' LIST THE PAYOFF VALUES FOR THE PROJECTS, SEPARATED BY CO
      1MMAS:'/)
27     FORMAT(/' WHAT IS THE AVAILABILITY OF RESOURCE ',I2,':'$)
28     FORMAT(/' LIST THE AMOUNT OF RESOURCE ',I2,' NEEDED FOR'/' EACH PR
      1OJECT, SEPARATED BY COMMAS:'/)
29     FORMAT(/' OPTIMUM PAYOFF IS ',F10.2,//' DO THE FOLLOWING PROJECTS
      1')
291    FORMAT(I3)
292    FORMAT(/' THE AMOUNT OF RESOURCE ',I2,' NOT ALLOCATED IS ',F10.2,'
      1 UNITS.')
268    FORMAT(6(/),' DO YOU WANT TO CHANGE SOME OF THE OLD DATA AND RERUN
      1'/' THIS PROBLEM:'$)
269    FORMAT(////' DO YOU WANT TO RUN AN ENTIRELY NEW PROBLEM:'$)
271    FORMAT(/' DO YOU WANT TO CHANGE ANY PAYOFF VALUES:'$)
272    FORMAT(/' LIST THE PROJECTS FOR WHICH YOU WANT TO CHANGE THE PAYOF
      1FS,'/' SEPARATED BY COMMAS:'$)
273    FORMAT(/' PAYOFF FOR PROJECT ',I2,' IS NOW ',F10.2,'.'//' NEW PAYO
      1FF FOR PROJECT ',I2,' IS:'$)
274    FORMAT(/' DO YOU WANT TO CHANGE THE AVAILABILITY OF ANY RESOURCE:'
      1$)
275    FORMAT(/' LIST THE RESOURCES FOR WHICH YOU WANT TO CHANGE THE AVAI
      1LABILITY,'/' SEPARATED BY COMMAS:'$)
276    FORMAT(/' AVAILABILITY OF RESOURCE ',I2,' IS NOW ',F10.2,' UNITS.'
      1//' NEW AVAILABILITY OF RESOURCE ',I2,' IS:'$)
277    FORMAT(/' DO YOU WANT TO CHANGE THE RESOURCE REQUIREMENTS FOR ANY
      1 PROJECTS:'$)
278    FORMAT(' FOR WHICH PROJECTS DO YOU WANT TO CHANGE THE RESOURCE RE
      1QUIREMENTS:'/$)
279    FORMAT(/' FOR WHICH RESOURCES WILL PROJECT ',I2,I4','S REQUIREMENT
      1S CHANGE:'/)
280    FORMAT(/' PROJECT ',I2,' NOW REQUIRES ',F10.2,' UNITS OF RESOURCE
      1',I2,'.'//' NEW REQUIREMENT OF PROJECT ',I2,' IS:'$)
281    FORMAT(/////' PROJECTS SELECTED IN BOTH THE RERUN AND THE PREVIOUS
      1 RUN ARE AS FOLLOWS')
282    FORMAT(//////' DO YOU WANT TO PRESERVE THE RERUN SELECTION, CHANGE
      1 SOME OF THE'/' DATA, AND RERUN THE PROBLEM:'$)
       WRITE(4,21)
       READ(4,22)V
       IF(V.EQ.'Y')WRITE(4,23)
```

```
307     WRITE(4,24)
        READ(4,2)N
        WRITE(4,25)
        READ(4,2)M
        WRITE(4,26)
        READ(4,2)(C(J),J=1,N)
        DO 3 I=1,M
        WRITE(4,27)I
        READ(4,2)B(I)
        WRITE(4,28)I
3       READ(4,2)(A(I,J),J=1,N)
314     DO 31 J=1,N
31      X(J)=1
9       DO 4 I=1,M
        S(I)=-1
        DO 41 J=1,N
41      S(I)=S(I)+A(I,J)/B(I)*X(J)
4       IF(S(I).LT.0)S(I)=0
        DO 42 I=1,M
42      IF(S(I).GT.0)GO TO 43
        PAYOFF=0
        DO 10 J=1,N
10      PAYOFF=PAYOFF+X(J)*C(J)
        DO 294 I=1,M
        S(I)=B(I)
        DO 294 J=1,N
294     S(I)=S(I)-A(I,J)*X(J)
        DO 296 J=1,N
        Y(J)=0
296     IF(X(J).EQ.0)Y(J)=1
297     XMAX=0
        DO 298 J=1,N
        XMAX=AMAX1(XMAX,(C(J)*Y(J)))
298     IF(XMAX.EQ.(C(J)*Y(J)).AND.XMAX.NE.0)K=J
        IF(XMAX.EQ.0)GO TO 299
        DO 300 I=1,M
300     IF(S(I).LT.A(I,K))GO TO 301
        PAYOFF=PAYOFF+C(K)
        DO 302 I=1,M
302     S(I)=S(I)-A(I,K)
        X(K)=1
301     Y(K)=0
        GO TO 297
299     WRITE(4,29)PAYOFF
        DO 293 J=1,N
293     IF(X(J).EQ.1)WRITE(4,291)J
        DO 305 I=1,M
305     WRITE(4,292)I,S(I)
        IF(RERUN.NE.'Y')GO TO 317
        WRITE(4,281)
        DO 318 J=1,N
        IF(X(J).EQ.SAVEX(J).AND.X(J).EQ.1)WRITE(4,291)J
318     SAVEX(J)=0
        WRITE(4,282)
        READ(4,22)RERUN
        IF(RERUN.EQ.'Y')GO TO 306
        GO TO 319
```

```
317     WRITE(4,263)
        READ(4,22)RERUN
        IF(RERUN.EQ.'Y') GO TO 306
319     WRITE(4,269)
        READ(4,22)V
        IF(V.EQ.'Y')GO TO 307
        STOP
306     DO 309 J=1,N
309     SAVEX(J)=X(J)
308     WRITE(4,271)
        READ(4,22)V
        IF(V.EQ.'N')GO TO 310
        WRITE(4,272)
        READ(4,2)(CHANGE(J),J=1,N)
        DO 311 J=1,N
        IF(CHANGE(J).EQ.0)GO TO 310
        K=CHANGE(J)
        CHANGE(J)=0
        WRITE(4,273)K,C(K),K
311     READ(4,2)C(K)
310     WRITE(4,274)
        READ(4,22)V
        IF(V.NE.'Y')GO TO 312
        WRITE(4,275)
        READ(4,2)(CHANGE(I),I=1,M)
        DO 313 I=1,M
        IF(CHANGE(I).EQ.0)GO TO 312
        K=CHANGE(I)
        CHANGE(I)=0
        WRITE(4,276)K,B(K),K
313     READ(4,2)B(K)
312     WRITE(4,277)
        READ(4,22)V
        IF(V.NE.'Y')GO TO 314
        WRITE(4,278)
        READ(4,2)(CHANGE(J),J=1,N)
        DO 315 J=1,N
        IF(CHANGE(J).EQ.0)GO TO 314
        K=CHANGE(J)
        WRITE(4,279)K
        READ(4,2)(CHANG(I),I=1,M)
        DO 316 I=1,M
        IF(CHANG(I).EQ.0)GO TO 315
        KK=CHANG(I)
        CHANG(I)=0
        WRITE(4,280)K,A(KK,K),KK,K
316     READ(4,2)A(KK,K)
315     CHANGE(J)=0
        GO TO 314
43      DO 5 J=1,N
        G(J)=0
        DO 51 I=1,M
51      G(J)=A(I,J)/B(I)*X(J)*S(I)+G(J)
5       IF(G(J).NE.0)G(J)=C(J)/G(J)
        K=1
        DO 6 J=2,N
6       IF(X(J).EQ.1.AND.G(J).LT.G(K)) K=J
        X(K)=0
        GO TO 9
        END
```

PROGRAM 4.1 2 × 2 MARKOV PROCESS

```
      DIMENSION P(4)
      DATA YES,NO/'Y','N'/
      REAL NO
 1 FORMAT(' 2X2 MARKOV PROCESS'//' IF IN STATE 1, P(STATE 1):'$)
 2 FORMAT(' IF IN STATE 2, P(STATE 1):'$)
 3 FORMAT(' TRANSITION MATRIX FOR TIME PERIOD ',I2//4X,'P(1,1)=',
     1F6.4,3X,'P(1,2)=',F6.4//4X,'P(2,1)=',F6.4,3X,'P(2,2)=',F6.4/)
 4 FORMAT(' TRANSITION MATRIX (0 FOR NONE)?:'$)
 5 FORMAT(' STEADY-STATE MATRIX?:'$)
 6 FORMAT(' DO YOU WISH TO ENTER A STATE VECTOR:'$)
 7 FORMAT(' S1:'$)
 8 FORMAT('+S2:'$)
 9 FORMAT(' VECTOR AT END OF PERIOD ',I2/)
10 FORMAT(' S1=',F10.2,3X,'S2=',F10.2/)
11 FORMAT(' VECTOR AT END OF PERIOD (0 FOR NONE)?:'$)
12 FORMAT(' DO YOU WISH THE STEADY-STATE VECTOR?:'$)
13 FORMAT(' STEADY-STATE MATRIX'//4X,'P(1,1)=',F6.4,3X,'P(1,2)=',F6.4
     1//4X,'P(2,1)=',F6.4,3X,'P(2,2)=',F6.4/)
14 FORMAT(' DO 2X2 MARKOV AGAIN?:'$)
15 FORMAT(G)
16 FORMAT(A1)
17 WRITE(4,1)
      READ(4,15) P(1)
      A=P(1)
      P(2)=1.-P(1)
      WRITE(4,2)
      READ(4,15) P(3)
      B=P(3)
      P(4)=1.-B
      K=1
18 WRITE(4,3) K,(P(I),I=1,4)
      WRITE(4,4)
      READ(4,15) K
      IF(K.EQ.0) GO TO 19
      CHECK=0.
23 P(1)=(B+(1.-A)*(A-B)**K)/(1.-A+B)
      P(2)=1.-P(1)
      P(3)=B*(1.-(A-B)**K)/(1.-A+B)
      P(4)=1.-P(3)
      IF(CHECK.EQ.1.) GO TO 24
      GO TO 18
19 WRITE(4,5)
      READ(4,16) ANSWER
      IF(ANSWER.EQ.NO) GO TO 20
25 P(1)=B/(1.-A+B)
      P(2)=1.-P(1)
      P(3)=P(1)
      P(4)=P(2)
      IF(CHECK.EQ.2) GO TO 24
      WRITE(4,13) (P(I),I=1,4)
```

```
20 WRITE(4,6)
   READ(4,16) ANSWER
   IF(ANSWER.EQ.YES) GO TO 21
27 WRITE(4,14)
   READ(4,16) ANSWER
   IF(ANSWER.EQ.YES) GO TO 17
   STOP
21 WRITE(4,7)
   READ(4,15) S1
   WRITE(4,8)
   READ(4,15) S2
   K=1
22 CHECK=1.
   GO TO 23
24 SS1=S1*P(1)+S2*P(3)
   SS2=S1*P(2)+S2*P(4)
   IF(CHECK.EQ.2) GO TO 26
   WRITE(4,9) K
   WRITE(4,10) SS1, SS2
   WRITE(4,11)
   READ(4,15) K
   IF(K.GT.0) GO TO 22
   CHECK=2.
   WRITE(4,12)
   READ(4,16) ANSWER
   IF(ANSWER.EQ.YES) GO TO 25
26 WRITE(4,10) SS1, SS2
   GO TO 27
   END
```

PROGRAM 10.1   MINIMAL SPANNING TREE

```
      INTEGER SN(31), EN(31), UB, ARC(30), SCHDUL(30), NODE(60)
      REAL LENGTH(31)
      DATA YES/'Y'/
      UB=30
 1 FORMAT(' MINIMAL SPANNING TREE'//' ENTER ARCS AS FOLLOWS:'//
    1' STARTING NODE, ENDING NODE, DISTANCE'//' STOP INPUT BY TYPING:0,
    20,0'//)
 2 FORMAT('+ARC ',I2,':'$)
 4 FORMAT(' DONE'//' THE M. S. T. CONSISTS OF THE FOLLOWING ARCS:'/)
 6 FORMAT(/' DO YOU WISH TO DO ANOTHER PROBLEM?:'$)
 7 FORMAT(' SORRY, BUT THE PROGRAM CAN CURRENTLY ACCEPT AT MOST ',I2,
    1' ARCS.'//' GOODBYE')
 8 FORMAT(3G)
 9 FORMAT(A1)
21 FORMAT(' ARC ',I2,'(',I2,',',I2,')')
10 WRITE(4,1)
      UB=UB+1
      DO 11 N=1,UB
      WRITE(4,2) N
      READ(4,8) SN(N), EN(N), LENGTH(N)
      IF(SN(N)) 12,12,11
11 CONTINUE
      UB=UB-1
      WRITE(4,7) UB
      STOP
12 N=N-1
      UB=UB-1
13 DO 14 I=1,N
14 SCHDUL(I)=0
      UB=UB*2
      DO 24  J=1,UB
24 NODE(J)=0
      UB=UB/2
      NODE(1)=1
      L=0
15 MINARC=0
      DO 16 I=1,N
      IF(SCHDUL(I).EQ.1) GO TO 16
      J=SN(I)
      K=EN(I)
      IF(NODE(J).EQ.1.XOR.NODE(K).EQ.1) GO TO 18
      GO TO 16
18 IF(MINARC) 19,19,20
19 MINARC=I
      GO TO 16
20 IF(LENGTH(MINARC).GT.LENGTH(I)) GO TO 19
16 CONTINUE
      IF(MINARC.EQ.0) GO TO 23
      L=L+1
      ARC(L)=MINARC
      SCHDUL(MINARC)=1
      J=SN(MINARC)
      K=EN(MINARC)
      NODE(J)=1
      NODE(K)=1
      GO TO 15
23 WRITE(4,4)
      DO 22 II=1,L
      I=ARC(II)
22 WRITE(4,21) I, SN(I), EN(I)
      WRITE(4,6)
      READ(4,9) ANSWER
      IF(ANSWER.EQ.YES) GO TO 10
      STOP
      END
```

PROGRAM 10.2   OPTIMUM CASH REPLENISHMENT, LUMPY DEMAND

```
      DIMENSION  D(52)
      DATA YES/'Y'/
    1 FORMAT(24H OPTIMUM CASH MANAGEMENT//26H DO YOU WANT THE TUTORIAL:$
     1)
    2 FORMAT(A1)
    3 FORMAT(73H THIS PROGRAM WILL CALCULATE THE OPTIMUM CASH BALANCE RE
     1PLENISHMENT UNDER/35H CONDITIONS OF TIME-VARYING DEMAND.//56H YOU
     2 WILL BE ASKED TO PROVIDE THE FOLLOWING INFORMATION://64H 1) THE O
     3PPORTUNITY COST OF HOLDING CASH, THAT IS, WHAT INTEREST/50H RATE Y
     4OUR CASH COULD EARN YOU INVESTED ELSEWHERE,/73H 2) THE FIXED TRANS
     5ACTION COST OF OBTAINING A CASH BALANCE REPLENISHMENT,/   69H 3) T
     6HE NUMBER OF TIME PERIODS IN ADVANCE FOR WHICH YOU HAVE THE CASH/2
     78H BALANCE DEMAND INFORMATION,/50H 4) THE FORECASTED DEMAND FOR CA
     8SH IN EACH PERIOD,/68H AND 5) WHETHER OR NOT ALL CASH NEEDED IN A
     9 PERIOD MUST BE AVAILABLE/28H AT THE START OF THE PERIOD.//)
    5 FORMAT(63H ENTER THE OPPORTUNITY COST OF HOLDING CASH (DECIMAL FRA
     1CTION):$)
    6 FORMAT(68H ENTER THE FIXED TRANSACTION COST OF OBTAINING A CASH RE
     1PLENISHMENT:$)
    7 FORMAT(69H ENTER THE NUMBER OF TIME PERIODS FOR WHICH YOU HAVE FOR
     1ECASTED DATA:$)
    8 FORMAT(49H ENTER CASH BALANCE DEMANDS FOR PERIODS 1 THROUGH,I3,1H,
     1/21H SEPARATED BY COMMAS:$)
    9 FORMAT(46H MUST ALL CASH NEEDED IN A PERIOD BE AVAILABLE/28H AT TH
     1E START OF THE PERIOD:$)
   10 FORMAT(32H OPTIMUM CASH REPLENISHMENT IS $,F10.2,1H.//19H THIS WIL
     1L RUN OUT ,F5.2,37H TIME PERIODS FROM THE STARTING DATE.)
  101 FORMAT(//54H DO YOU WISH TO CALCULATE THE NEXT CASH REPLENISHMENT:
     1$)
   11 FORMAT(12(/),41H DO YOU WANT TO LOOK AT ANOTHER FORECAST:$)
   12 FORMAT(G)
   13 FORMAT(50G)
   22 FORMAT(46H NEXT REPLENISHMENT WILL OCCUR SOMETIME AFTER ,I2,22H PE
     1RIODS HAVE ELAPSED.//40H MORE DATA IS NECESSARY IN THE FORECAST.)
      WRITE(4,1)
      READ(4,2) V
      IF(V.EQ.YES)  WRITE(4,3)
  181 WRITE(4,5)
      READ(4,12) C
      WRITE(4,6)
      READ(4,12) S
      WRITE(4,7)
      READ(4,12) N
      WRITE(4,8) N
      READ(4,13) (D(J), J=1,N)
      WRITE(4,9)
      READ(4,2) V
      IF(V.EQ.YES) GO TO 14
      EOQSUM=0
      K=1
      T=0
      XM=2*S/C
   18 TOLD=T
      EOQOLD=EOQSUM
   15 DO 16 J=K,N
      X=(J-T)**2*D(J)
   16 IF(X.GT.XM) GO TO 17
      GO TO 173
```

```
17      T=TOLD+SQRT(XM/D(J))
        CHECK=FLOAT((J-1))
        IF(T.LT.CHECK) T=CHECK
        K=J
        EOQ=0
        I=INT(T)
        IF(I.EQ.0) GO TO 170
        DO 171 J=1,I
171     EOQ=EOQ + D(J)
        EOQSUM=EOQ + (T-I)*D(I+1)
        EOQ=EOQ + (T-I)*D(I+1) - EOQOLD
        GO TO 172
170     EOQ=T*D(1) - EOQOLD
        EOQSUM = T*D(1)
172     WRITE(4,10) EOQ,T
        IF(K.EQ.N) GO TO 182
        WRITE(4,101)
        READ(4,2) V
        IF(V.EQ.YES) GO TO 18
182     WRITE(4,11)
        READ(4,2) V
        IF(V.EQ.YES) GO TO 181
        STOP
173     WRITE(4,22) N
        GO TO 182
        STOP
14      XM=S/C
        K=0
21      G=XM
        IEOQ=0
        DO 20 J=K+1,N
        IEOQ=IEOQ+D(J)
        X=(J-K)**2*D(J+1)
        IF(X.GT.G)  GO TO 19
20      G=G+(J-K)**2*D(J+1)
19      T=J
        EOQ=FLOAT(IEOQ)
        WRITE(4,10) EOQ,T
        K=J
        IF(K+1.GT.N) GO TO 182
        WRITE(4,101)
        READ(4,2) V
        IF(V.EQ.YES) GO TO 21
        GO TO 182
        END
```

PROGRAM 10.3   WAREHOUSE LOCATION (GRANGE'S METHOD)

```
C
C
C     WAREHOUSE LOCATION HEURISTIC
C
C     REFERENCE:  SHANNON, R. E., AND IGNIZIO, J. P., "A HEURISTIC
C     PROGRAMMING ALGORITHM FOR WAREHOUSE LOCATION," AIIE TRANSACTIONS
C     VOL. II, NO.4, P. 334.
C
C     NOTATION MORE OR LESS FOLLOWS THE ABOVE REFERENCE.
C
      DIMENSION  A(100), T(20), ASTAR(20), THETA(20), S(20), X(20), F(20
     1), NEXTB(20), Y(20)

      DATA YES/'Y'/
      INTEGER THETA, X, Y
    1 FORMAT(45H WAREHOUSE LOCATION FOR MINIMUM SHIPPING COST//26H DO YO
     1U WANT THE TUTORIAL:$)
    2 FORMAT(A1)
    3 FORMAT(71H THIS PROGRAM LOCATES A NUMBER OF WAREHOUSES TO MINIMIZE
     1 SHIPPING COSTS/62H TO CUSTOMERS.  THE PROGRAM REQUIRES THE FOLLOW
     2ING INPUT DATA://6X,50H1) MAXIMUM NUMBER OF WAREHOUSES THAT MAY BE
     3 BUILT,/6X,63H2) TOTAL NUMBER OF POSSIBLE SITES FOR WAREHOUSES (MU
     4ST EQUAL OR/9X,51HEXCEED THE NUMBER OF WAREHOUSES THAT MAY BE BUIL
     5T),/6X,61H3) NUMBER OF CUSTOMERS TO BE SERVICED (ONLY ONE WAREHOUS
     6E MAY/9X,21HSERVE EACH CUSTOMER),/6X,60H4) ANNUAL COST OF SUPPLYIN
     7G EACH CUSTOMER FROM EACH POSSIBLE/9X,61HWAREHOUSE SITE: COSTS ARE
     8 DETERMINED ON THE BASIS OF CUSTOMER/9X,63HORDER VOLUMES (TONS/YEA
     9R), DISTANCES (MILES), AND FREIGHT RATES/9X,13H($/TON-MILE).//)
    4 FORMAT(60H WHAT IS THE MAXIMUM NUMBER OF WAREHOUSES THAT MAY BE BU
     1ILT:$)
    5 FORMAT(30G)
    6 FORMAT(45H HOW MANY POSSIBLE WAREHOUSE SITES ARE THERE:$)
    7 FORMAT(/66H THE NUMBER OF POSSIBLE SITES IS EXCEEDED BY THE MAXIMU
     1M NUMBER OF/30H WAREHOUSES THAT MAY BE BUILT.//53H DO YOU WANT TO
     2 READ THE TUTORIAL AGAIN (IF NO, DATA/21H INPUT WILL RESTART):$)
    8 FORMAT(35H HOW MANY CUSTOMERS MUST BE SERVED:$)
    9 FORMAT(48H LIST THE ANNUAL SHIPPING COSTS TO EACH CUSTOMER/21H FRO
     1M WAREHOUSE SITE ,I2,22H, SEPARATED BY COMMAS:/)

C
C
C     INPUT
C
      WRITE(4,1)
      READ(4,2) ANSWER
      IF(ANSWER.EQ.YES) WRITE(4,3)
   11 WRITE(4,4)
      READ(4,5) K
      WRITE(4,6)
      READ(4,5) N
      IF(K.LE.N) GO TO 10
      WRITE(4,7)
      READ(4,2) ANSWER
      IF(ANSWER.EQ.YES) WRITE(4,3)
      GO TO 11
   10 WRITE(4,8)
      READ(4,5) M
      I=0
      DO 12 J=1,N
      I2=J*M
      I1=(J-1)*M+1
      WRITE(4,9) J
      READ(4,5) (A(I), I=I1,I2)

C
C
C     SELECT FIRST LOCATION
C
      T(J)=0
      DO 13 I=I1,I2
   13 T(J)=T(J)+A(I)
      IF(J-1) 14,14,15
   15 IF(T(J) - TSTAR) 14,14,12
   14 TSTAR=T(J)
      THETA(1)=J
   12 CONTINUE
```

```
C
C           SET-UP ASTAR COLUMN AND BUILDING ORDER VECTOR THETA
C
          J=THETA(1)
          Y(J)=1
          I1=(J-1)*M
          DO 16  I=1,M
          I1=I1+1
          X(I)=J
   16 ASTAR(I)=A(I1)
          KL=1
C
C           SELECT NEXT LOCATION WITH SAVINGS
C
   22 SMALLS=0.0
          KL=KL+1
          DO 17   J=1,N
          IF(Y(J) - 1) 13,17,18
   18 S(J)=0
          I1=(J-1)*M+1
          I2=I1+M-1
          I3=0
          DO 19 I=I1,I2
          I3=I3+1
          IF(A(I) - ASTAR(I3)) 20,19,19
   20 S(J)=S(J) + A(I) - ASTAR(I3)
   19 CONTINUE
          IF(S(J) - SMALLS) 21,17,17
   21 SMALLS = S(J)
          THETA(KL) = J
   17 CONTINUE
          J=THETA(KL)
          Y(J)=1
C
C           NEW ASSIGNMENT IN ASTAR
C
          I1=(J-1)*M
          DO 24 I=1,M
          I2=I1+I
          IF(A(I2) - ASTAR(I)) 251,24,24
  251 ASTAR(I)=A(I2)
          X(I)=J
   24 CONTINUE
          IF(K.EQ.2) GO TO 40
          IF(KL-2) 22,22,23
C
C           COMBINATION IMPROVEMENT (ELIMINATION COST)
C
   23 IF(SMALLS.EQ.0) GO TO 40
          DO 25 K1=1,KL
          E(K1)=0.0
          DO 26 I=1,M
          IF(X(I).NE.THETA(K1)) GO TO 26
          K3=0
          DO 27 K2=1,KL
          IK=(THETA(K2) - 1)*M +I
          IF(K1.EQ.K2) GO TO 27
          K3=K3+1
          IF(K3.GT.1) GO TO 28
          RS=A(IK)
          NEXTB(I)=THETA(K2)
   28 IF(RS.LT.A(IK)) GO TO 27
          RS=A(IK)
          NEXTB(I)=THETA(K2)
   27 CONTINUE
          E(K1)=RS-ASTAR(I)+E(K1)
   26 CONTINUE
          IF(K1.GT.1) GO TO 30
          SMALLE=E(K1)
          LASTK=1
   30 IF(SMALLE.LT.E(K1)) GO TO 25
          SMALLE=E(K1)
          LASTK=K1
   25 CONTINUE
```

```
C
C        ELIMINATION CHECK
C
      IF(LASTK.EQ.KL) GO TO 31
C
C        LAST ASSIGNED SITE DOES NOT HAVE SMALLEST ELIMINATION COST
C
C        REVISE ASTAR COLUMN WITHOUT THETA(LASTK)
C
      I1=(THETA(LASTK) - 1)*M
      DO 32 I=1,M
      IF(X(I).NE.THETA(LASTK)) GO TO 32
      NB=NEXTB(I)
      X(I)=NB
      I1=(NB-1)*M+I
      ASTAR(I)=A(I1)
   32 CONTINUE
C
C        ELIMINATE THETA(LASTK) FROM THE BUILDING ORDER ROW
C
      DO 33 J=LASTK,KL
      NEXTK=J+1
   33 THETA(J)=THETA(NEXTK)
      KL=KL-1
      GO TO 22
C
C        LAST ASSIGNED SITE HAS SMALLEST ELIMINATION COST, BUT HAVE
C        ENOUGH SITES BEEN ASSIGNED WAREHOUSES?
C
   31 IF(KL.LT.K) GO TO 22
C
C        FINISHED
C
   34 FORMAT(41H BUILD WAREHOUSES ON THE FOLLOWING SITES:/)
   35 FORMAT(/I8)
   36 FORMAT(//64H IF INSUFFICIENT FUNDS ARE AVAILABLE TO BUILD ALL THE
     1 WAREHOUSES/52H IMMEDIATELY, BUILD THEM IN THE ORDER GIVEN ABOVE./
     2/)
   37 FORMAT(17H SUPPLY CUSTOMER ,I2,16H FROM WAREHOUSE ,I2,20H AT ANNUA
     1L COST OF $,F10.2)
   38 FORMAT(50H TOTAL ANNUAL COST OF SHIPPING FROM ALL WAREHOUSES/22H T
     10 ALL CUSTOMERS IS $,F15.2)
   40 WRITE(4,34)
      WRITE(4,35) (THETA(J), J=1,KL)
      WRITE(4,36)
      WRITE(4,37) (I, X(I), ASTAR(I), I=1,M)
      TOTCST=0.0
      DO 39 I=1,M
   39 TOTCST=TOTCST + ASTAR(I)
      WRITE(4,38) TOTCST
      STOP
      END
```

PROGRAM 11.1   MAX-FLOW, MIN-CUT NETWORK

```
      COMMON/NET/F(20,20),C(20,20),N
      DIMENSION L(20,2)
      INTEGER F,C,S(20)
    1 FORMAT(' MAX-FLOW MIN-CUT'//' ENTER ARC DATA AS:  SOURCE, SINK,
     1 CAPACITY; END WITH 0,0,0'/)
    2 FORMAT(3G)
    3 FORMAT(/' NET AT START'/)
    4 FORMAT(//' NET AT BREAKTHROUGH'/)
    5 FORMAT(//' NET AT OPTIMUM'/)
      WRITE(4,1)
      N=0
      DO 12 I=1,20
      DO 12 J=1,20
   12 C(I,J)=0
    7 READ(4,2) I,J,K
      IF(I.EQ.0) GO TO 8
      C(I,J)=K
      F(I,J)=0
      N=MAX0(I,J,N)
      GO TO 7
    8 WRITE(4,3)
   18 CALL OUTPUT
      DO 10 I=1,N
      S(I)=0
      L(I,1)=0
   10 L(I,2)=0
      L(1,1)=-1
      L(1,2)=999999
   20 DO 11 I=1,N
      IF(L(I,1).NE.0.AND.S(I).EQ.0) GO TO 21
   11 CONTINUE
      WRITE(4,5)
      CALL OUTPUT
      STOP
   21 DO 13 J=1,N
      IF(C(I,J).EQ.0.OR.L(J,1).NE.0.OR.F(I,J).EQ.C(I,J)) GO TO 14
      L(J,1)=I
      L(J,2)=MIN0((C(I,J)-F(I,J)),L(I,2))
      GO TO 13
   14 IF(C(J,I).EQ.0.OR.L(J,1).NE.0.OR.F(J,I).EQ.0) GO TO 13
      L(J,1)=-I
      L(J,2)=MIN0(F(J,I),L(I,2))
   13 CONTINUE
      IF(L(N,1).NE.0) GO TO 15
      S(I)=1
      GO TO 20
   15 WRITE(4,4)
      I=N
   19 J=IABS(L(I,1))
      IF(L(I,1)) 22,22,23
   22 F(I,J)=F(I,J)-L(N,2)
      GO TO 24
   23 F(J,I)=F(J,I)+L(N,2)
   24 I=J
      IF(J-1) 18,18,19
      END
      SUBROUTINE OUTPUT
      COMMON/NET/F(20,20),C(20,20),N
    1 FORMAT(' FROM NODE',5X,'TO NODE',5X,'CAPACITY',5X,'FLOW'/)
    2 FORMAT(5X,I2,11X,I2,8X,I5,6X,I5)
      WRITE(4,1)
      DO 3 I=1,N
      DO 3 J=1,N
      IF(C(I,J).GT.0) WRITE(4,2) I,J,C(I,J),F(I,J)
    3 CONTINUE
      RETURN
      END
```

PROGRAM 11.2   SHORTEST PATH FROM NODE 1 TO ALL OTHERS

```
      DIMENSION F(20), F1(20)
      INTEGER SN(21), EN(21), UB
      DATA YES/'Y'/
      REAL LENGTH(21)
      UB=20
    1 FORMAT(' SHORTEST PATH FROM NODE ONE TO ALL OTHERS'//' ENTER ARCS
     1 AS:  STARTING NODE, ENDING NODE, DISTANCE'//' STOP INPUT BY TYPI
     2NG: 0,0,0'/)
    2 FORMAT('+ARC ',I2,':'$)
    3 FORMAT(//' STATUS OF NETWORK AT ITERATION ',I2/)
    4 FORMAT(' FROM NODE',5X,'TO NODE',5X,'DISTANCE')
    5 FORMAT(5X,'1',11X,I2,9X,F7.2)
    6 FORMAT(/' STATUS OF NETWORK AT OPTIMUM'/)
    7 FORMAT(/' THE SHORTEST PATH FROM NODE 1 CONSISTS OF:'/)
   24 FORMAT(' ARC(',I2,',',I2,')')
   10 FORMAT(A1)
    8 FORMAT(/' DO ANOTHER?:'$)
    9 FORMAT(3G)
   11 FORMAT(' SORRY, BUT THE PROGRAM CAN CURRENTLY ACCEPT AT MOST ',I2,
     1' NODES OR ARCS.'//' GOODBYE')
   12 WRITE(4,1)
      MAXNOD=0
      UB=UB+1
      DO 13 I=1,UB
      WRITE(4,2) I
      READ(4,9) SN(I), EN(I), LENGTH(I)
      IF(EN(I).GT.MAXNOD) MAXNOD=EN(I)
      IF(MAXNOD.GT.UB) GO TO 15
      IF(SN(I)) 14,14,13
   13 CONTINUE
   15 UB=UB-1
      WRITE(4,11) UB
      STOP
   14 UB=UB-1
      N=I-1
      K=1
      WRITE(4,3) K
      WRITE(4,4)
      DO 16 I=1,N
      J=EN(I)
      IF(SN(I).NE.1) GO TO 17
      WRITE(4,5) J, LENGTH(I)
      F1(J)=LENGTH(I)
      GO TO 16
   17 IF(F1(J).EQ.0.) F1(J)=999999.
   16 F(J)=F1(J)
   18 K=K+1
      WRITE(4,3) K
      DO 19 I=1,N
      J=SN(I)
      JJ=EN(I)
      IF(F(J).GT.(F1(JJ)+LENGTH(I))) F(J)=F1(JJ)+LENGTH(I)
      IF(F(JJ).GT.(F1(J)+LENGTH(I))) F(JJ)=F1(J)+LENGTH(I)
   19 CONTINUE
      WRITE(4,4)
      DO 22 J=2,MAXNOD
      IF(F(J).NE.999999.) WRITE(4,5) J, F(J)
   22 F1(J)=F(J)
      IF(K.LT.(MAXNOD-1)) GO TO 18
      WRITE(4,6)
      WRITE(4,4)
      DO 23 J=2,MAXNOD
      IF(F(J).LT.999999.) WRITE(4,5) J, F(J)
   23 CONTINUE
      WRITE(4,7)
      DO 25 I=1,N
      J=SN(I)
      K=EN(I)
      IF(LENGTH(I).EQ.(F(K)-F(J))) WRITE(4,24) J,K
   25 CONTINUE
      WRITE(4,8)
      READ(4,10) ANSWER
      IF(ANSWER.EQ.YES) GO TO 12
      STOP
      END
```

Index